# Digital Afterlife

# Chapman & Hall/CRC
# Artificial Intelligence and Robotics Series
**Series Editor:** Roman V. Yampolskiy

**Intelligent Autonomy of UAVs**
Advanced Missions and Future Use
*Yasmina Bestaoui Sebbane*

**Artificial Intelligence**
With an Introduction to Machine Learning, Second Edition
*Richard E. Neapolitan, Xia Jiang*

**Artificial Intelligence and the Two Singularities**
*Calum Chace*

**Behavior Trees in Robotics and AI**
An Introduction
*Michele Collendanchise, Petter Ögren*

**Artificial Intelligence Safety and Security**
*Roman V. Yampolskiy*

**Artificial Intelligence for Autonomous Networks**
*Mazin Gilbert*

**Virtual Humans**
*David Burden, Maggi Savin-Baden*

**Deep Neural Networks: WASD Neuronet Models, Algorithms, and Applications**
*Yunong Zhang, Dechao Chen, Chengxu Ye*

**Introduction to Self-Driving Vehicle Technology**
*Hanky Sjafrie*

For more information about this series please visit: https://www.crcpress.com/Chapman--HallCRC-Artificial-Intelligence-and-Robotics-Series/book-series/ARTILRO

# Digital Afterlife

## Death Matters in a Digital Age

Edited by

**Maggi Savin-Baden**
**Victoria Mason-Robbie**

CRC Press
Taylor & Francis Group
Boca Raton London New York

CRC Press is an imprint of the
Taylor & Francis Group, an **informa** business

A CHAPMAN & HALL BOOK

CRC Press
Taylor & Francis Group
6000 Broken Sound Parkway NW, Suite 300
Boca Raton, FL 33487-2742

International Standard Book Number-13: 978-0-367-33716-2 (Paperback)
International Standard Book Number-13: 978-0-367-33791-9 (Hardback)

**Visit the Taylor & Francis Web site at**
http://www.taylorandfrancis.com

**and the CRC Press Web site at**
http://www.crcpress.com

# Contents

Acknowledgements, ix

Editors, xi

Contributors, xiii

Introduction    1

MAGGI SAVIN-BADEN AND VICTORIA MASON-ROBBIE

CHAPTER 1 ▪ Perspectives on Digital Afterlife    11

MAGGI SAVIN-BADEN AND VICTORIA MASON-ROBBIE

CHAPTER 2 ▪ Social Media and Digital Afterlife    27

ELAINE KASKET

CHAPTER 3 ▪ Posthumous Digital Material:
Does It 'Live On' in Survivors'
Accounts of Their Dead?    39

MÓRNA O'CONNOR

CHAPTER 4 ▪ The Transition from Life to the Digital
Afterlife: Thanatechnology and Its Impact
on Grief    57

CARLA SOFKA

CHAPTER 5 ▪ Profit and Loss: The Mortality
of the Digital Immortality Platforms    75

DEBRA BASSETT

CHAPTER 6 ■ The 'New(ish)' Property, Informational
Bodies, and Postmortality    89

EDINA HARBINJA

CHAPTER 7 ■ Digital Remains: The Users' Perspectives    107

TAL MORSE AND MICHAEL BIRNHACK

CHAPTER 8 ■ Legal Issues in Digital Afterlife    127

GARY F. RYCROFT

CHAPTER 9 ■ Building a Digital Immortal    143

DAVID BURDEN

CHAPTER 10 ■ Philosophical Investigations
into Digital Afterlife    161

JOHN READER

CHAPTER 11 ■ Postdigital Afterlife: A Philosophical
Framework    173

PETAR JANDRIĆ

CHAPTER 12 ■ Digital Afterlife Matters    189

VICTORIA MASON-ROBBIE AND MAGGI SAVIN-BADEN

GLOSSARY, 203

INDEX, 205

# Acknowledgements

This book has been a challenge to create in these liquid times of moving technologies and shifting perceptions of the afterlife. We are grateful to the initial reviewers of the proposal, including Steve Fuller, who was very positive about this project, and also to Debra Bassett for allowing us to use her term *Digital Afterlife* in the title.

We also wish to thank the chapter authors and Randi Cohen at CRC Press/Taylor & Francis Group for being so supportive of this project.

Finally, thanks are due to our families and in particular to John Savin-Baden and Neil Robbie for providing support, and for being our sounding boards.

Any mistakes, in this life at least, are ours.

# Editors

**Maggi Savin-Baden** is Professor of Education at the University of Worcester and has researched and evaluated staff and student experience of learning for over 20 years and gained funding in this area (Leverhulme Trust, JISC, Higher Education Academy, MoD). She has a strong publication record of over 50 research publications and 17 books which reflect her research interests on the impact of innovative learning, digital fluency, cyber-influence, pedagogical agents, qualitative research methods, and problem-based learning. In her spare time, she runs, bakes, climbs, and attempts triathlons.

**Victoria Mason-Robbie** (PhD CPsychol CSci AFBPsS FHEA) is a chartered psychologist with a range of research interests within the fields of Health Psychology and Education who has published widely in psychology, medical, and teaching journals. She is an experienced lecturer having worked in the Higher Education sector for over 15 years. Her current research focuses on evaluating web-based avatars, pedagogical agents, and virtual humans.

# Contributors

**Debra Bassett** gained her PhD from the University of Warwick. Her qualitative research into human–computer interaction looks at how the Internet enables the creation of posthumous digital memories and messages with blogs, vlogs, avatar creation, and social network sites and how this digital endurance may affect how people grieve.

**Michael Birnhack** is professor and associate dean (research) at the Faculty of Law, Tel Aviv University. His research focuses on information law, especially privacy and intellectual property. His 2010 book, *Private Space* (Hebrew), won the Israeli Political Scientists Association Annual Prize.

**David Burden** has been involved in AI, VR, and immersive environments since the 1990s. David set up Daden Limited in 2004 to help organisations explore and exploit the social and commercial potential of using chatbots, AI, and virtual environments and has authored over a dozen papers on virtual worlds and AI.

**Edina Harbinja's** principal areas of research and teaching are related to the legal issues surrounding the Internet and emerging technologies. Edina is a pioneer and a globally recognised expert in post-mortem privacy, that is, privacy of the deceased individuals. Her research has a policy and multidisciplinary focus and aims to explore different options of regulation of online behaviours and phenomena, including privacy and data protection, IP, contract law, property and succession.

**Petar Jandrić** (PhD) is professor at the Zagreb University of Applied Sciences, Croatia. His previous academic affiliations include the Croatian Academic and Research Network, National e-Science Centre at the

University of Edinburgh, Glasgow School of Art, and Cass School of Education at the University of East London. He is Editor-in-Chief of the *Postdigital Science and Education* journal (https://www.springer.com/journal/42438) and book series (https://www.springer.com/series/16439).

**Elaine Kasket** is a writer, keynote speaker and counselling psychologist, and a long-time scholar of death and the digital. She is the author of *All the Ghosts in the Machine: The Digital Afterlife of Your Personal Data* and serves as Bereavement Lead for the Digital Legacy Association.

**Tal Morse** teaches at Hadassah Academic College in Jerusalem. His research focuses on media and death, especially mediated death rituals. His book, *The Mourning News: Reporting Violent Death in a Global Age* was published by Peter Lang (New York) in 2017.

**Mórna O'Connor** is a final-year doctoral candidate at the Nottingham Centre for the Advancement of Palliative, Supportive and End-of-Life Care (NCARE) at the University of Nottingham. Mórna's PhD thesis, *The Digital Memories Study,* explores the role played by potentially vast and varied posthumous digital material in modern grieving.

**John Reader** is a Senior Research Fellow with the William Temple Foundation and honorary senior lecturer with the Institute of Education at the University of Worcester. Recent publications include *A Philosophy of Christian Materialism: Entangled Fidelities and the Public Good* cowritten with Christopher Baker and Thomas A. James (Routledge 2015) and *Theology and New Materialism: Spaces of Faithful Dissent* (Palgrave Macmillan 2017). He has also cowritten *Technology Transforming Theology: Digital Impacts* with Maggi Savin-Baden for the William Temple Ethical Dialogue series.

**Gary Rycroft** studied Law at the University of Manchester 1991–1994, obtained a post graduate diploma in legal practice from the College of Law at Chester in 1995 and qualified as a solicitor in England & Wales in 1998. He is the senior partner of Joseph A. Jones & Co, a law firm based in Lancaster. Gary is a former chair of The Law Society Private Client Section Advisory Committee, which supports solicitors who specialise in Wills, Trusts & Probate. He was a trustee of the National Council of Palliative care until the charity merged with Hospice UK in 2017 and continues to chair the Dying Matters Forum for Hospice UK. Gary is often asked to write and comment on the law in newspapers, magazines, radio, and television and is the resident legal expert on the BBC1 consumer affairs programme *Rip Off Britain*.

**Carla Sofka** is professor of social work at Siena College. She began writing about the impact of the Internet and technology on death education and grief counselling in the mid-1990s, coining the term 'thanatechnology' in 1996. Her recent research has investigated the role of digital and social media in dealing with life-threatening and terminal illness, death, and grief. In addition to co-editing and authoring several chapters in *Dying, Death, and Grief in an Online Universe* (2012), she has recently published and presented on issues related to digital immortality and digital legacy.

# Introduction

Maggi Savin-Baden and Victoria Mason-Robbie

Despite the range of studies into grief and mourning in relation to the digital, research to date largely focuses on the cultural practices and meanings that are played out in and through digital environments. As yet, there is little understanding of what seems to be the emergence of different ways of 'creating' digital immortality and the ways in which these result in digital legacies. This book draws together a group of leading experts in the field to present the diverse understandings of digital immortality, and examines the impact that a Digital Afterlife has on recipients and on the wider society.

The possibilities for creating digital immortality have become more sophisticated through technological advances, for example, virtual assistants such as Siri that provide voice and conversational interfaces. There are companies dedicated to creating digitally immortal personas (LifeNaut, 2017; Eternime, 2017), and Facebook has now put in place measures to control the post-mortem data on their site (Brubaker & Callison-Burch, 2016). Steinhart (2014) has examined personality capture, mind uploading, and levels of simulation, arguing for a computationally inspired theory of life after death that will change the future of religion radically. However, there is a need for clarity in the lexicon being used (Bassett, 2015; 2018) and an understanding of how the dead, despite being dead, still survive in society (Walter, 2017).

In this book we argue that the effects of the use of digital media and the creation of digital immortality require investigation, for whilst it appears to be changing understandings of grief and the afterlife, there has been no sustained research that has examined its consequences. The desire for continued existence after death may be understandable, but the development of the digitised forms being created, and the effects of these new technologies, require further research. Companies such as Etern9 and LifeNaut allow 'creators' to build a virtual copy of themselves, training their immortals through daily interactions prior to death. The claim that it is possible to 'live on' through such technological innovations has the potential to change the religious landscape radically, and recent developments suggest socio-political and psychological impacts in understandings about embodiment, death, the social life of the dead, and new forms of post-mortem veneration.

This book presents a comprehensive overview of this rapidly developing field combined with philosophical issues and debates, practical advice on legal and ethical concerns, ways of creating a digital immortal, dealing with the bereaved, and issues pertaining to the persistence of social media after death. It covers a variety of matters which have been neglected in other research texts, for example:

a. The impact of creating a digital immortal on relatives and friends.

b. The consequences of persistent digital legacies.

c. The ways digital media are currently being used to expand the possibilities of commemorating the dead and managing the grief of those left behind.

d. The extent to which digital media are complementing or replacing well-established formal structures and religious rituals.

e. The legal and ethical impact of creating a digital immortal.

## OUR STANCE

This booked emerged from discussions about Digital Afterlife as result of our work on virtual humans (Savin-Baden, Burden, Bhakta, & Mason-Robbie, 2019). As we examined the possibilities for creating a virtual copy of a person, we became fascinated by the idea that we could create our own digital immortal without the use of proprietary software. However, we soon realised that it was not just about creating a digital immortal because the issues stretched out into a larger concept—Digital Afterlife—that included law, ethics, and philosophy, and was affected by our own stories:

*Maggi:* Early in my career I worked as an occupational therapist on an oncology ward. Discussing death or avoiding discussions about it were a daily occurrence as I dealt with terrified relatives and resigned patients trying to protect their loved ones. I became interested in death and with how people chose to deal with it, whether doctors, patients or relatives. Then, and now, it seems people's responses to death, whatever their faith and belief is markedly different. The digital seems to have prompted shifts away from many of the taboos about death; however, ministers and funeral directors, in the main, seem ill-equipped to deal with issues associated with death and the digital. At the same time our global society seems to have moved beyond physical age manipulation (plastic surgery) towards the need to remain, and keep remains, beyond the grave. My interest in digital afterlife stems from my fascination with death and technology, as well as an inquisitiveness about what it is that makes want people to create a Digital Afterlife.

*Victoria:* As a Psychologist, I am interested in both the practical and philosophical issues surrounding the way we communicate with others and the extent to which our intentions are reasoned choices or spontaneous acts. My interest in Virtual Humans first came about through a serendipitous encounter on the University campus which has led to my involvement in the research to test the development of Virtual Human technology. This has raised questions about the possible implications of creating a digital copy of oneself and what would happen to this following death, and the impact it would have on others (children, spouse, parents, siblings, wider family, friends and acquaintances). I am also interested, both personally and professionally, in how people choose to present themselves online, and how this shapes the way other people view them. This may represent only the public dimension of our digital footprint and I am reminded of a box in the attic containing diaries written in my early 20s that my family is under strict instruction to destroy if anything should happen to me. Whilst they may choose to ignore my wishes, this has strong parallels with how we feel about our digital legacy, and how comfortable we are with this being shared in its entirety. Just as we leave traces of our physical selves, whether consciously or not, all of us who engage with technology inevitably leave a digital footprint—in some form or another—that will continue to exist when we cease to.

The book comprises 12 chapters from a broad range of perspectives. Each one addresses the questions emerging from the intended, unintended, planned, or unplanned persistence of our digital footprint and includes research and ideas that capture the significant impact of this on society. Questions raised are likely to require answers that evolve in parallel with technological developments in this field. The focus is on 'Digital Afterlife', particularly in the context of the technology around developing a digital copy of an individual, a so-called digital immortal; however, depending on context, other terms such as 'digital immortality' will also be referred to.

## Chapter 1 Perspectives on Digital Afterlife – Maggi Savin-Baden and Victoria Mason-Robbie

The research and literature around an active Digital Afterlife and the impact of this on relations, friends, colleagues, and institutions is examined. In particular, three perspectives are focused on. First, pre-servers of digital media, who are those that use memories and artefacts to create a digital legacy, such as a memorial site or digitally immortal persona, and may include the deceased themselves before death. Second, receivers of digital media, who receive the memories and artefacts, including memorial sites, digital messages, and/or digitally immortal persona; and third, mediators, who are professionals, such as religious leaders, lawyers or bereavement counsellors, who support these people pre-death to create digital legacies of themselves, and the bereaved who receive or encounter legacies, memorial sites, or digitally immortal persona.

## Chapter 2 Social Media and Digital Afterlife – Elaine Kasket

Warnings about disclosures on social media often invoke the perceived *persistence* of online information—what we post lasts 'forever'. Further encouraging this impression, the social media giant Facebook memorialises the profiles of its deceased users by default, positioning itself as both site and steward for digital remains for an indefinite period of time. The English Victorians bought their burial plots 'in perpetuity', a perpetuity that was reduced to 75 years when finances and space shortages required it. Are today's social media users facing a similar situation, in which 'forever' may actually mean 'until corporations fail, data storage systems prove insufficient, and/or technological obsolescence hits'? Will we achieve a Digital Afterlife or fall into the shadows of a 21st century Dark Ages, and how should we respond in the face of these polarised possibilities? This chapter will contextualise, critique, and problematise the concept of immortality via social media and will provide an argument for how we should now proceed differently, in service of preserving our lasting legacies.

## Chapter 3 Posthumous Digital Material: Does It 'Live On' in Survivors' Accounts of Their Dead? – Mórna O'Connor

This chapter explores how digital traces of the in-life activity and correspondence of the dead figure in survivors' posthumous storying of their dead, and whether the technical possibility for the afterlife of such material bears out in practice for grievers. To explore this, longitudinal qualitative data are presented from four interviews with a bereaved young woman, Sarah, as she told the story of her late sister, Leah, and their relationship, with respect to the sisters' extensive text correspondence. The central argument of this chapter is that, for this survivor, the technical potential for digital traces of her dead to 'live on' is only realised to the extent that material is woven into a posthumous account crafted around the griever's ongoing life and experiences. It is this survivor's creative narration of this digital material into a living posthumous account, blending history of the dead with ongoing story of the bereaved, which accords it continuing currency, relevance and vitality; and the potential to 'live on'.

## Chapter 4 The Transition from Life to the Digital Afterlife: Thanatechnology and Its Impact on Grief – Carla Sofka

Thanatechnology, the concept that digital and social media that are used during times of life-threatening illness, tragedy, and death, is changing the way that society copes with grief. This chapter will explore the ways that an individual's ongoing and potentially evolving online presence or 'digital legacy' has the possibly of having an impact on the experiences of the bereaved and those who hope to provide them with emotional support. In addition to summarising the issues around the use of thanatechnology, this chapter will argue that there is a need to create new strategies to educate the public about the netiquette during times of crisis and loss.

## Chapter 5 Profit and Loss: The Mortality of the Digital Immortality Platforms – Debra Bassett

The quest for immortality is nothing new; we humans have sought to defy death by surviving beyond our biological existence for millennia. However, in many societies the fountain of eternal life was only available to the rich, famous, or infamous. The Internet and the digital societies it enables has changed this: Digital Afterlives are now available to many, and everyday technologies such as smart phones ensure many of us are now 'accidentally' or 'intentionally' creating digital memories and messages that can be inherited by others after we die. But how immortal is a Digital Afterlife? This chapter presents recent research which tracks the longevity and failure of service providers and suggests the term digital endurance may be a more appropriate term for digital immortality. This chapter discusses the ramifications of the demise of the service providers and how the fear of losing the data of the dead is creating a new anxiety for the bereaved in the form of 'second loss'.

### Chapter 6 The 'New(ish)' Property, Informational Bodies, and Postmortality – Edina Harbinja

This chapter will examine the concept of digital assets and immortality from novel angles, not explored holistically in the literature so far. Most legal scholars have considered digital assets either from a perspective of succession and probate, the intersection of property and intellectual property, sometimes referring to data protection, but they have not fully explored theory and conceptualisations that go beyond these. This chapter, therefore, aims to use digital assets as a case study and to test concepts of property (digital assets as the 'new property'), postmortem privacy, and informational bodies and afterlife, looking at how these could be utilised as justifications for a more appropriate regulatory regime, and legislation around digital assets and death. The chapter then relates these concepts to the ideas around postmortal society, introducing the new concept of postmortal privacy. This conceptualisation is then used to explore some of the existing legal and policy regimes around the transmission of digital assets.

### Chapter 7 Digital Remains: The Users' Perspectives – Tal Morse and Michael Birnhack

As our lives go digital, so will, inevitably, our death. Emails we send, pictures we post, and thoughts we share are all stored digitally. These are users' digital remains that reflect their digital personalities and make up the memories for friends and family. After death, the social norms and legal rules regarding access to digital remains are no longer clear. A conflict might arise between the privacy expectations of the user, and his or her family and friends' wish to utilise the digital remains for mourning and commemoration. Some IT corporations have recently addressed the quandaries of digital remains, and legal systems are slowly beginning to follow. As these technological and legal responses emerge, we should not neglect the users themselves. What do users want? How do users wish to manage access to their digital remains? Based on a national survey of Israeli population, this chapter reveals the multiplicity of users' perspectives, perceptions, and practices regarding access to digital remains—their own and others. The chapter points to the emergence of new social perspectives on posthumous privacy and commemoration in the contemporary digital age, and comments on their relevance to policymaking.

## Chapter 8 Legal Issues in Digital Afterlife – Gary F. Rycroft

Digital assets and the law is an emerging area. As technology and the digital footprint of our everyday lives expands, so lawyers are trying to contain and manage digital assets within existing legal frameworks and also explore how the law should develop. Like any asset where there is protection and regulation by the law, digital assets are assets which have value of some kind; be that financial, social, sentimental, or intellectual. This chapter will explore which assets may be classed as digital assets of value and also look at who actually owns what and who has legal rights and responsibilities in respect of those assets. A particular flash point in law has arisen with which digital assets can and cannot be passed on, on death. The chapter will look at how some digital assets can be transferred on death and others may not so easily. The chapter will have a UK law focus but will look at how other jurisdictions in other countries are tackling this area of law and are seeking to develop a new legal approach.

## Chapter 9 Building a Digital Immortal – David Burden

This chapter will examine the approaches and technologies involved in building a digital immortal. These would be considered against the different types of digital immortal (e.g., active/passive) and against how these technologies are likely to mature over the coming decades. The chapter explores the current Digital Afterlife technology available and evaluates their state of maturity. A blueprint for a digital immortal design at different stages of development will be provided. The chapter will particularly focus on how the immortal may obtain long-terms goals that give reason to its immortality, and how it may be able to communicate, and even exert influence and power, in order to move towards those goals.

## Chapter 10 Philosophical Investigations into Digital Afterlife – John Reader

The events which marked the 100th anniversary of the ending of the Great War provided a powerful example of ways in which traces of those who had perished were 'brought to life'. Many communities published brief accounts of those who died and some even marked the houses where they had lived. This raises the question of what we might mean by a trace and how the impact of digital technology could change this. New possibilities of traces are now available which challenge traditional understandings of how the human interacts with the non-human and there is a need for a different conceptualisation to underpin this. Such concepts are to be found within ideas stemming from New Materialism and its engagement with Christian Realism. This chapter will explore concepts such as assemblages, distributed agency, plasticity, technology as pharmakon, and how the digital might create new experiences of time itself as these traces potentially construct unexplored spaces and the possibility of continued engagements. Does the digital short-circuit such engagements or raise the potential for deeper engagements?

## Chapter 11 Postdigital Afterlife: A Philosophical Framework – Petar Jandrić

What is a human being? Who can be considered human, and under which circumstances? During history, the humankind has answered these questions in different ways. Arguably, slaves in ancient Athens (who could not freely move, work, or vote) were considered less human than their free, voting masters; in various places and historical periods, the same can be said for women, people of different races, and minorities. More often than not, these inequalities had been 'scientifically' justified. During the last few centuries, for instance, 'pseudo-scientific theories such as scientific racism, and their more proactive siblings such as eugenics, have been closely associated with poisonous social systems and politics such as slavery, apartheid, and fascism' (Peters and Jandrić, 2019, p. 198). Based on a long history of exclusion, Steve Fuller argues that '"human" began—and I believe should remain—as a normative not a descriptive category' (Fuller and Jandrić, 2019). It is argued that:

> Following Fuller's argument, our question becomes: under which circumstances should we accept living machines as (equal to) human beings? It is extremely hard to quantify humanity,

and it would take genius of (at least) Alan Turing's calibre to give a satisfactory answer. Therefore, we finally settle at a more down to earth question: how should we treat living machines of the moment, and their potentially more advanced successors in the future?

(PETERS AND JANDRIĆ, 2019. p. 202)

This chapter expands previous work on normative aspects of equality, and/or symmetry, between human and non-human agents, in our postdigital world (Jandrić et al., 2018). Using a range of posthumanist literature, the chapter asks: under which circumstances should we accept digital immortals as (equal to) human beings? and, more broadly, how should we treat digital immortals in our postdigital society?

### Chapter 12 Digital Afterlife Matters – Victoria Mason-Robbie and Maggi Savin-Baden

In this final chapter, we summarise and discuss some of the key questions raised throughout the book. Some of the gaps in our understanding are identified, and how we need to address these to keep pace with the rapidly changing landscape of Digital Afterlife. We celebrate the multidisciplinary nature of the field of studies examining Digital Afterlife and argue that such diverse ways of approaching it are essential to fully appreciate the implications it has for society. Ultimately, our Digital Afterlives matter.

## SUMMARY

As technology advances and digital engagement increases the salience and relevance of our digital immortality, it becomes an intrinsic part of living and dying in society. With this in mind, capturing the experience of those wishing to create digital immortality, or those left behind is an essential part of situating digital immortality within a social, psychological, philosophical, moral, and legal context. Within the chapters that follow, key issues and perspectives are debated and discussed, and new questions and possibilities raised for this area that will eventually touch the lives of every digitally connected person living in society.

## REFERENCES

Bassett, D. (2015). Who wants to live forever? Living, dying and grieving in our digital society. *Social Sciences, 4,* 1127–1139.

Bassett, D. (2018). Digital afterlives: From social media platforms to Thanabots and beyond. In C. Tandy, (Ed.). *Death and anti-death, vol. 16: 200 years after Frankenstein.* Ann Arbor, MI: Ria UP.

Brubaker, J., & Callison-Burch, V. (2016). Legacy contact: Designing and implementing post-mortem stewardship at Facebook. In *Proceedings of the ACM Conference on Human Factors in Computing Systems* (pp. 2908–2919). Santa Clara, CA: ACM.

Eter9. (2017). Available https://www.eter9.com/

Eternime. (2017). Available http://eterni.me/

Fuller, S. & Jandrić, P. (2019). The postdigital human: Making the history of the future. *Postdigital Science and Education, 1*(1), 190–217. doi: https://doi.org/10.1007/s42438-018-0003-x.

Jandrić, P., Knox, J., Besley, T., Ryberg, T., Suoranta, J., & Hayes, S. (2018). Postdigital science and education. *Educational Philosophy and Theory, 50*(10), 893–899. doi: https://doi.org/10.1080/00131857.2018.1454000.

LifeNaut Project. (2017). Retrieved https://www.lifenaut.com/

Peters, M. A., & Jandrić, P. (2019). AI, human evolution, and the speed of learning. In J. Knox, Y. Wang, & M. Gallagher (Eds.), *Artificial intelligence and inclusive education: Speculative futures and emerging practices.* Singapore: Springer Nature.

Savin-Baden, M., Burden, D., Bhakta, R., & Mason-Robbie, V. (2019). An evaluation of the effectiveness of using pedagogical agents for teaching in inclusive ways. In Y. Wang, M. Gallagher, J. Knox (Eds.). (2019) *Speculative futures for artificial intelligence and educational inclusion.* London: Springer.

Steinhart, E. C. (2014). *Your digital afterlives.* Basingstoke, UK: Palgrave MacMillan.

Walter, T. (2017). How the dead survive: ancestors, immortality, memory. In M. H. Jacobsen (Ed.), *Postmortal society: Towards a sociology of immortality.* London: Routledge.

# CHAPTER 1

# Perspectives on Digital Afterlife

Maggi Savin-Baden and Victoria Mason-Robbie

## CONTENTS

Introduction 11
Background 12
Social and Psychological Impact of Digital Afterlife 15
Religion and the Digital Afterlife 15
The Death-Tech Industry 16
    DeadSocial (http://deadsocial.org) 17
    Eter9 (https://www.eter9.com) 17
    LifeNaut (https://www.lifenaut.com) 18
    Eternime (http://eterni.me) 19
    Daden 20
Perspectives on Digital Afterlife 20
    Preservers of Digital Media 21
    Mediators 21
    Receivers of Digital Media 22
The Impact of Digital Afterlife Creation 22
    Posthumous Digital Etiquette 22
    Unintended Consequences 23
Conclusion 23
References 23

## INTRODUCTION

This chapter examines the concept of Digital Afterlife and explores research into the emotional and social impact it may have on relations, friends, colleagues, and institutions. It provides an overview of the various types of Digital Afterlife and suggests a need for greater clarity about the use of terminology. The use of different media to support, create, and maintain Digital Afterlife will also be presented and critiqued. The final section of the chapter raises challenging issues that will be explored across the book as a whole.

## BACKGROUND

The concept of Digital Afterlife is defined here as the continuation of an active or passive digital presence after death (Savin-Baden, Burden, & Taylor, 2017). Other terms have been used to describe Digital Afterlife, including *digital immortality*. 'Afterlife' assumes a digital presence that may or may not continue to exist, whereas 'immortality' implies a presence, in some form at least, *ad infinitum*. Whilst these terms may be used interchangeably, afterlife is a broader and more flexible construct as it does not contain assumptions about the duration or persistence of the digital presence.

Advances in *data mining* and *artificial intelligence* are now making an active presence after death possible, and the dead remain part of our lives as they live on in our digital devices (Bassett, 2015). Recent developments seem to suggest shifts in understandings about embodiment, death, and afterlife (Walter, 2017). For example, digital media are currently being used to expand the possibilities of commemorating the dead and managing the grief of those left behind, complementing and sometimes replacing the well-established formal structures and rituals of Christianity and other faiths. It is now possible to light online memorial candles and create augmented coffins and tombstones with QR codes (Quick Response Codes—machine-readable labels that contain information about the person). Despite increasing interest and research into death online (Hutchings, 2017) there is little exploration of the impact of the use of digital media and the creation of digital immortals on religious practices and grief management. There is also little understanding of the value of digital media in restoring family relationships or the impact it has on the mental well-being of the bereaved. Whilst *Digital Afterlife* tends to be used as an overarching term, it can be broken down into the components presented in Table 1.1.

Research to date has focused on the wider implications of media death, the idea that all our media, from photographs to social network posts are deleted. Thus, it is important at the outset to define different types of Digital Afterlife and explore the impact of these differences.

TABLE 1.1  Features of Digital Afterlife

| Term | Definition | Example/s | Related Research |
|---|---|---|---|
| Digital traces | Digital footprints left behind through digital media | Play lists Blog posts Website searches | Mayer-Schönberger (2009) |
| Digital legacy | Digital assets left behind after death | Things that are static once the user has died | Maciel and Pereira (2013) |
| Digital death | Either the death of a living being and the way it affects the digital world or the death of a digital object and the way it affects a living being | The impact of left behind digital traces on family or the need for people to delete digital media because of its impact on everyday life | Pitsillides, Waller, and Fairfax (2012) |
| Digital Afterlife | The idea of a virtual space, where information, assets, legacies, and remains reside as part of the cyber soul | The platform DeadSocial enables people to schedule posts after they have passed away. Not really a virtual heaven or a place for souls to reside but it creates some of the illusion of this | Bassett (2018a) |
| Digital remains | Digital content and data which was accumulated and stored online during our lifetime that reflect our digital personality and memories | They are not uniform: these remains can be intangible assets, intellectual property, information about physical or tangible property, or personal data | Birnhack and Morse (2018) |
| Posthumous personhood | The idea of a model of a person that transcends the boundaries of the body | Someone being able to tweet or be reanimated though an avatar | Meese, Nansen, Kohn, and Arnold (2015) |
| Second death | The deletion of digital remains | The grief experienced if/ when someone's Facebook profile is deleted after death without consulting friends and family | Stokes (2015) |
| Second loss | The loss experienced due to the deletion of digital remains | People not upgrading their phones because they are afraid to lose voice messages from dead loved ones | Bassett (2018b) |

*(Continued)*

TABLE 1.1 *(Continued)*   Features of Digital Afterlife

| Term | Definition | Example/s | Related Research |
|---|---|---|---|
| Technologically mediated mourning | The use of social networking sites to mourn and memorialise those who have died physically | The setting up of blogs and social media for the purposes of grief management sites after event such as the Manchester Arena bombing in the United Kingdom in 2017 | Kasket (2012) |
| Digital endurance | The creation of a lasting digital legacy and being posthumously present through digital reanimation | Using sites such as SocialEmbers or the KeepTheirMemoryAlive mobile phone app or an existing system which lives on after their death, such as a person's in-life profile that has been put into memorialised/ remembering status in services such as Facebook | Savin-Baden and Burden (2018) |
| Digital resurrection | The use of dead people in media after death | Oliver Reed's role in *Gladiator* was finished using a digitally constructed face mapped onto a body double during editing as he died just before the final shoot of the film | Sherlock (2013) |
| Digital inheritors | Those who inherit digital memories and messages following the death of a significant other | People who expectedly or unexpectedly 'inherit' the social media profiles and messages following death of close friends and relative and may or may not be able to delete them | Bassett (2018a) |
| Digital mourning labour | This is activity undertaken by corporate brands who use social media to share (and gain from) emotions of grief and nostalgia about dead celebrities | After the death of David Bowie, the music and fashion industry shared their grief on social media using images such as the thunderbolt, the signature sign of Bowie | Kania-Lundholm (2019) |

## SOCIAL AND PSYCHOLOGICAL IMPACT OF DIGITAL AFTERLIFE

Over time, our digital footprint becomes larger, and people leaving their footprint behind are not necessarily aware of the impact this may have on people left behind after their death. This footprint is after all, a construction of a living person with public and private dimensions, not a carefully constructed and intentional legacy for people to pour over once we are no longer living (for most people at least). The informal norms and values for using death-related digital media have not yet fully emerged, and our understanding of the impact of digital media on the mental well-being of the bereaved is a relatively new field of inquiry. The idiosyncratic response to loss and bereavement (e.g., Worden, 2008) is also likely to be mirrored in the response of the bereaved to experiencing, and being exposed to, the Digital Afterlife of a loved one. The intentions of the person who has died, may not be in line with the feelings and expectations of the bereaved. Moreover, it may not be possible to predict the response of the bereaved to being witness to the digital legacy of their loved ones.

## RELIGION AND THE DIGITAL AFTERLIFE

Marking the end of life today increasingly includes memorials, whether sites of roadside crashes, family and friends 'saying a few words', or listening to the deceased's favourite music during services. This shift in practices illustrates why this project is needed, especially given the increasing reification of the bodily form in the 21st century compared with the past focus on the transition of the soul to the afterlife. This reification also characterises the creation of Digital Afterlife as it is essentially treating the digital presence as if it is both a representation of the deceased person, but also that it in some way exists and has form beyond merely leaving behind letters, diaries, and personal effects. The growth of personality capture, mind uploading, and computationally inspired life after death have huge implications for the future of religion, understandings of the afterlife, and the influence of the dead surviving in society. Wagner (2012, p. 4) notes '[b]oth religion and virtual reality can be viewed as manifestations of the desire for transcendence, the wish for some mode of imagination or being, that lies just beyond the reach of our ordinary lives'.

Yet few Christian and other faith leaders have examined the potential for the positive impact of digital media and Digital Afterlife creation in religious contexts. This sense of investment in flesh (through the incarnation) results in a perception that what happens in the digital context is disembodied and therefore less real, less incarnational, less faith-related (O'Donnell, 2019). Gooder's (2016) work on the body sees resurrection as a continuation of this life, prioritising a resurrection of the material body, and is therefore committed to the flesh of this life carrying over into the resurrected life. One of the central difficulties is that Christianity and other faiths find Digital Afterlife disconcertingly disembodied and it is not clear whether it promotes particular views about bodily forms in the afterlife. Afterlife and resurrection remain troublesome because they are couched in mystery, and philosophical and theological discourse cannot explain resurrection of the body, because the human body itself is not reducible to simple description or ready comprehension. Chauvet (1995), for example, sees the human as a subject whose corporality is a 'triple body' comprised of culture, tradition, and nature. Furthermore, Digital Afterlife may prevent us from being free to die (Davies, 2008, p. 106), as well as introducing questions about how 'the dead' might be classified.

The increasing move away from traditional funeral services focusing on the transition of the deceased into the future world beyond, and the rise in popularity of memorial content within funerals and commemorative events heralds shifts in afterlife beliefs by replacing them, to all intents and purposes by attitudes to this life. Irrespective of religious belief, most present at memorials can reflect on a person's life and find something worth recalling. It is a shared act that induces a sense of singleness of purpose without introducing divisive beliefs. In a post-modern context of mixed religious beliefs and secular outlooks this affords a safe ritual space (Brock, 2010, p. 64). As technology develops, Digital Afterlife represents the next quantum leap, in creating potentially everlasting memorials which will enable increasing levels of interaction for those left behind.

It is not yet evident what the impact Digital Afterlife may have on conceptions and theologies of death. Nor is it clear about the extent to which Digital Afterlife is enabling people to tell their story in a world that has lost a sense of religion but not a sense of the sacred. In Chapter 10, John Reader discusses the idea of the digital traces left by the dead as unexplored spaces, and the impact this has on the possibility of continued, and possibly deeper, engagements.

## THE DEATH-TECH INDUSTRY

With developments in Digital Afterlife creation there is an increasing interest in the management of death online despite much of the current software being an embellishment of the true possibilities. For example, the use of virtual assistants, such as Siri, that provide voice and conversational interfaces, the growth of machine learning techniques to mine large data sets, and the rise in the level of autonomy being given to computer-controlled systems, all represent shifts in technology that enhance the creation of Digital Afterlife. This section offers an overview of the developments in the Death-tech industry.

DeadSocial (http://deadsocial.org)

DeadSocial argue they are seeking to change the way society think about and prepare for death online by providing digital legacy and digital end of *life-planning tutorials*. This site offers a number of tutorials which include preparing for death on social media sites (Facebook, Twitter, Instagram) and ways of downloading your media and data from social networks. It also offers 'funeral-tech tutorials' which includes arranging your own funeral and suggestions such as 'What "Game of Thrones" can teach us about funeral planning'. The end of life-planning tutorial offers useful suggestions about passing on passwords and a section which offers an offline legacy builder which includes creating a will and social media will. In reality, such sites only tend to be accessed by those consciously and deliberately preparing for death, beyond the common cultural practices of creating a will and, for some, planning or expressing wishes about a funeral. It also has parallels with the idea of appointing a digital executor discussed later in the book.

Eter9 (https://www.eter9.com)

Eter9 (2017) describes itself as 'is a social network that relies on artificial intelligence as a central element' and that 'Even in your absence, the virtual beings will publish, comment and interact with you intelligently'. A key element is Counterparts:

> 'Your Virtual Self that will stay in the system and interact with the world just like you would if you were present. Your Counterpart will learn more with each action you take. The more you interact in the new social network, the more your Counterpart will learn!'

Such a Counterpart is able to continue to post and interact with others on the network after you are dead (Morse, 2015). In practice users post tweet style messages ('thinking into Eternity') which can be read by other users of the system (if set to 'public' or 'connections'), and also, it is assumed, start to build the knowledge base of the Counterpart (although how this happens is not detailed). There are also 'Eternilisations', effectively favourite posts. Eliza Nine, the host bot has 54467 connections (as of 3 July 2018), which is probably a reasonable estimate of the user-base to date, although there are fewer active users. There is no obvious way in which you can access your own or other's Counterparts in order to see how well they are developing, if at all. Again, sites like this would only be accessed and used by those with a keen interest in their continued online presence. The consequent impact on those left behind could be both considerable and unpredictable.

LifeNaut (https://www.lifenaut.com)

LifeNaut works on a similar principle to Eter9, enabling people to create mindfiles by uploading pictures, videos, and documents to a digital archive, but this is an explicit process rather than a background one as with Eter9. It also enables the user to create a photo-based avatar of the person that will speak for them, although there is the choice of only a single male and female voice which are both US English. LifeNaut is a product of the Terasem Movement Foundation (http://www.terasemmovementfounda-tion.com/) which describes its work on LifeNaut as being to investigate the Terasem Hypotheses which state that:

1. A conscious analog of a person may be created by combining sufficiently detailed data about the person (a 'mindfile') using future consciousness software ('mindware').

2. Such a conscious analog can be downloaded into a biological or nanotechnological body to provide life experiences comparable to those of a typically birthed human.

In practice LifeNaut offers a number of ways to build a 'mindfile'. These include:

- Just talking to a few sample bots, although the conversations seem nonsensical and they appear to ignore what you say.

- Filling out some interview questionnaires, including some 'validated' personality profiles, including a 486 question personality survey measuring cautiousness, conscientiousness, cooperation, gregariousness, and nurturance.

- Talking to your own avatar so it learns from what you say, although this appears to require an explicit 'correction' action.

- Manually adding favourite things and URLs, although your bot does not appear to learn them once added.

It is, however, also possible to have your mindfiles beamed continually into space for later, potential, interception, and recreation by alien intelligences. It is notable that much of the site functionality is implemented using the now deprecated Adobe Flash and so is hard to access from modern web-browsers, and completely unsupported by the end of 2020 (Mackie, 2017). The grandiosity of some of the claims made here are not all empirically testable. Furthermore, the idea of creating a digital archive for future use raises questions about the impact of life stage at death, as the experiences of people at different stages of the life span will impact on the legacy left behind such that an afterlife may become 'stuck' at a particular stage without moving forward with those who are left behind. This idea is taken-up by Reader in Chapter 10.

## Eternime (http://eterni.me)

When using Eternime the individual is expected to train their immortal prior to death through daily interactions. Data are *apparently* mined from Facebook, Fitbit, Twitter, e-mail, photos, video, and location information with the individual's personality being developed through algorithms through pattern matching and data mining. Eternime (2017) is currently in a private stage, (as of July 2018), so it is not yet possible to verify any claims or really understand what technology is in use. As of 3 July 2018, 40,497 people were signed up for their waiting list.

Given the practical state of Eter9 and LifeNaut, and the continued 'private Alpha' of Eternime, it would seem that there is more hype than substance to much of the current media coverage of such digital immortalisation systems. There are also other high-profile android/chatbot projects which should be approached with caution. For example, in Autumn 2017 Sophia, a humanoid robot gave a 'speech' at the United Nations (United Nations, 2017) and has even been granted citizenship of Saudi Arabia (Griffin, 2017). Whilst this may encourage recognition of the fact that there needs to be more debate, as well as legislation in this area, the level of technical accomplishment actually shown is hotly debated (Ghosh, 2018). Related to this, Jandrić discusses the status we should give to such robots in Chapter 11.

## Daden

The work of Daden and the University of Worcester (Burden & Savin-Baden, 2019) in the United Kingdom aims to create a virtual human, which is a digital representation of some, or all, of the looks, behaviours, and interactions of a specific physical human. This prototype system contains relevant memories, knowledge, processes, and personality traits of a specific real person, and enables a user to interact with that virtual persona as though they were engaging with the real person. The virtual persona has the individual's subjective and possibly flawed memories, experiences, and view of reality. The information provided by the individual is in a curated form and, as such, only data the individual chooses to share and be included in the virtual persona has been used so far. Whilst the project has focused around the use of such persona within the sphere of corporate knowledge management, the mere existence of the virtual persona immediately raises issues around its Digital Afterlife. The virtual persona projects are described in more detail in a forthcoming paper (Mason-Robbie et al., forthcoming) and in Chapter 9, Burden discusses approaches and technologies involved in building a digital immortal.

## PERSPECTIVES ON DIGITAL AFTERLIFE

The use of digital media in managing the Digital Afterlife appears to be both evocative and troublesome, affecting emotions and the ability to grieve and manage legacies. Kasket (2012, p. 252) notes 'mourning on Facebook, and the "repurposing" of in-life profiles as continuing spaces to connect with the dead, is a relatively new phenomenon and a young area of research'. Most current research merely focuses on grief and mourning, with little research exploring the sociocultural and sociopolitical impacts. Further, there is little evidence about the impact of eternal endurance and instant vanishment on recipients, family, friends, and religious leaders, nor its effect on mourning practices. Preserving oneself or being preserved by someone else may affect both the dying person's peace of mind and the well-being of the bereaved. Further, it is not clear whether the possibility of Digital Afterlife and the use of digital media alters thoughts about the mind-body connection, and whether interaction with a person's Digital Afterlife alters one's spiritual journey through grief. Distinguishing between those who preserve their own or another's Digital Afterlife, those that mediate the experience of others, and those that receive the Digital Afterlife of a deceased person is important when considering the intended and unintended consequences of the very existence of Digital Afterlives.

## Preservers of Digital Media

Preservers are those who use memories and artefacts to create a digital legacy, such as a memorial site or digitally immortal persona, and may include the deceased themselves before death. Three potential types of creators of Digital Afterlives can be identified:

- Memory creators—Those creating passive digital memories and artefacts pre and post the subject's death. These have already been considered above in examples such as virtual venerations, digital commemoration, digital memorisation and durable biographies, and are typically not created by the subject.

- Avatar creators—Those creating a representative interactive avatar pre-death, typically by the subject, which is able to conduct a limited conversation with others but has a very limited capability to learn, grow, act on, and influence the wider world around it (and hence could be considered a virtual humanoid in the typology identified by Burden & Savin-Baden, 2019). It has minimal likelihood of being mistaken for a still-living subject. An example of this is the virtual persona created by Daden described earlier and discussed in more detail in Burden's Chapter 9.

- Persona creators—Those creating a digitally immortal persona pre-death that learns and adapts over time and can influence and act on the wider world around it (and hence could be considered a virtual human or even ultimately a *virtual sapien* (Burden & Savin-Baden, 2019). It has a high likelihood of being mistaken for a still-living subject.

## Mediators

Mediators are professionals, such as bereavement counsellors, religious leaders, or lawyers who support both people pre-death to create digital legacies of themselves, and the bereaved who receive or encounter legacies, memorial sites or digitally immortal persona. An understanding of multiple perspectives, including the wishes and desires of the person pre-death, and the potential idiosyncratic response of the receivers experiencing the Digital Afterlife of the deceased person is becoming more important to this group.

## Receivers of Digital Media

These are people who receive the memories and artefacts, including memorial sites, digital messages, and/or digitally immortal persona. As highlighted earlier, reactions to the Digital Afterlife of the deceased may be highly idiosyncratic and unpredictable, and indeed may change over time. The perspective of this group should be an important consideration, in the cultural context within which they are embedded.

## THE IMPACT OF DIGITAL AFTERLIFE CREATION

In an emerging area of research, it is becoming increasingly important to consider the impact of Digital Afterlives on those who are left behind. For example, whilst the living person may consent to their Digital Afterlife existing, the loved ones of the deceased may hold a different perspective on experiencing this. Furthermore, in Chapter 5, Bassett discusses the concept of the fear of 'second loss' where the bereaved fear losing the data left by the dead. Therefore, the bereaved person is faced with the original loss of the loved one, and the emotional concomitants of exposure to their digital legacy, followed by the actual or potential loss of this digital legacy in the future. Yet currently there is little literature or guidance about post-humous digital etiquette or the impact of the unintended consequences of Digital Afterlife creation.

## Posthumous Digital Etiquette

Cuminskey and Hjorth (2018) explore representing, sharing, and remembering of loss. They suggest that mobile media results in a form of entanglement with the dead that are both private and public. What is of both interest and concern is who owns the data, what is the relationship between privacy and commemoration, and whether since there are few guidelines there needs to be an etiquette about how death online is managed. Shifting cultural norms towards an increase in sharing personal stories online and the expression of grief and mourning online are important to consider here. We are a long way from Victorian mourning etiquette and the rules that governed appropriate behaviour. Wagner (2018) reviews a range of studies exploring mourning online and highlights that norms are constantly changing and renegotiated by users of social media. A distinction is also made between those who are mourning themselves, and reactions to the mourning of others, highlighting the need to consider the needs of both mourners, and the users of social media who are reacting to expressions of grief online.

## Unintended Consequences

Work in this area, such as Kasket (2019), introduces questions about the unintended consequences of the digital on death, suggesting that the dead continue to 'speak' themselves. Further she asks pertinent questions about how we manage our own data and what might occur when corporations compete with us for control of these data? It is possible that the intentions of the person pre-death become distorted and reshaped such that they no longer resemble the thoughts and wishes of that person. Hence, agency is called into question as the deceased is no longer able to act according to their will and agency is taken over by the corporation/s that control the data. This in turn raises concerns about to what ends the data might be used. It is already clear that commercial companies are using digital mourning labour to sell their products by capitalising on the grief and mass mourning following the death of celebrities.

## CONCLUSION

The effects of the use of digital media and the creation of Digital Afterlives require careful examination. For while it appears to be changing understandings of grief and the afterlife, there has been no sustained research that has examined its effects on faith, faith rituals, mental health, and family relationships pre- and post-death. In the chapters that follow, issues pertaining to these important aspects of culture and society are considered. As with any emerging field, we are left with unanswered ethical, moral, and spiritual questions that will require ongoing consideration and debate as the technological advances gather pace.

## REFERENCES

Bassett, D. (2015). Who wants to live forever? Living, dying and grieving in our digital society. *Social Sciences*, 4, 1127–1139.

Bassett, D. (2018a). Ctrl+Alt+Delete: The changing landscape of the uncanny valley and the fear of second loss. *Current Psychology*. https://doi.org/10.1007/s12144-018-0006-5.

Bassett, D. (2018b). Digital afterlives: From social media platforms to Thanabots and beyond. In C. Tandy, (Ed.), *Death and anti-death* (Vol. 16: 200 Years After Frankenstein). Ann Arbor, MI: Ria UP.

Birnhack, M., & Morse, T. (2018). Regulating access to digital remains – research and policy report. Israeli Internet Association. Available online https://www.isoc.org.il/wp-content/uploads/2018/07/digital-remains-ENG-for-ISOC-07-2018.pdf.

Brock, B. (2010). *Christian ethics in a technological age*. Grand Rapids, Michigan: Wm B Eerdmans Publishing Co.

Burden, D., & Savin-Baden, M. (2019). *Virtual humans: Today and tomorrow.* Florida, US: Taylor and Francis.

Chauvet, L. M. (1995). *Symbol and sacrament: A sacramental reinterpretation of Christian existence,* trans. Patrick Madigan and Madeleine Beaumont. Collegeville, MN: Liturgical Press.

Cuminskey, K., & Hjorth, L. (2018). *Haunting hands.* Oxford, UK: Oxford University Press.

Davies, J. D. (2008). *The theology of death.* London: Continuum.

Eter9. (2017). Available online https://www.eter9.com/

Eternime. (2017). Available online http://eterni.me/

Ghosh, S. (2018). *Facebook's AI boss described Sophia the robot as 'complete b——t' and 'Wizard-of-Oz AI'.* Business Insider UK. Available online https://www.businessinsider.in/facebooks-ai-boss-described-sophia-the-robot-as-complete-b-t-and-wizard-of-oz-ai/articleshow/62391979.cms

Gooder, P. (2016). *Body: Biblical spirituality for the whole person.* London: SPCK Publishing.

Griffin, A. (2017). *Saudi Arabia Grants Citizenship to a Robot for the first time ever.* The Independent. Available online https://www.independent.co.uk/life-style/gadgets-and-tech/news/saudi-arabia-robot-sophia-citizenship-android-riyadh-citizen-passport-future-a8021601.html

Hutchings, T. (2017). We are a united humanity: Death, emotion and digital media in the church of Sweden, *Journal of Broadcasting & Electronic Media, 61*(1), 90–107.

Kania-Lundholm, M. (2019). Digital mourning labor: Corporate use of dead celebrities on social media. In T. Holmbery, A. Jonsson, & F. Palm. (Eds.). *Death matters: Cultural sociology of mortal life.* Cham, Switzerland: Palgrave Macmillan.

Kasket, E. (2012). Continuing bonds in the age of social networking: Facebook as a modern-day medium. *Bereavement Care, 31*(2), pp. 62–69.

Kasket, E. (2019). *All the ghosts in the machine: Illusions of immortality in the digital age.* London: Robinson.

LifeNaut Project. (2017). Available online https://www.lifenaut.com/

Maciel, C., & Pereira, V. (2013). *Digital legacy and interaction.* Heidelberg, Germany: Springer.

Mackie, K. (2017). Adobe and browser makers announce the end of flash. Redmond Magazine. Available online https://redmondmag.com/articles/2017/07/25/adobe-ending-flash-support.aspx Accessed 6th December 2019

Mayer-Schönberger, V. (2009). *Delete: The virtue of forgetting in the digital age.* Princeton, NJ: Princeton University Press.

Meese, J., Nansen, B., Kohn, T., & Arnold, M., & Gibbs, M. (2015). Posthumous personhood and the affordances of digital media. *Mortality, 20*(4), pp. 408–420.

Morse, F. (2015). Eter9 social network learns your personality so it can post as you when you're dead. BBC Newsbeat website. Available online http://www.bbc.co.uk/newsbeat/article/34015307/eter9-social-network-learnsyour-personality-so-it-can-post-as-you-when-youre-dead. Accessed 6th December 2019

O'Donnell, K. (2019). *Digital theology: Constructing theology in a digital age.* London: Bloomsbury.

Pitsillides, S., Waller, M., & Fairfax, D. (2012). Digital death, the way digital data affects how we are (re)membered. In S. Warburton, & Stylianos Hatzipanagos, (Eds.). *Digital identity and social media,* pp. 75–90. IGI Global.

Savin-Baden, M., & Burden, D. (2018). Digital immortality and virtual humans. *Journal of Post digital Science and Education, 1*(1), pp 87–103 (Published online July 2018).

Savin-Baden, M., Burden, D., & Taylor, H. (2017). The ethics and impact of digital immortality. *Knowledge Cultures, 5*(2), 11–19.

Sherlock, A. (2013). Larger than life: Digital resurrection and the re-enchantment of society. *The Information Society, 29*(3), pp. 164–176.

Stokes, P. (2015). Deletion as second death: The moral status of digital remains. *Ethics and Information Technology, 17*(4), pp. 237–248.

United Nations. (2017). Speech by 'Sofia'.

Wagner, A. J. M. (2018). Do not click "Like" when somebody has died: The role of norms for mourning practices in social media. Social Media + Society. https://doi.org/10.1177/2056305117744392.

Wagner, R. (2012). *Godwired: Religion, ritual and virtual reality.* New York: Routledge.

Walter, T. (2017). How the dead survive: Ancestors, immortality, memory. In M. H. Jacobsen (Ed.), *Postmortal society. Towards as sociology of immortality.* London: Routledge.

Worden, J. W. (2008). *Grief counseling and grief therapy: A handbook for the mental health practitioner* (4th ed.). New York: Springer.

# CHAPTER 2

# Social Media and Digital Afterlife

**Elaine Kasket**

## CONTENTS

Introduction 27
Physical and Digital Remains 28
Digital Afterlives and the Fantasy of Immortality 29
Digital Legacies 30
Coming to Terms with Our Finite Digital Afterlives 35
Conclusion 37
Notes 37
References 37

## INTRODUCTION

Warnings about disclosures on social media invoke the perceived *persistence* of online information, and we are often warned that what we post lasts 'forever'. Further encouraging this impression, the social media giant Facebook memorialises the profiles of its deceased users by default when not instructed otherwise, explicitly positioning itself as both site and steward for digital remains for an indefinite period of time. While physical remains were once assured a permanent 'home' in many countries, with burial plots being purchased in perpetuity, this perpetuity was amended to considerably less time when finances and space shortages required it. Are today's social media users facing a similar situation, in which 'forever' may actually mean 'until corporations fail, data storage systems prove insufficient and/or technological obsolescence hits'? Will we achieve a Digital Afterlife or be obscured in the shadows of a 21st century Dark Ages, and how should we respond in the face of these polarised possibilities? This chapter will contextualise, critique, and problematise the concept of afterlife via social media and will provide an argument for how we might proceed differently, in service of preserving our lasting legacies.

## PHYSICAL AND DIGITAL REMAINS

Each time I have encountered a dead body, I knew it was about to happen and I could have opted out. Such is the luxury of choice and control in places where death is highly managed, where the care of the sick and the dead is carried out largely by professionals. As I come from a culture where open caskets are common (Harper, 2010) and viewing the body in the funeral home is often a social requirement (Walter, 2005), those physical remains that I have seen were embalmed, and carefully made up for highly ritualised public view by people licensed by the state, perhaps graduates of mortuary science programmes. Proceedings were organised by the employees of the funeral home, and mourners were directed through the process by people who have done it many times before.

While the customs and contexts vary from place to place, most people's experience of encountering physical remains will be similar to my own: infrequent confrontations with silent entities prepared and looked after by people with well-established roles. My experience of encountering digital remains is a different story. Online, I am surprised when I bump into the dead in places where I do not expect them or flummoxed when I cannot find them where they once were. The digital remains of the dead are usually easily located on any connected device, but these remains are often not as tame, quiet, or tidied up as their physical correlates. A posthumously persistent Facebook profile, for example, is nowhere near as orderly or predictable as the funeral home. It is often not clear exactly who is in charge, but one thing is certain: there is no training for how to manage the online dead, no digital mortuary science degree, and no code of ethics. There is no rulebook for digital remains, although some are endeavouring to write it.

It is not surprising that exposure to death, in whatever form, often discomfits us. The industrial and medical revolutions drove a wedge between the living and the dead, shunting the dying into hospitals and the deceased into climate-controlled mortuaries and large, purpose-built cemeteries in the suburbs. The late historian Philippe Ariès (1976) called the last 200 years 'The Age of Forbidden Death', an era in which death gradually became ever more distant, spatially confined, and monitored. Ariès argued that during the 19th and 20th centuries, death receded from us not only physically, but psychologically too. Assumptions held about death being a 'taboo' are likely to come from this time period. But is it still true?

When Ariès died in 1984, he had no reason to believe that the Age of Forbidden Death would draw to a close anytime soon. However, the following year was a watershed moment in time, the start of an era that would eventually mark a shift away from 'forbidden death' culture in the West. In Prensky's (2001) terminology, if you were born before 1985, you are a 'digital immigrant'. If you arrived into the world after that year, you can be considered a 'digital native'. Ariès died before he ever had the chance to become a digital immigrant; he never had to adjust to the new normal. Digital natives capture, store, and share digital data as naturally as they breathe, never having known anything else. Given that this state of affairs is relatively new, the current proprietor of the online World Wide Cemetery says that we have 'baby Internet' (Kasket, 2019)[1]. As such, perhaps it is not surprising that few data processors and controllers give much thought to the end point. What happens to all of these data when the people associated with them *die*?

No virtual carrion beetles traverse the Internet, nibbling away all traces of us after we have breathed our last. No consistent guidelines exist for whether and when to cull the data associated with entities who are no longer here, and there is no foolproof way of even identifying who is 'dead' and who is 'alive' online. No existing laws of succession, data protection laws, or contract laws are truly fit to coherently guide us on what to do with digital remains. No professional body trains and registers people to manage digital remains, although this has been mooted as a career of the future. There are only vague terms and conditions, rampant confusion, and bitter disputes over the ownership and management of the data of the deceased, of which there is an increasing amount (Öhman & Watson, 2019).

## DIGITAL AFTERLIVES AND THE FANTASY OF IMMORTALITY

So it is that, courtesy of the digital revolution, we suddenly find ourselves in the middle of a reunion bash for the living and the dead: those who breathe and those who have not mingled in the same places and spaces so much since the 18th century (Ariès, 1976; Kasket, 2019). Needless to say, this is a surprise party that the hosts did not realise they were organising, and for which they are not well provisioned. Things really got started in 2006, when YouTube marked its first anniversary and Twitter and Facebook were born, and when millions of us began, in earnest, to compile digital reflections of ourselves. Those reflections often remain accessible, for at least a time, after our physical bodies shuffle off this mortal coil.

Images of death and tragedy now appear daily in our news feeds. Deceased Facebook friends usually remain on the platform, in memorialised

'Remembering' form or otherwise, and thanks to profile cloners, there may even be the occasional friend request from a dead person. We receive emails from lost loved ones, courtesy of hackers and spammers. No wonder that one Danish scholar believes the Age of Forbidden Death to be over. With the grim reaper constantly staring us in the face from our phone screens and tablets, he says, it is the Age of Spectacular Death (Jacobsen, 2016), in which we can all watch death from a position that is closer and further away at the same time, framed and mediated by our technologies. Portable, omnipresent devices like mobile phones amplify and help us to process our emotional experiences of loss, while simultaneously affording us opportunities to distance and distract ourselves from our pain and from the realities of mortality (Cumiskey & Hjorth, 2017).

Jacobsen (2016) argues persuasively that we are currently in the Age of Spectacular Death, and I would add that, given the popular discourse of online material lasting forever, we are also in the Age of Apocryphal Immortality. This conceit of immortality is not entirely new, but it hearkens back to Victorian fantasies. The Victorians liked memorialising the dead 'in perpetuity', and when the City of London Cemetery and Crematorium was founded, all of the grave plots and columbarium niches were sold 'in perpetuity'. The current superintendent of that cemetery complains that he is still keeping up graves that the cemetery received a handful of pounds to maintain back in 1902. '[Perpetuity] is not particularly good, in business terms', he comments (Kasket, 2019, p. 165)[2]. Permanent memorialisation was so bad for the balance books, in fact, that the London Cemetery Company went bust in the early 1970s, and the laws around disturbing human remains had to change. 'Perpetuity' was slashed to 75 years. As the century wore on and the popularity of cremation increased, the discourse of 'forever' was diluted.

## DIGITAL LEGACIES

When the digital revolution came along, with its megabytes and then gigabytes and then terabytes of inexpensive storage, its seemingly infinite 'cloud', its backups and copies, and its potential to retain hundreds and thousands of images that could remain undimmed by the passage of years. With the digital age it became possible to comprehensively document and even *reflect* an individual's life. Not only do we deliberately capture, store, and share information across multiple platforms and on multiple devices, but we also fail to switch off the automatic data-capturing settings that lie buried deep in our devices, like the iPhone feature that tracks everywhere you have ever been (Zahradnik, 2019). In fewer than two decades, we have moved from no digital trace at all, to digital 'footprints', to well-developed digital identities. As artificial intelligence (AI) advances, phenomenon like the 'Be Right Back' episode of *Black Mirror* (Brooker & Harris, 2013)—in which an artificially intelligent humanoid robot is created from the digital remains of a woman's dead partner—may become possible too.

Unsurprisingly, with all of these developments, the discourse of 'forever' is back with a vengeance. How often have you heard, or even conveyed yourself, the cautionary maxim that 'online is forever'? Concerned about their future university admissions or their employability, we remind our children: online is forever. Witnessing the downfall of relationships, reputations, or political careers due to damning online material, we remind ourselves: online is forever. Somewhere along the line, this seems to have morphed from a just-in-case admonition to an accepted truth.

Occasionally our belief in 'forever' is challenged by the loss of important data, but somehow we manage to forget again: the twin sirens of convenience and capacity lure us back, and once again we entrust 'the cloud' with our most precious personal and sentimental data. Believing in the relative security of online storage, we shed our material stuff. We cast off the untidy shackles of the paper office and digitise all of our documents. Even the most ardent sock-rolling fans of Marie Kondo's (2014) KonMari method may feel concerned about disposing of family photographs, but they find reassurance in their scanner. Our homes may be tidy and our physical possessions sparser, but online we are all extreme hoarders.

A score of 'digital legacy' companies have attempted to capitalise on the idea that online is forever, promising users to safeguard their information and their memories until the end of time. Some enterprises, like Eternime, offer to help us 'live' on forever as digital avatars. But even sites with eternity worked into their name, like Perpetu, often close up shop a few years shy of 'forever'. In 2011, I watched as one academic and designer presented an animated slide on the life cycle of legacy websites. One by one, at the click of her remote, the full-colour logos of digital-immortality-promising services appeared onscreen along the arrow of her timeline. At another click, the logos of all the enterprises that had since died off faded to grey. In mid-2019, one of the early digital-legacy preservation companies, SafeBeyond, emailed its users to let them know about the uncertain future of the company (Bassett, personal communication, June 2019).

Digital legacy services are designed for the express purposes of memorialisation and preservation, but they are mere minnows next to the gigantic blue whale of a platform that never set out to be a digital cemetery in the first place. Facebook could find itself hosting the digital remains of 4.9 billion dead people by the end of the century (Öhman & Watson, 2019). This is—needless to say—a social and practical responsibility for which this particular platform was not designed.

Nevertheless, Facebook has gamely accepted responsibility for preserving the data of the deceased. It ceased its delete-after-death policy following the Virginia Tech massacre of 2007, in which over 30 people died, and has memorialised deceased users' profiles ever since (Brubaker, 2015). Facebook recognises that the digital remains on its site are often particularly coherent, vivid, and biographical representations of the lost person, and as such they remain extremely important to many mourners. The commercial incentives behind profile preservation must exist but are unspoken and likely varied—customer relations, retention of living users who do not wish to lock themselves out of the digital cemetery, and use of deceased users' data for such purposes as market insights and training new models (Öhman & Watson, 2019).

In the first quarter of 2019, Facebook announced in a press release that they were 'Making it Easier to Honor a Loved One on Facebook After They Pass Away' (Sandberg, 2019). The new raft of memorialisation features was designed to make the site 'even more supportive', but I had reservations about some of them. Using AI to detect profiles of deceased users and to stop birthday reminders from those accounts, for example, would only be helpful to those mourners who *wanted* birthday reminders to cease, unlike one grieving mother I interviewed (Kasket, 2019). The granting of greater editorial powers to legacy contacts would only be favourable if legacy contacts were prepared and equipped to moderate a Facebook profile for years to come.

Technology companies, it seems, are telling us what the easiest and best ways are for us to honour our loved ones, a moral and psychological judgement that, one could argue, they are not best placed to make, particularly given the idiosyncrasy of grief. The co-founder of Facebook has criticised the fact that the platform is able to make such powerful decisions based on the personal values of individuals (Hughes, 2019), and this is one such example. When I interviewed one of the main forces behind memorialisation at Facebook, I asked him about Facebook's role in managing deceased users' data and the needs of the bereaved. 'The metaphor of the funeral director is not far off, right?' he said. 'We don't ask the bereaved to go and embalm their loved ones. A lot of that complexity [can be] taken away. Call it an example of good design, so that people make choices that meet them where they're at' (Kasket, 2019, p. 157)[3].

It would not have been possible to predict that Facebook would one day function, and see itself, as the funeral director of our online digital remains. But for better or for worse, our encounters with the dead are now framed through the power and the design choices of socially influential big technology companies like Google, Apple, and Facebook. If death is the spectacle, big tech is the lens. But for any particular individual's digital remains, how quickly might that spectacle fade?

On an occasion when I went to the offices of *The Observer* to be interviewed for a feature, the photographer asked about the subject of my book. When I explained, he told me a story about the Digital Railroad. He and many of his colleagues once stored their images on this site, which billed itself as a secure place for professional photographers to back up their precious bodies of work. At 5 p.m. in October 2008, however, an email arrived with an abrupt message. The company had been forced to cease operations, it explained, and Digital Railroad subscribers had 24 hours to download their material. Just 10 hours later, however, the website had closed, leaving many photographers with no apparent recourse to retrieve their images (Ngo, 2008). More recently, in a November 2018 blog post, Flickr announced (Stadlen, 2018) that it had changed its T&Cs and would shortly begin culling photographs from free accounts, a process that started in February 2019 (Kleinman, 2019). 'Storing tens of billions of Flicker members' photographs is staggeringly expensive', Flicker's blog said (Stadlen, 2018).

One of the people I interviewed in the course of my research was a filmmaker based in Los Angeles. As someone who works in digital media and who cares about the preservation of his own work, he is haunted by the possibility of its loss. 'We've gone tapeless now, right, and so everything is filed on cards or drives', he said. 'If you have money and your private studio then there's mainframe backups and stuff like that. But if you're the average person, just trucking along and making your stuff and shooting photos, you're relying on spinning discs and now more solid-state stuff. You're relying on things to preserve that media in a way that's not built to be long lasting' (Kasket, 2019, p. 227)[4]. My interviewee cited several fellow artists who had lost significant portions of their bodies of work when their laptops 'died'.

I am one of those average people myself, trucking along and making my stuff and shooting photos. You probably are too. My photographs are all on iCloud, behind layers of password protection. Other than what is published in paperback form, and scribbled in a handful of notebooks, most of my writing is digitally stored. Largely because I am an expatriate, far from my home, I have used Facebook to chart the first eight years of my daughter's life, and I am reliant on email and messenger apps to communicate with family. But I would do well to remember that hardware, software, and coding will inevitably change. Companies will fail. Terms and conditions will alter. And companies will jettison data when they become too expensive to store, making their decisions based on the bottom line. Sometimes I will find out in advance and will be able to act. Sometimes I will not.

Sobered by the extent to which big tech now controls our information, Sir Tim Berners-Lee (2018), the inventor of the Internet, has argued for a decentralised Web. Perhaps there is no better illustration of big tech's control over us than the fact that they often continue governing our information even when we die. There are doubtless well-intentioned people at Facebook, ethical people who want to build better systems for managing the data of the dead. Ultimately, however, anything they develop will still constitute big tech's writing the rules, maintaining ultimate control over how—and how long—we and our loved ones will be remembered in the world. Companies like this are not governed by sentiment, philanthropy, or a commitment to preserving the historical records of ordinary people's lives. At the point where our posthumously persistent data drain the coffers too much, social media will likely abandon the burgeoning digital cemeteries to ruin and vanishment.

My mother has boxes of family documents, going back many generations: photographs, letters, legal documents, and family trees. I store my own information almost exclusively in digital form. Unless I go 'old school' and start printing things out into more stable, controllable formats, there is a good chance that my descendants will know more about my great grandmother than they know about me. There is a good chance that I will lose access to images of and correspondences with deceased friends, unless I download them from the places where they are currently stored. There is a good chance that the historians of the future will find it easier to access an ancient Egyptian papyrus scroll than a MySpace account from 2004, especially in light of massive data losses from that site in early 2019 (Day, 2019). There is a good chance that the amateur genealogists of the future—far from being overwhelmed by surplus data—might be unable to locate any information *at all* about their 21st century ancestors, finding that it is in an unreadable format or has been culled from overheating servers.

Online is not forever. Immortality is not possible, and leaving something of your life behind is not necessary or required. Nevertheless, it may be something that you would like to do, for the benefit of your loved ones, your descendants, or even history. If that is the case, be wary of putting all your memory eggs into one digital basket, especially if that basket is being carried by a big technology company. Even the biggest redwood can fall, chopped down by an axe or gradually rotted from the inside. Imagine that one fine morning, a few years hence, you awake to a notification on your phone. You don't even *have* Facebook notifications enabled on your phone, and yet somehow there it is.

*Dear Facebook User,* this imagined notification might read. *For 20 years, we've been there as you shared good times and memories with your Facebook friends. But all good things must eventually come to an end. Click here for instructions and a full press release…*

## COMING TO TERMS WITH OUR FINITE DIGITAL AFTERLIVES

The author of *With the End in Mind* calls 'legacy' a 'loaded word' (Mannix, 2019, p. 233). Loaded, indeed, for it overflows with meanings and forms. We may carefully plan and craft our legacies, consciously designing them. Others may define our legacy for us, interweaving what we left behind with what we meant to them. Legacies may be tangible or intangible, financial or sentimental, material or digital. If legacy is a loaded word, then *digital legacy* is a loaded concept. The question of whether our Digital Afterlives are beneficial to individuals and society seems to be one of the dilemmas of our age.

Many of us associate digital legacy or Digital Afterlives with the social media profiles that often outlive their users. Perhaps our minds gravitate there because heavily-used social media are like digital autobiographies, full of personal information with emotional and relational significance. If you lack a Facebook, Twitter, or Instagram account, however, do not imagine that you have no digital legacy. Nearly everyone has digitally stored assets, documents, and online accounts of financial and pragmatic significance to their heirs. The contents of email account(s) and the text-message threads on computers and phones are highly personal, sometimes sensitive, archives of material. Our devices can track all the locations we have ever been; our browsers keep logs of the websites we have visited; and our search engines store the search terms that we use. Our devices and cloud storage accounts are full of text documents, images, audio, and video that trace the stories of our lives. On one hand, the stringent password protections that adopt in service of data protection can mean everything is inaccessible after we've gone, by accident or design. On the other, our loved ones may experience suffering through having too *much* access to private information.

When our digitally stored material is available to loved ones after we have gone, or when it is not, is that for good or for ill? Depending as it does on individual situations and perspectives, there is no straightforward answer, and a number of tricky issues can arise. Grief is idiosyncratic, and a digital legacy that is critically important for one mourner may be exquisitely painful for another. Legacies can be a mixed bag—for example, a Facebook profile containing important sentimental material may also have troubling elements. Many of us overestimate the amount of control or ownership that we have over our digital material; for example, the contents of an iTunes library cannot be bequeathed or transferred. The wishes of the deceased can conflict with that of mourners—for example, someone may arrange to send emails to loved ones posthumously, which may or may not be welcome and could be aversive.

The form, function, and management of digital legacies are all rapidly evolving. Sometimes they are controlled and managed by technology companies, rather than people who knew the deceased. It is tempting to throw up our hands and assume that there is nothing that we can do to assert a greater level of control. There are, however, a number of general principles that we can follow and adapt to our wishes and circumstances. Where control over, access to, or ownership of digital material are concerned, we must always assess, never assume. Digital legacies are often not subject to the same laws and systems as physical possessions. If the contents of an online account are important to current and/or future generations and the ownership of that account is nontransferable, those contents must be moved to a different place and/or translated into a different format if they are to be preserved. Entrusting the long-term management of precious personal data to third parties is likely not the safest option.

Second, we have become digital hoarders through both intent and through default. The digitally stored materials we leave behind are often voluminous archives of essential and unimportant data jumbled together. Consider capturing and storing less data, cleaning your digital house frequently, and deleting extraneous files. Organise important data into clearly labelled locations and ensure that they are accessible to their intended stewards after you are gone.

The word 'legacy' is derived from the Latin word 'legatus', meaning 'person delegated'. A large percentage of the remains we leave behind in the world may be in digital form, so include conversations about your wishes for your digital remains within your general estate planning. Identify a trusted person to be your 'digital executor' but ensure that this is done with discussion and consent. This is not yet a legal role, and it is potentially a complex and enduring one, especially in comparison with executing a physical estate. Consider what a digital executor may need to carry out your instructions—the access password to your smartphone, for example.

## CONCLUSION

Remember that online is *not* forever. Your digitally stored material will likely be most important to your loved ones in the immediate and medium term, but it may vanish entirely when hardware, software, and company fortunes inevitably change and evolve. Curated material legacies in more stable formats—photo books, paper documents, sentimental physical possessions—may better stand the test of time, as may oral stories and traditions passed down the generations. Legacy is multifaceted. Even if your entire digital archive and all of your physical possessions were to vanish, you would still have a legacy. 'Whatever actions they may take with the deliberate intention of shaping their legacy', Mannix says, speaking of people who are dying, 'they may well be unaware of the multiple, nuanced effects that they have already had on people's lives' (Mannix, 2019, p. 233). The same will be true of you, when your time comes.

## NOTES

1. Personal communication from Marc Saner, as interviewed by Elaine Kasket and published in Kasket (2019).
2. Personal communication from Gary Burks, as interviewed by Elaine Kasket and published in Kasket (2019).
3. Personal communication from Jed Brubaker, as interviewed by Elaine Kasket and published in Kasket (2019).
4. Personal communication from Greg King, as interviewed by Elaine Kasket and published in Kasket (2019).

## REFERENCES

Ariès, P. (1976). *Western attitudes toward death: From the middle ages to the present.* London: Marion Boyars Publishers Ltd.

Berners-Lee, T. (2018, September 29). One small step for the Web...[Blog Post]. *Medium: Technology.* Accessed 12 June 2019. Available on https://medium.com/@timberners_lee/one-small-step-for-the-web-87f92217d085

Brooker, C. (Writer), &Harris, O. (Director) (2013, 11 February). *Be right back* [Television Series Episode]. In *Black Mirror,* Channel 4, UK.

Brubaker, J. (2015). *Death, identity and the social network* [Doctoral Thesis]. UC Irvine. ProQuest ID: Brubaker_uci_0030D_13596. Merritt ID: ark:/13030/m5mh29sx. Available on https://escholarship.org/uc/item/6cn0s1xd

Cumiskey, K. M., & Hjorth, L. (2017). *Haunting hands: Mobile media practices and loss*. New York: Oxford University Press.

Day, H. (2019, March 20). How the world responded to the MySpace data loss: And whatever happened to Friendster, Bebo and Vine? [Online article] *BBC3*. Accessed 17 June 2019. Available on https://www.bbc.co.uk/bbcthree/article/8935e719-174b-42fc-a37f-6d4441214d9a

Harper, S. (2010). Behind closed doors? Corpses and mourners in English and American funeral premises. In J. Hockey, C. Komaromy, & K. Woodthorpe (Eds.), *The matter of death: Space, place and materiality* (pp. 100–116). Basingstoke, Hampshire, UK: Palgrave Macmillan.

Hughes, C. (2019, May 19). Opinion: It's time to break up Facebook. *The New York Times*. Accessed 12 June 2019. Available on https://www.nytimes.com/2019/05/09/opinion/sunday/chris-hughes-facebook-zuckerberg.html

Jacobsen, M. H. (2016). 'Spectacular Death': Proposing a new fifth phase to Philippe Ariès's admirable history of death. *Humanities*, 5(2), 1–20. https://doi.org/10.3390/h5020019

Kasket, E. (2019). *All the ghosts in the machine: Illusions of immortality in the digital age*. London: Robinson/Little, Brown UK.

Kleinman, Z. (2019, February 5). Flickr starts culling users' photos [Online News Story]. *BBC News: Technology*. Accessed 12 June 2019. Available on https://www.bbc.co.uk/news/technology-47130138

Kondo, M. (2014). *The life-changing magic of tidying: A simple, effective way to banish clutter forever*. London: Vermillion.

Mannix, K. (2019). *With the End in Mind: How to Live and Die Well*. London: William Collins.

Ngo, D. (2008, October 29). Photo site Digital Railroad derailed completely [Online News Story]. *C/Net*. Accessed 12 June 2019. Available on https://www.cnet.com/news/photo-site-digital-railroad-derailed-completely/

Öhman, C. J., & Watson, D. (2019). Are the dead taking over Facebook? A big data approach to the future of death online. *Big Data & Society*. https://doi.org/10.1177/2053951719842540

Prensky, M. (2001). Digital natives, digital immigrants (Part 1). *On the Horizon*, 9(5), 1–6. https://doi.org/10.1108/10748120110424816

Sandberg, S. (2019, April 9). Making it easier to honor a loved one on Facebook after they pass away [Online Press Release]. Accessed 12 June 2019. Available on https://newsroom.fb.com/news/2019/04/updates-to-memorialization/

Stadlen, A. (2018, November 1). Why we're changing Flickr free accounts [Blog Post]. *FlickrBlog*. Accessed 12 June 2019. Available on https://blog.flickr.net/en/2018/11/01/changing-flickr-free-accounts-1000-photos/

Walter, T (2005). Three ways to arrange a funeral: Mortuary variation in the modern West. *Mortality*, 10(3), 173–192. https://doi.org/10.1080/13576270500178369

Zahradnik, F. (2019, 21 February) How to find your location history in Google Maps or iPhone: Here's how to see your location history and opt in or out [Online Article]. *Lifewire*. Accessed 12 June 2019. Available on https://www.lifewire.com/location-history-google-maps-iphone-1683392

# CHAPTER 3

# Posthumous Digital Material

## *Does It 'Live On' in Survivors' Accounts of Their Dead?*

Mórna O'Connor

## CONTENTS

| | |
|---|---|
| Introduction | 39 |
| Literature and Background | 40 |
| Material Objects in Grief and Posthumous Accounts | 42 |
| Digital Objects in Grief and Posthumous Accounts | 43 |
| The Research | 43 |
| Findings | 44 |
| Non-Engagement Narrated as Relational Strength | 44 |
| Deceased and Relationship Narrated as Greater Than Their Digital Parts | 46 |
| Material Relativised to Protect Narrative | 48 |
| Material Narrated as Fuelling Harmful Hagiography | 49 |
| Discussion | 51 |
| Conclusion | 54 |
| Acknowledgements | 54 |
| References | 54 |

## INTRODUCTION

Contemporary grief theory accentuates the possibility for the bereaved of retaining a relationship with their dead, wherein a posthumous account of the deceased with which to continuingly relate is central. Bereaved people's posthumous accounts of their dead are not, however, about recounting agreed histories and objective facts about lives lived. Rather, they involve grievers' open-ended, creative storying of their departed; drawing on the life of the dead, but told through the prism of the ongoing, changing experiences of their socio-culturally situated bereaved. The availability of digital records of the life and relationships of their dead to today's bereaved would appear to disrupt the creative blending of history and story entailed in these posthumous accounts.

This chapter explores how digital traces of the in-life activity and correspondence of the dead figure in survivors' storying of their dead, and whether the technical possibility for the afterlife of such material bears out in practice for grievers. To explore this, longitudinal qualitative data are presented from four interviews with a bereaved young woman, Sarah, as she told the story of her late sister, Leah, and their relationship, with respect to the sisters' extensive text correspondence. The central argument of this chapter is that, for this survivor, the technical potential for digital traces of her dead to 'live on' is only realised to the extent that this material is woven into a posthumous account crafted around the griever's ongoing life and experiences. It is this survivor's creative narration of this digital material into a living posthumous account, blending the history of the dead with the ongoing story of the bereaved, which accords it continuing currency, relevance and vitality; and the potential to 'live on'.

## LITERATURE AND BACKGROUND

Central to the *Continuing Bonds* model in contemporary grief theory, is the development by bereaved people of representations of their dead with which to continue the bond. If grieving is about living *with* the dead rather than *without* them, survivors need a representation of their deceased to integrate into their continuing lives and with which to ongoingly relate (Howarth, 2007; Walter, 1996). In Walter's original (1996) exposition of the role of survivors' representations of their dead in grief and bond continuation, the development by the bereaved of a biography of their dead was central. Durability of posthumous biographies was tied to their accuracy, verisimilitude and agreement amongst other bereaved, with the aim of communally 'reconstruct[ing] what the deceased was actually like, what they actually did and how they actually died' (Walter, 1996 p. 19).

Since Walter's pivotal paper, the significance of posthumous representations of the dead in bond continuation has been widely accepted in grief scholarship and practice. However, whether grievers' posthumous representations of their dead need be true, accurate, or agreed upon has shifted. Following critique from Stroebe (1997), Walter retracted his 1996 invocation of truth, accuracy, and agreement with respect to grievers' representations of their dead; a posthumous biography 'need not be true or agreed. All it needs is to be good enough for practical purposes' (1997, p. 263). Academic and grief counselling contributions have since further challenged this relationship between 'the truth' about a life, and what is needed by the bereaved, as they story their dead (Árnason, 2000; Caswell, 2011; Hedtke & Winslade, 2016; Pearce, 2011).

In Árnason's (2000) extension to Walter's model, truth, accuracy, and agreement are secondary to survivors' ability to forge stories of their dead that are malleable to their ongoing needs, values, and experiences. Rather, they are fluid, creative acts of storytelling, wherein grievers ongoingly narrate their deceased and their relationship to them in light of their unfolding experience. Binding biography and autobiography, truth and testimony, these 'creative achievements of "emplottment" and characterisation' (Árnason, 2000, p. 189) are as much about narrator as narrated, such that 'in constructing a biography of the deceased the bereaved simultaneously create a story of themselves and their relationship with the deceased'. Árnason also emphasised the significance of socio-cultural influences in the development of posthumous stories; they are shaped by cultural expectations about what constitutes good relationships and lives, and forged in dialogue with other bereaved. Thus, per Árnason (2000, p. 202), rather than biographies of the dead, survivors' formulations of their dead are better conceived as 'stories of the bereaved'.

In their grief counselling text 'The Crafting of Grief', Hedtke and Winslade (2016) conceive of grief and posthumous storying as a craft that bereaved people live out rather than achieve. In this account, survivors craft stories of their dead and grief from the raw materials of their shifting preferences, principles, and value systems, those of other mourners, socio-cultural repositories and tropes of grief and posthumous storying, and in the company of, and in dialogue, with their imagined dead. The open-endedness of posthumous stories, and their inextricable tie to the ongoing life of the bereaved, are expressed in Hedtke and Winslade's terminology. Stories of grief and of the dead are crafted in the course of being lived out; a 'lived story of grief', rather than a creative achievement (2016, p. 19). These creative, narrative, relational accounts of the dead, which interweave history and story, fact and construct, record and rendering, make for posthumous representations that live on because they are born of, and continuingly pertinent to, survivors' ongoing lives.

Material Objects in Grief and Posthumous Accounts

> She's everywhere and nowhere. She lives in things. Her hand-
> writing scrawled on notes in postcards sent. She lives in trinkets
> collected, the tattoos on my arms, in the jeans I still wear, she's
> in this jumper, but that's just a turtleneck from Next, is it really
> her?
>
> (PERKIN, 2019, P. 53)

Established bodies of anthropological, psychological, psychiatric, and sociological literature provide accounts of the role of material objects relating to the dead in grieving and bond continuation. Diverse material culture relating to the dead—chairs, photographs, watches, books, let-ters, remote controls, rolling pins, rings, cars, hairbrushes, teddies, and turtlenecks from Next—can play a role for survivors. They can function as linking objects between bereaved and departed (Volkan, 1972; Wheeler, 1999), as metonyms for dead people and relationships past (Dasté, 2007; Gibson, 2004) and evoke memories of the dead (Pollack, 2007; Turley & O'Donohoe, 2012). They can also represent sites for negotiation of post-humous narratives amongst grievers (Gibson, 2008); and entail shifting narratives and registers of meaning and value over time (Gibson, 2010). Further, material effects can bridge corporeal presence and absence (Worden, 1991), represent absence and the absent (Aytemiz, 2013), and embed the deceased into the continuing lives and conversations of grief communities (Gibson, 2008; Hallam & Hockey, 2001).

Though the role, meaning, and significance of objects of the dead varies within and across grief experiences, the importance of material objects in bond continuation and development of posthumous accounts of the dead is clear.

The active role that the physical 'stuff' of the dead can have for survi-vors has been termed an 'afterlife' (Simpson, 2014, p. 1), wherein objects can have 'active life presences' (Turkle, 2007, p. 9) and be 'active partners with bereaved people' (Turley & O'Donohoe, 2012, p. 1333). Since mate-rial objects are embedded in the biographies and identities of individuals (Hoskins, 2006), and mediate relationships, entailing what Komter (2001, p. 59) called 'trajectories between persons', they are natural, physical sites for posthumous formulations of, and continuing relationships with, the corporeally absent to whom they relate.

Digital Objects in Grief and Posthumous Accounts

Claims about the long-term posthumous persistence of the digital remains of lives and relationships have been tempered, as impermanence of data formats and machine architectures, incompatibilities between old and ever-new media, and shifts in language comprehension over time undercut the indefinite accessibility, legibility, and comprehension of material (Bryson, 2012; Jones, 2004; Kasket, 2019). Moreover, even when material persists in the short term, its form and availability for survivors is by no means given or fixed, and gaining and maintaining access to the accounts, profiles, and devices of the dead can be a byzantine affair (Kasket, 2019).

However, notwithstanding what survivors *cannot* access, there are, in most cases, digital traces of the lives and relationships of their recently departed that grievers *can* access. Remains of the deceased's in-life digital activity, and grievers' digital correspondence with them, can, in the short term at minimum, remain varyingly and idiosyncratically available to those with whom the deceased was digitally connected in life, on the platforms, accounts, and devices they used to interact with the dead. This presents an interesting new strand to theories of posthumous storying, which involve, as the scholarship suggests, socio-culturally situated survivors crafting relational accounts of their dead that weave together history and story. If, in theory, we 'not only "live on" through our estate and in the memories of those we love but on their servers and in their hard disks' (Pitsillides, 2016, p. 114), how does this technical capacity for material to outlive people translate into the experiences of grievers as they story their dead? In practice, it is not clear how the availability of potentially extensive, detailed, searchable, sound-and-vision digital records relating to the dead and deceased-bereaved relationships plays into bereaved people's posthumous accounts of their dead. This chapter presents data from primary research exploring this, using the example of a young bereaved woman who, across four interviews, told the story of her late sister and the sisters' relationship with reference to their text correspondence.

## THE RESEARCH

This was a longitudinal, qualitative inquiry undertaken for my doctorate, wherein I conducted up to four semi-structured interviews with recently bereaved adults (18 years old or more and five years or less post-bereavement), grieving deceased adults with a range of death types. Serial interviews explored participants' uses and experiences over time of digital material relating to in-life activity of, and communication with, their deceased, to which respondents had access.

Given a paucity of empirical study of this phenomenon and the inquiry's exploratory ethos, I drew on a sociological approach that takes bereavements as study units and explores diverse material culture identified by grievers, and their longitudinal roles in grieving (Gibson, 2008). Therefore, rather than focusing on particular types or categories of digital material (e.g., intended for post-mortem consumption, generated peri-mortem, particular services, platforms, or devices), I asked broadly what digital culture relating to the deceased's in-life activities and communications was of use and significance for bereaved participants over time.

Using constructivist grounded theory (Charmaz, 2014), concurrent data collection and analysis identified many of lines of inquiry. This chapter presents data from one inquiry line: the role of digital records of the deceased's in-life activity and communication in bereaved participants' posthumous accounts of their dead. I show data from four interviews, conducted over 11 months in 2017/18, with a 29-year-old Scottish woman (Sarah, pseudonym), bereaved of her 23-year-old sister (Leah, pseudonym), who died suddenly and accidentally. Interviewing began six months post-bereavement, occurring at 12 to 16-week intervals.

## FINDINGS

Across four interviews, Sarah discussed a vast range of digital material relating to her late sister, with material fluctuating in role and significance over time. This chapter focuses on one piece of digital material, which featured in all four interviews: approximately five years of text messaging correspondence with Leah, including messages, images, links, and videos. Sarah changed phone shortly after Leah's death, turning off the old one and putting it safely away. Across her interviews, Sarah deliberated about turning on this old, powered-off mobile phone and looking through the texts. The following section presents four ways in which Sarah narrated these texts—and the possibility of reading them—in her four interviews.

### Non-Engagement Narrated as Relational Strength

This section illustrates how Sarah uses her choice not to view the texts as a narrative device in support of an emerging account of her sister and their relationship. This account is shaped by Sarah's wish to avoid the imagined pain of viewing the messages, and in relation to the grief of her remaining sister, Betty.

In her first interview, six months after Leah's death, Sarah was ambivalent about this old phone and the text correspondence with Leah on it. She had taken steps to keep the phone, yet did not know if she wanted to turn it on and look at the messages.

> …they were doing some phone drive at work…but I didn't want to give mine away because I know I have messages from Leah…I haven't turned it on since I got my new phone but I might, I might not. I don't know.

Having these messages allayed Sarah's fear that she would forget details about Leah and the sisters' relationship over time. The texts were a soothing antidote to this fear, offering an external, objective, and authentic record of Leah and their relationship; the most 'real' rendering of Leah now possible. Though unable to look through the texts at this point, Sarah was comforted by the thought that this material— and the unadulterated view of Leah and their relationship she felt they held—would be available to her in an imagined future when she needs these jogs to memory.

> I just don't feel able [to turn on the phone] now but I am very comforted by the fact that it will be there y'know…when I do need it… maybe…that I'd forget how her laugh sounds or I'd forget what she looks like or…and I'll need it then.

Though citing the pain of seeing such vivid portrayals of Leah and their relationship as what precludes her from engaging with the texts, Sarah also narrates this non-engagement with the messages as indicating the strength of the sisters' relationship. Owing to the strength of her in-life bond with Leah, Sarah does not need this material to evoke what she already knows. Sarah further supported this narrative by drawing a comparison with her other sister, Betty's, greater need for digital material relating to Leah. In Sarah's telling, Betty is much more reliant on, and regularly engages with, all digital material relating to Leah available to her because of her and Leah's sometimes-difficult relationship. In Sarah's view, Betty's greater need for this material is because she is grieving a more complicated relationship. Sarah's need for the material is less, as she and Leah 'were always very close'.

> I don't think I'd put as much importance on it that Betty would…
> She doesn't want to let go of a thing whereas…I'd have a less…less, you know, a need for it

Sarah narrates her non-reliance on the text messages in a relational way. It not only signifies her bond with Leah in its own right, but is amplified when compared to Betty's relative dependence on the Leah-related digital material available to her; the sisters' respective uses of material mapping onto their in-life relationships with Leah. Sarah narrates her non-engagement with the messages as supporting a building narrative about the comparative strength of her and Leah's relationship. This narrative fortifies Sarah's choice not to view these painful messages, and is, therefore, set into her unfolding needs (to avoid exposure to painful material), as well as set into her ongoing relationships (comparison with her remaining sister, Betty).

### Deceased and Relationship Narrated as Greater Than Their Digital Parts

At interview two, Sarah deploys her wish to avoid these too-vivid messages, and consequent confidence in her own memories of Leah, in service of her emerging account of her late sister and their relationship. Ten months after Leah's death, Sarah is still deliberating about turning on the phone and she unpacked the significance of one particularly important message on it. Leah and Sarah attended a music festival together two years prior to Leah's death. The following year, unable to attend the festival, Leah texted Sarah during it:

> …she wasn't able to come home for festivals and stuff, so she texted me at [festival name] last year at the exact same date and said 'Do you remember this time last year, we were running round the field? We'd taken mushrooms and were pretending to be horses' It was just like 'yeah, we'll do it again next year'

The significance of this message for Sarah is layered. It is connected to Leah having written the message: 'even the words of that message', and the enactment of the sisters' relationship it entails; Leah remembered this time fondly and made the effort to communicate this to Sarah.

Given the layers of detail, meaning, and memory in this message, Sarah articulated a growing feeling that not accessing it, and forgetting these painful relational minutiae, might be a good thing. She begins to narrate the loss of these previously treasured records of Leah and their relationship as preferable to the pain of their availability. Now, on her previously held fear of forgetting Leah and the sisters' relationship, Sarah said:

> I don't think I have that anymore, like I've thought about that and sometimes I think 'fuck, it would be better to forget than this', it might make it easier

Wedded to this turn towards forgetting painful digital detail is an attendant narrative about Leah and the sisters' relationship as having been greater than their digital traces.

This narrative also entails a burgeoning trust in Sarah's own memory of Leah and the sisters' relationship, over the digital remains of them. Though still viewed as imprecise and subjective, Sarah now articulates a confidence in her own memory of Leah and their relationship as providing what she needs.

> I'm starting to come to an understanding, that I don't think you'll ever forget and whatever you remember, that's what you need really…I'm definitely not scared of it [forgetting] now

Sarah also connects this turn towards forgetting painful detail with her budding narrative about Leah and the sisters' relationship. Again, Sarah narrates her inclination away from viewing these painful messages as illustrative of the strength of her and Leah's relationship. Despite having such vivid evocations of Leah and the sisters' relationship at her disposal in these texts, Sarah describes a greater trust in her own memories. Though more fallible and subjective, Sarah describes her memories as better placed to evoke and represent an individual and relationship of such depth, dimension and duration, only fragments of which are contained in this digital material.

> I don't need that stuff to remember, I have what I need of her myself…up here [points to head] cos we had great times…were great friends and it was a lot more than just…just online

Here, Sarah weaves her non-engagement with these painfully vivid texts, and her growing trust in her own memory, into an account of Leah and the sisters' relationship as having been more rich, multi-faceted, and comprehensive than the texts' detailed and evocative record of them.

## Material Relativised to Protect Narrative

In order to protect her account from information that might undercut it, here Sarah challenges the existence of any objective truth about Leah and the sisters' relationship. Instead, she narrates the digital material, and any truth it might support, as relative, and casts her own truth of Leah and their relationship as uniquely tailored to her particular needs.

Fourteen months after Leah's death, at Sarah's third interview, she has decided not to turn on the phone and read the messages; doing so would be too painful. However, she does not want the phone's contents cleared, nor for the phone to be recycled, instead considering a ceremony to mark the end of the texts' availability:

> Should I do some sort of ceremonial thing around it? I actually don't think I'd want to turn it on…I just think that it would be sad to read those things. Like I can almost imagine what would have been said in the different messages and different photographs and videos and things. But to have a smashing of the phone or something like that

Unlike her earlier fear of forgetting, Sarah now feels that losing these finer points about Leah and their relationship would be preferable to the pain of remembering, or engaging with content that would remind her of these painful nuances.

However, Sarah's wish to end the availability of this material is not just about closing the door on painful, high-fidelity memories of positive dimensions of Leah and their relationship. It is also rooted in the possibility that these unseen messages might furnish an unwanted view of Sarah and her interactions with Leah.

> …imagining some of them [texts] and I was like, 'Oh, god, don't even look at it, what if you said something bitchy like, you know?' Because I'm an awful bitch sometimes and I'm their big sister and I'm so bossy to them. Yes, so for my own kind of sense of self I was like, 'Don't look at them'…rose-tinted memories, yes

Not engaging with the texts enables Sarah to retain a soft-focus view of her relationship with Leah, guarding her emerging construct of their relationship and her role in it. This knowingly idealised rendering of the relationship, and suppression of detail that might upend it, shows a shift away from Sarah's earlier narration of the digital material as a repository of real, objective detail. Not viewing the texts both leaves narrative room for Sarah's personally tailored truth about their relationship, and guards it against inconsistent and dissonant information that might destabilise it.

> ...who's it [viewing the texts] for, like, everyone has their own truth...I just think I need to form my own sort of personal like, what she was, whether that's the truth either or not. Like, my own truth about it

To protect 'rose-tinted memories' of her role in the sisters' relationship, and her ongoing 'own kind of sense of self' from contradictory digital material, Sarah challenges the very notion of a single, objective truth about Leah and their relationship. She narrates truth itself, and the digital material that might convey it, as relative. Furthermore, Sarah narrates the subjectivity and inexactness of her own relative truth about Leah and their relationship as more uniquely suited to her needs than the digital material, as it is a function of her idiosyncratic view on, and relationship with, her late sister.

## Material Narrated as Fuelling Harmful Hagiography

Here, Sarah recruits the texts into a narrative about digital material being partial and unbalanced. She counteracts an unduly glowing account of Leah—propagated by the digital material relating her—that clashes with Sarah's account of her late sister, is damaging to the remaining sisters and draws on a narrative trope that is inconsistent with her account of Leah.

At her final interview, 17 months after Leah's death, Sarah has the phone in a safe place; she has not turned it on, wiped it, nor destroyed it ceremonially. From time to time, she checks it's there but has decided not to turn it on. Now, unable to recall specifics of the sisters' correspondence, Sarah minimises the messages' significance; they are likely stupid, general, and organisational.

> I don't know what we were talking about and I don't want to know...I can't remember what's on it...It was probably stupid conversations around arranging things, or just general chitchat or sharing info or whatever

This underplaying of the texts' significance takes root in a wider concern, described by Sarah, about the perils of overstating the significance of such material. Sarah is critical of others' use of Leah-related digital material to represent, remember, and evoke her, as, in her view, this fuels an uneven narrative, wherein positive representations of Leah dominate, and less favourable elements are underrepresented.

> …it's a tough one, Facebook, because people only put up what's in their control…, you know, it's easy to kind of adulate someone or glorify someone and it's all the good times…she was an awful bitch at times as well

For Sarah, other grievers' (particularly Leah's friends') lack of knowledge about the full complexity of Leah's character, and their focus on digital material relating to Leah that does not portray these unflattering aspects, is resulting in a false posthumous hagiography of her sister. This hagiography is not only troubling because of the disparity between the Leah Sarah knew and the angelic Leah being portrayed. More than this, in Sarah's view, this posthumous glorification, propagated by one-dimensional digital material, is causing harm to her and her other sister, Betty. This overly positive posthumous account of Leah gives credence to a harmful diminutive comparison with Betty and Sarah, the remaining 'shit sisters'.

> Everybody always talked about how great Leah was and how brilliant she was and a couple of months after she died, Betty would say 'Do you know, the shit sisters are left'

Furthermore, Sarah described this one-dimensional rendering of Leah—bolstered by unbalanced digital material relating to her—as even more potentially damaging for Betty, as it airbrushed out unsavoury elements of Betty and Leah's relationship, and Leah's character, that had negatively impacted Betty. Sarah worried that this posthumous whitewashing curtailed Betty's capacity to recognise the full dimensionality of Leah and their relationship, and therefore grieve the real Leah, rather than an exalted account of her.

> Leah was horrible to Betty at times…I think if there is anything bad [digitally], it would almost be a good thing…I almost wish it wasn't as great about her [Leah]…obviously, no one knew that

bitchy side of Leah more than us at home…I think all the good stuff is hard, especially for Betty…it was shit there was so much, how much fun she [Leah] was, how brilliant she was and all this. It wasn't the complete picture and I think that's just the way of social media and digital, you get a view that's controlled

Sarah's narration of the sisters' texts as low in value is tied into this broader concern about the dangers of using digital material as one-to-one representations of the dead, and the false, harmful post-death aggrandising it fosters. Casting the texts, and digital material generally, in this way, therefore conserves Sarah's own narrative about Leah (she wasn't an angel), counters an ill-fitting narrative trope (the dead are angels), protects herself and Betty from portrayal as 'the shit sisters', and diminishes a hagiography that glosses over Betty's actual experience. Thus, Sarah recruits the digital into a narrative that is shaped by her ongoing self-account, her ongoing relationships, and her socio-cultural setting.

## DISCUSSION

Across her interviews, Sarah harnesses the same unseen material as different narrative devices, which, depending on the given plotline, serve to underscore, undermine, suppress, buttress, and guard particular accounts of Leah and the sisters' relationship. Material portrayed in the first interview as evidence of the sisters' bond, and deployed in that narrative, is, in interview three, cast as insignificant, partial and unbalanced, when it threatens the narrative. Across the interviews, Sarah is creative with this material's truth-value. She tacks adroitly between narrating the material as a source of unassailable truth, and as biased and untrustworthy, depending on the narrative.

It is Sarah's creativity with the truth-value of this material that allows her to craft an account of Leah and their relationship around her continuing experience, with different strands of this experience influencing the narrative at different times. In the above illustration, these strands include: Sarah's fear of forgetting details of her sister and their relationship, her eventual forgetting and trust in her memory; her need to avoid painful material; her self-account about the sister she was, is and wishes to be; her value that one ought to tell the warts-'n'-all truth about their dead; her critique of a cultural tendency to posthumously idolise, and her ongoing relationships (comparison with, care for, and protection of her remaining sister).

This illustration builds to the central argument of this chapter; that the technical and theoretical capability for digital material emanating from lost lives and relationships to have an afterlife does not necessarily equate to an afterlife in the experience of survivors. Rather, in light of this illustration, I suggest that it is this survivor's creative deployment of this digital material in a shifting account of her dead—told through the prism of her own continuing, dynamic, and situated experiences—that breathes continued life into it. This survivor's deft interweaving of digital material into a posthumous narrative that blends history of the dead with ongoing story of the bereaved is what accords it continuing relevance, vitality, and meaning for her and therefore, the capacity to 'live on'.

This argument leads to some wider observations about the afterlife of digital material as it relates to the bereaved, and the emerging scholarship about it, and comments about its contribution to theories of posthumous storying. Despite the availability of precise, detailed, and voluminous digital material that would appear to disrupt creative posthumous storying, this chapter's illustration suggests that this material can be creatively narrated *into* grievers' posthumous accounts of their dead. Indeed, the very characteristics of the material that would seem to challenge creative storying (e.g., its detail about deceased-bereaved relationships), are themselves recruited into the narrative (i.e., not needing this detail is testament to our bond). In this sense, the practice of creative posthumous storying by socio-culturally situated survivors remains, but with digital material relating to the dead representing another element out of which story is wrought, and which presents novel opportunities for creative narration by the bereaved. It is thus an 'age-old practice in the "new world"' (Taylor & Harper, 2002, p. 439).

Relatedly, survivors' creative use of this material may take unexpected forms within particular grief experiences, which do not fit construal of the afterlife of digital material based on technical existence, persistence and accessibility. In this chapter's illustration, the digital material in question 'lives on' in the narrative of this bereaved sister despite, and perhaps *because*, it is never actually accessed. The texts' role in Sarah's narrative hinges on her rejecting its availability. Therefore, not only does this chapter's illustration suggest that a technically possible Digital Afterlife does not export simply into grievers' experience, it also suggests that the technical affordances that offer this afterlife in the abstract are themselves changed in the practice of posthumous storying. The material and its characteristics are modified in the course of being harnessed into the narrative—to serve and reflect the embedded social phenomenon—such that use in social practice mutates the imagined functionalities of the media. Thus, though the media here does enable, facilitate, and shape this practice, per the concept of mediatisation (Hepp, 2013), the practice simultaneously shapes the media (Refslund Christensen & Sandvik, 2016). This further undermines the contention that a technical capacity for material to have an afterlife can be transported unchanged into situated cultural practice.

Since the advent of electronic communication, technology has kindled hopes of persistence of, and communication with, the dead, wherein 'fantastic accounts of media presence...emphasized powers of the technology itself and suggested that its rational applications would eventually lead to ever more incredible boundaries between life and death' (Sconce, 2000, pp. 10–11). As we develop conceptions about the afterlife of digital material emanating from the lives of the departed, we must take care not to similarly overstate this material's power, by according it extraordinary properties abstracted from the meaning and use of these properties by situated human agents. In this time of exciting new technical possibilities that fire our cultural and scholarly imaginations, we must not fetishise these media and their capabilities in respect of a Digital Afterlife, forgetting the importance of human agency, and the role of people, cultures, and systems that construct and infuse such material with value, significance, and meaning (Steiner, 2001).

This chapter shows that, as with material objects of the dead, bereaved people's uses and experiences of digital objects of their dead are inextricable from particular temporalities, contexts, relationships, and sociocultural settings. The findings above shed light on this particularity in the case of one woman's experience over time, and therefore illustrates that the afterlife of digital material cannot be construed as universally applicable to, or uniform for, all grievers. Conceiving of digital traces of the dead as uniformly entailing an afterlife for survivors homogenises these particularities, and draws on normative, universalising discourses that flatten grief's diversity.

As to this, in this nascent area of scholarship, we must be aware that our concepts about post-death material imply particular notions about grieving, which may filter into clinical, social, and cultural understandings of it. Indeed, the phasic, linear model of grief that emerged from Kübler-Ross' (1969) descriptions of Genevan cancer patients' experiences of dying—though indirectly related to grief—have crystallised into a harmful, widely-cited prescription for 'normal' grieving. In contributing to the emerging discourse about the afterlife of digital material, we must recognise that professionals and lay people may calibrate their ideas and experiences of digital-age grieving against expectations drawn from our work. Thus, it is critical that our conceptions of the Digital Afterlife of the remains of lives lost and relationships past remain steeped in, and inextricable from, the particular and idiosyncratic contexts of their production. By doing this, we will protect and promote grief's diversity and be deliberate about not 'offering yet another model that could be taken up as a rigid prescription' (Hedtke & Winslade, 2016, p. 14).

## CONCLUSION

Today's grievers can have at their disposal digital records of lives of, and relationships with, their dead, which would appear to disrupt the construction of creative, relational, and shifting posthumous accounts of these dead. Given this seeming clash between creative posthumous storying and detailed digital records, this chapter explored how the technical capacity for digital material relating to the dead to 'live on' bears out as grievers posthumously construct their dead. Citing the longitudinal experiences of one grieving sister, I illustrated the thesis of this chapter, that whether and how digital material emanating from lost lives and relationships can be said to 'live on' for the recently bereaved is a function of its creative narration into living accounts by grievers in particular and fluid socio-cultural, experiential, and relational contexts.

## ACKNOWLEDGEMENTS

I would like to acknowledge Sarah's contribution to this research, particularly during this difficult time. I also wish to acknowledge the guidance and insights of my doctoral supervisors, Prof. Kristian Pollock, Prof. Heather Wharrad and Dr. Glenys Caswell, and external advisor, Dr. Elaine Kasket. The doctorate during which I undertook this research was funded by the University of Nottingham's Vice-Chancellor's Scholarship for Research Excellence (European Union).

## REFERENCES

Árnason, A. (2000). Biography, bereavement, story. *Mortality*, 5(2), 189–204.
Aytemiz, P. (2013). *Representing absence and the absent one: remembering and longing through mourning photography*. (PhD), Bilkent University, Ankara. Retrieved from http://repository.bilkent.edu.tr/handle/11693/17122

Bryson, J. J. (2012). Internet memory and life after death. *Bereavement Care*, *31*(2), 70–72.

Caswell, G. (2011). Personalisation in Scottish funerals: Individualised ritual or relational process? *Mortality*, *16*(3), 242–258. doi:10.1080/13576275.2011. 586124.

Charmaz, K. (2014). *Constructing grounded theory: A practical guide through qualitative analysis* (2nd ed.). London: Sage.

Dasté, O. (2007). The suitcase. In S. Turkle (Ed.), *Evocative objects: Things we think with* (pp. 244–249). Cambridge, MA: MIT Press.

Gibson, M. (2004). Melancholy objects. *Mortality*, *9*(4), 285–299. doi:10.1080/ 13576270412331329812.

Gibson, M. (2008). *Objects of the dead: Mourning and memory in everyday life*. Melbourne, AU: Melbourne University Press.

Gibson, M. (2010). Death and the transformation of objects and their value. *Thesis eleven*, *103*(1), 54–64. doi:10.1177/0725513610388988.

Hallam, E., & Hockey, J. (2001). *Death, memory and material culture*. Oxford: Berg.

Hedtke, L., & Winslade, J. (2016). *The crafting of grief: Constructing aesthetic responses to loss*. London: Routledge.

Hepp, A. (2013). *Cultures of mediatization*. Cambridge: Polity.

Hoskins, J. (2006). Agency, biography and objects. In C. Tilley, W. Keane, S. Küchler, M. Rowlands, & P. Spyer, (Eds.), *Handbook of material culture* (pp. 74–84). London: Sage.

Howarth, G. (2007). *Death and dying: A sociological introduction*. Cambridge: Polity.

Jones, S. (2004). 404 not found: The internet and the afterlife. *OMEGA - Journal of Death and Dying*, *49*(1), 83–88. doi:10.2190/8uuf-gleg-x6t5-unjm.

Kasket, E. (2019). *All the ghosts in the machine*. London: Robinson.

Komter, A. (2001). Heirlooms, nikes and bribes: Towards a sociology of things. *Sociology*, *35*(1), 59–75. doi:10.1017/S0038038501000049.

Kübler-Ross, E. (1969). *On death and dying*. New York: Macmillan.

Pearce, C. (2011). Girl, interrupted: An exploration into the experience of grief following the death of a mother in young women's narratives. *Mortality*, *16*(1), 35–53. doi:10.1080/13576275.2011.536000.

Perkin, J. (2019). *I'm not ready*. Bristol, UK: Self-published.

Pitsillides, S. (2016). Death and memory in the twenty-first century. In S. Groes (Ed.), *Memory in the twenty-first century: New critical perspectives from the arts, humanities and sciences* (pp. 113–118). London: Palgrave Macmillan.

Pollack, S. (2007). The rolling pin. In S. Turkle (Ed.), *Evocative objects: Things we think with* (pp. 224–231). Cambridge, MA: MIT Press.

Refslund Christensen, D., & Sandvik, K. (2016). Introduction: Mediating and remediating death. In D. Refslund Christensen, & K. Sandvik (Eds.), *Mediating and remediating death* (pp. 17–36). London: Routledge.

Sconce, J. (2000). *Haunted media: Electronic presence from telegraphy to television*. Durham, NC: Duke University Press.

Simpson, J. M. (2014). Materials for mourning: Bereavement literature and the afterlife of clothes. *Critical studies in fashion & beauty*, *5*(2), 253–270. doi:/10.1386/csfb.5.2.253_1.

Steiner, C. (2001). Rights of passage: On the liminal identity of art in the border zone. In F. Myers (Ed.), *The Empire of Things: Regimes of Value and Material Culture* (pp. 207–231). New Mexico, US: School of American Research Press.

Stroebe, M. (1997). From mourning and melancholia to bereavement and biography: An assessment of Walter's New Model of Grief. *Mortality, 2*(3), 255–262. doi:10.1080/714892787.

Taylor, A. S., & Harper, R. (2002). *Age-old practices in the 'new world': a study of gift-giving between teenage mobile phone users.* Paper presented at the Proceedings of the SIGCHI Conference on Human Factors in Computing Systems, Minnesota, USA.

Turkle, S. (2007). *Evocative objects: Things we think with.* Cambridge, MA: MIT press.

Turley, D., & O'Donohoe, S. (2012). The sadness of lives and the comfort of things: Goods as evocative objects in bereavement. *Journal of Marketing Management, 28*(11–12), 1331–1353. doi:10.1080/0267257X.2012.691528.

Volkan, V. D. (1972). The linking objects of pathological mourners. *Archives of General Psychiatry, 27*(2), 215–221. doi:10.1001/archpsyc. 1972.01750260061009.

Walter, T. (1996). A new model of grief: Bereavement and biography. *Mortality, 1*(1), 7–25. doi:10.1080/713685822.

Walter, T. (1997). Letting go and keeping hold: A reply to Stroebe. *Mortality, 2*(3), 263–266. doi:10.1080/713685875.

Walter, T. (1999). *On bereavement: The culture of grief.* London: McGraw-Hill Education.

Wheeler, I. (1999). The role of linking objects in parental bereavement. *OMEGA - Journal of Death and Dying, 38*(4), 289–296. doi:10.2190/ e2x1-tm7g-gdcq-ulpw.

Worden, J. W. (1991). *Grief counselling and grief therapy: A handbook for the mental health practitioner.* New York: Springer.

# CHAPTER 4

# The Transition from Life to the Digital Afterlife

*Thanatechnology and Its Impact on Grief*

Carla Sofka

## CONTENTS

Introduction   57
The Transition from Life to the Digital Afterlife   58
Documenting the End of Life   59
Planning for One's Digital Afterlife: Digital Estate Planning   60
Contemplating Two-Way Immortality: Posthumous Personhood through a Digital Afterlife and the Impact on the Bereavement Process   61
Continuing Bonds   61
Second Loss: The Domino Effect   64
Communities of Remembrance and Support as an Element of the Digital Afterlife   65
Digital Survivor Advocacy: The Power of the Hashtag to Extend One's Digital Afterlife   67
Conclusion   68
References   70

## INTRODUCTION

When I began studying thanatology in 1983, public conversations about death and grief were largely taboo. This shifted drastically in the mid-1990s, as information about end of life care, death, and grief proliferated on the 'World Wide Web' and discussions about these topics became more prevalent using new types of 'thanatechnology' (Sofka, 1997). In 2004, Kastenbaum used the term 'assisted immortality' to capture new possibilities for technology-assisted survival and posed the following question: 'What would be a meaningful or essential form of survival, and would I make use of a technological assist, if available?' (p. 460). As the evolution of digital technology and artificial intelligence creates new and unique opportunities for achieving digital immortality (Sofka, Gibson, & Silberman, 2017), this question becomes increasingly relevant.

Today, according to Leland (2018), 'death is having a moment in the sun'. As part of the *Death Positive Movement*, people attend *Death Cafes* (www.deathcafe.com) and openly discuss their wishes about end of life care (https://theconversationsproject.org; https://www.mywishes.co.uk/). The dead are no longer sequestrated from the living (Brubaker, Hayes, & Dourish, 2013; Walter, Hourizi, Moncur, & Pitsillides, 2011–2012; Walter, 2015, 2017), and the expression of grief is more public (Sofka, Cupit, & Gilbert, 2012; Walter, 2008). 'Digital Death Day' events have been held, encouraging people to plan for their digital legacies and to contemplate their Digital Afterlives. There is a growing potential for a person's decisions about their Digital Afterlife to have an impact on their own and their loved ones' experiences with impending death and grief.

Thanatechnology is changing the way that our society deals with impending death, grief, and tragedy. This chapter will identify ways that digital and social media are being used by the dying to document their end of life experiences, resulting in the creation of a digital record of their journey and a component of their Digital Afterlife. The importance of digital estate planning is discussed, and resources to assist with this process are identified. Opportunities for an ongoing technology-mediated connection with the deceased and their impact on the bereaved, including the potential for experiencing second loss, are explored. New phenomena illustrating the involvement of strangers and the role of digital survivor advocacy in one's Digital Afterlife are described. The development of 'netiquette' to guide society in their use of thanatechnology is acknowledged, and implications for public death education and future research are presented.

## THE TRANSITION FROM LIFE TO THE DIGITAL AFTERLIFE

Imagine that you have just been diagnosed with a life-threatening or a terminal illness. In addition to making health-care related decisions, you must consider how to share the news with family and friends, whether or not you wish to document your experiences (privately and/or publicly), and contemplate issues related to planning for your Digital Afterlife.

## DOCUMENTING THE END OF LIFE

What factors influence a person's decision about how to share news regarding a life-threatening illness and whether or not to document their end of life journey? First, access to digital technology and/or online resources must be considered. The Pew Research Center (2018) reported that 95% of Americans own a cell phone, with 77% being smartphones. However, some Americans still report no Internet usage: 27% of adults 65 and older, 29% of those with less than a high-school education, and 18% of individuals who live in households earning less than $30,000 a year (Anderson, Perrin, Jiang, & Kumar, 2019).

Second, one's tendencies regarding the public *versus* private expression of personal experiences (Burkell, Fortier, Wong, & Simpson, 2014; Gibson, 2011) will have a significant impact on the presence of a public digital legacy. Options for technology-mediated sharing about one's end of life journey include blogging (Sofka, 2012), creating video logs ('vlogs'), posting on social networking sites (SNS), or utilising a website designed for this specific purpose (e.g., www.CaringBridge.org or www.HospiceJourney.org).

Digitally documenting one's end of life journey serves several purposes. In addition to providing practical benefits to one's caregivers (coordinating and asking for assistance with daily tasks), the postings provide a digital record for those whose geographic location precludes face-to-face involvement (Mehring, 2013). Along with the convenience of sharing information with multiple recipients, dying individuals and their caregivers receive psychological support, knowing that people care (Anderson, 2011).

Rachman's (2016) description of recent end of life memoirs and potential motives for documenting one's impending demise noted another motive: to create because nobody [physically] endures, and create in order that you endure. A highly visible example of documenting one's end of life journey while creating a Digital Afterlife is that of Randy Pausch, a Carnegie Mellon professor whose journey with pancreatic cancer between his diagnosis in 2006 and his death on July 25, 2008 was captured in an online blog (https://www.cs.cmu.edu/~pausch/news/index.html). In addition to the practical goal of communicating information expediently, Dr. Pausch was known for openness about his illness and his commitment to raising awareness (Rosenzweig, 2018).

Public awareness of his impending death skyrocketed in September 2007 when the video of his *Last Lecture* (a talk presumed to be a professor's final opportunity to impart their wisdom) went viral. Pausch noted that 'Under the ruse of giving an academic lecture, I was trying to put myself in a bottle that would one day wash up on the beach for my children' (Pausch & Zaslow, 2008), who were all under age 6 at the time. Dr. Pausch's Digital Afterlife continues via several Facebook pages and over 19 million YouTube views of his lecture.

This documentation becomes an important component of one's Digital Afterlife, especially as a means of connection with the deceased for individuals who were too young at the time to form their own memories. However, potential challenges and dilemmas related to these resources exist. Reaching agreement about their use can be difficult, particularly if different styles of coping with the dying process exist across family members. For example, the decision by this author's relative to use CaringBridge as a tool to update family members and obtain support was abruptly reversed following her realisation that the person who was ill (in addition to being extremely private and not a technology user) had become uncomfortable with this information-sharing mechanism. Disagreement about maintaining this type of site and/or to continue posting after a death could put this element of one's Digital Afterlife at risk.

Kasket's (2019) detailed account of Lucy Watt's efforts to document her experiences with a life-limiting illness identifies another challenge with preserving someone's Digital Afterlife. What steps would guarantee that Lucy's digital legacy would remain accessible?

## PLANNING FOR ONE'S DIGITAL AFTERLIFE: DIGITAL ESTATE PLANNING

Efforts to help people get their 'digital ducks in a row' began with Carroll and Romano (2011), who published one of the first books and created a website that provides information about the topic (www.thedigitalbeyond.com). Vered Shavit (n.d.) launched her 'Digital Dust' website with practical resources after the sudden death of her brother in 2011, and James Norris created the Digital Legacy Association (DLA) in 2015 (www.digitallegacyassociation.org).

Numerous companies to assist with digital asset management have emerged; however, some companies have disappeared very quickly. Although resources to assist with digital estate planning are available (see the DLA's website or https://www.everplans.com/digital-estate), data from the

2018 Digital Death Survey (DDS) indicates the need for public education to encourage people to engage in this process. Only 14% of respondents were familiar with the policies, laws, and regulations that address what happens to online accounts when a user dies, and only 5% had documented their wishes regarding their social media accounts following their death (Norris, Sofka, & Kasket, 2018). Efforts to increase awareness of the importance of planning ahead for one's digital legacy are encouraged among adults as well as young adults when they become new users of digital technology and social media (Sofka, 2017a; Sofka, Gibson, & Silberman, 2017).

## CONTEMPLATING TWO-WAY IMMORTALITY: POSTHUMOUS PERSONHOOD THROUGH A DIGITAL AFTERLIFE AND THE IMPACT ON THE BEREAVEMENT PROCESS

In light of advances in artificial intelligence that have led to 'two-way interactions' with a digital representation of the deceased (Sofka, Gibson, & Silberman, 2017), will this alter our definition of death? How might the opportunity for ongoing interaction with a digital 'proxy' impact on the process of adjusting to a significant other's physical absence and one's subsequent grief?

AI researchers in the MIT Media lab are creating mechanisms for 'augmented eternity', a program that builds upon a person's digital archive to create an 'augmented-eternity bot' that evolves after physical death occurs (Matei, 2017). When contemplating the development of chatbots that can imitate human speech patterns, Leddy (2019) stated: 'With such sophisticated technology, the question is no longer what's possible but what's morally permissible. In the grey area between preservation and personality theft, there is a danger of too much holding on and not enough letting go' (para. 32). As these interactions begin to occur, understanding their impact on the bereavement process becomes crucial. Although most people do not currently have access to these types of interactions, many bereaved individuals are using digital and social media to stay connected with significant others who are deceased. These technology-mediated continuing bonds and their impact on the bereaved will now be discussed.

## CONTINUING BONDS

While conceptions about the process of coping with grief have evolved over time, Klass (2018) notes that maintaining a connection with the dead— a 'continuing bond'—is a common aspect of bereavement in all current models of grief. A growing body of literature has documented the use of digital and social media for this purpose (Balk & Varga, 2018; Cesare & Branstad, 2018; Irwin, 2018; Kasket, 2012, 2018, 2019). What might influence a bereaved person's engagement in technology-mediated communication? Does the presence of a Digital Afterlife have a positive or a negative impact on survivors' process of coping with grief?

Consider Kyleigh Leddy's (2019) description of her use of digital technology and social media to maintain a connection with her sister, Kaitlyn, who vanished in 2014. Kyleigh valued being able to 'see' her sister when she wanted by looking at photos online, dialling her number when she needed to hear her voice ('she would tell me to leave a message'—para. 8), and sending her texts. Leddy stated: 'As the years pass—I am now the age she was when she disappeared—I have come to know her better from the quotes she posted in her bio, the songs she cued in her iPod, the comments she left on her friend's photos. It's like getting to know someone through glimpses in a window, but it's better than nothing' (para. 29). Although Kaitlyn has not been declared legally deceased, perhaps these interactions can be considered a Digital Afterlife 'in limbo'.

Do individuals who use thanatechnology to connect with the deceased expect a response? Beliefs about sentience and agency after death are relevant. Respondents to a Digital Death Survey (DDS) were asked to rate the likeliness that the deceased experience ongoing 1) consciousness or existence; awareness of 2) loved one's activities; 3) non-technology-mediated communication; and 4) activity online, including messages sent to them or posted on social media (Norris, Sofka, & Kasket, 2018; Sofka, 2019). In addition, beliefs regarding whether the deceased become 'angelic' beings who can watch over and protect the living were also assessed (Table 4.1).

When asked if they had ever sent a message to a deceased person using a smartphone, social media, or any type of technology, 13% of the respondents said 'Yes'. Qualitative comments described reaching out on birthdays, the date of death, or events during which the deceased's presence was missed. For one respondent, sending messages on Facebook mirrored their communication when his friend was alive: 'I felt closer to him and less alone as I processed the pain of his loss'. Another respondent noted that while using virtual communication, the absence of a reply from the deceased felt 'less empty than real life'. Individuals who had not used technology-mediated communication described this behaviour as

TABLE 4.1    Personal Beliefs about Sentience and Agency after Death

| (N = 306) | Extremely likely | Somewhat likely | Unsure | Somewhat unlikely | Extremely unlikely |
|---|---|---|---|---|---|
| There is some form of ongoing consciousness or existence after death | 30.39% | 30.39% | 15.69% | 7.19% | 16.34% |
| The deceased experience some form of ongoing awareness of the activities of surviving loved ones | 20.26% | 30.39% | 19.61% | 10.78% | 18.95% |
| The deceased are aware of communication through non-technology-mediated means (e.g., talking to their picture, visiting their grave) | 15.03% | 24.18% | 21.90% | 14.38% | 24.51% |
| The deceased are aware of our activity online, including messages we send or post on social media | 5.23% | 10.13% | 27.12% | 18.95% | 38.56% |
| The deceased become "angelic" beings who can watch over and protect the living | 13.73% | 28.10% | 22.22% | 12.75% | 23.20% |

'bizarre', 'despicable', 'morbid', and an indicator of being 'unable to accept death' highlighting the idiosyncratic nature of grief.

Individuals who wish to reach out after death (labelled 'digital creators' by Bassett, 2018) can create and send text or video-based 'intentional' messages to significant others ('digital inheritors') through services such as SafeBeyond (marketed as 'Emotional Life Insurance') and GoneNotGone. These messages can be posted on the deceased's social media as a last farewell, or they can be sent to specific recipients on future dates, events, or locations (triggered by social media postings when the survivor visits a specific place). Approximately 14% of the DDS respondents reported being likely to create online messages such as this, with 21% being unsure and 65% being unlikely to do so. Masterson (2015) notes the wisdom of one company's decision to limit the delivery interval to 25 years to prevent descendants from being hassled by long-dead ancestors.

The impact of sending and/or receiving these types of messages and the inheritance of a deceased loved one's digital legacy—emails, social media accounts, and any other digital files—is beginning to be explored (see Bassett, 2018). Will 'digital initiators' prepare 'digital inheritors' in advance, or will this 'gift' be a surprise? Will receipt of someone's digital legacy be welcomed or create a burden? Do survivors have a moral duty to preserve someone's 'digital remains', and if not, would deletion count as 'harm to the deceased user' (Stokes, 2015)? For those with complicated relationships during life, will communication received after death exacerbate someone's grief? These questions merit attention.

## SECOND LOSS: THE DOMINO EFFECT

Psychoeducation about common reactions to loss and factors that impact on those reactions was an important component of my work with the bereaved and those who hoped to support them. This included validating the reality that the initial loss was accompanied by secondary losses—tangible or intangible (also known as psychosocial or symbolic losses) that coincided with or developed as a consequence of the initial loss (Rando, 1993). These secondary losses can be described as a 'domino effect' since that analogy captures the chain reaction of losses that frequently accompanies a death.

Bassett (2017) suggested the term 'second loss' to capture how the loss or deletion of digital memories would impact the bereaved, and Stokes (2015) contemplated the impact of the deletion of 'digital remains' or 'second death'. Based on information from the mass media, academic research, and anecdotal evidence, Kasket (2018) noted that 'we are seeing more and more anxiety about whether the online legacy of our dead will continue to be preserved' (p. 338).

Leddy's (2019) ability to maintain her technology-mediated bond with her sister changed unexpectedly after receiving a response to a text message that she sent to Kaitlyn's phone. Following a hopeful moment of thinking her sister was alive, she learned that the phone number had been reassigned, resulting in the need to mourn this additional loss. At one point, her mother suggested that Kaitlyn's Facebook account be deleted, wondering if it was inappropriate for Kaitlyn's online life to be 'paused with her random thoughts and photos on public display' (para. 27). Leddy stated: 'Ultimately we decided not to. It brings me too much comfort' (para. 28).

The list of new phenomena created by the use of thanatechnology to cope with grief continues to expand. As a result, the need becomes more urgent for helping professionals to be trained to provide support and guidance to the bereaved as they navigate these new situations (Sofka, 2017a, 2018a).

## COMMUNITIES OF REMEMBRANCE AND SUPPORT AS AN ELEMENT OF THE DIGITAL AFTERLIFE

The role of social media in relation to memorialisation/commemoration of the dead and the receipt of support while coping with grief is perhaps the most widely explored aspect of thanatechnology (for extensive reference lists, see Kasket, 2019; Sofka, 2018a; Wagner, 2018; Gotved, 2014; Sofka, Cupit, & Gilbert, 2012; and Walter, Hourizi, Moncur, & Pitsillides, 2011–2012). Figure 4.1 summarises the roles of digital and social media in coping with impending death and loss. Furthermore, the benefits and risks of their use to cope with grief are summarised in

FIGURE 4.1  Roles of digital and social media in coping with impending death and loss (Sofka, 2015, 2019*). *Note: Figure originally presented in 2015; revised for this chapter.

Sofka (2018a). Online communities of bereavement become a significant component of the deceased's Digital Afterlife and have an impact on the grief of those who knew them. Research has also recognised that a person's Digital Afterlife can involve individuals who did not know the deceased in life. Two of these phenomena—emotional rubbernecking and memorial trolling—and their potential impact on the bereaved will now be described.

DeGroot (2014) coined the term 'emotional rubberneckers' to describe 'online voyeurs who visit the Facebook memorials of strangers or distant acquaintances to read what others write and to post their own messages of grief' (p. 79). She noted that 'although the term rubbernecking has a negative connotation, emotional rubberneckers are not always seen as negative elements' (p. 82). Klastrup (2015) and Gibson (2015) both note that familiarity with the deceased can be created by media coverage of a death, with Klastrup (2015) using the term 'parasocial mourning' to describe the social media involvement that is prompted by curiosity.

However, when given the opportunity to describe their motives for participating in social media, strangers report being able to personally relate to some aspect of the situation such as identifying with the deceased's age or the cause of death (Sofka, 2018b). One survey respondent, unfamiliar with anyone in a car crash that occurred in this author's community (subsequently referred to as the '518 case'), posted messages of support to the bereaved on social media since his cousin died in an accident while he was in high school. I propose using the term 'experiential empathy' to capture the social media users' motive for becoming involved due to their ability to relate to other grievers based on a similar loss experience. Sadly, grieving the death of a stranger in cyberspace may be more socially acceptable than it is to express one's deep and heartfelt grief for a loved one in real life, where many people are ill-equipped to be supportive. In addition to alleviating feelings of loneliness and isolation, interacting with strangers in cyberspace is often perceived by the bereaved as helpful (Cesare & Branstad, 2018; Gibson, 2016; James, 2014; Sandberg & Grant, 2017).

On the other hand, there are times when the presence of strangers can be extremely distressing. According to Phillips (2015), memorial trolling or RIP trolling occurs when online instigators post abusive comments or insensitive images on SNS or social media. Her interviews with memorial trolls revealed that different beliefs about the appropriateness of publicly sharing one's grief, particularly by individuals who did not personally know the deceased, sometimes called 'grief tourists', appear to be at the heart of this phenomenon. Unlike this author's appreciation of the expression of 'experiential empathy' as beneficial to both the 'stranger' and the recipient, trolls described this behaviour as disingenuous, motivated by boredom, and 'a pathological need for attention masquerading as grief' (p. 84).

Even though the driver who caused the fatal crash in the '518 case' was speeding and texting at the time, one teen described 'inconsiderate people (who) took it upon themselves to use social media as a platform to accuse Chris (the deceased driver of the vehicle that was struck) of driving drunk, saying it was his fault'. One grieving friend was upset by a post on Chris' memorial page stating that 'he should have been a better driver'.

Anecdotal evidence suggests that the presence of strangers in online communities of bereavement has both benefits and potentially negative consequences. Additional research is merited in this area.

## DIGITAL SURVIVOR ADVOCACY: THE POWER OF THE HASHTAG TO EXTEND ONE'S DIGITAL AFTERLIFE

Some who survive traumatic loss channel their grief into preventive action (Trauma Foundation, 2001). In addition to adding a unique dimension to their significant other's Digital Afterlife, these 'survivor advocates' hope to prevent others from experiencing a similar loss through efforts that educate, raise awareness, and change behaviour and/or policy. Although non-technology-assisted survivor advocacy efforts have occurred for years, research about the impact of using digital and social media to achieve these goals is limited (For additional case studies involving death with dignity and the prevention of hate crimes, distracted driving, and suicide, see Sofka, 2017b).

Students who survived the mass shooting at Marjory Stoneman Douglas High School (MSD) in Parkland, Florida on 14 February 2018 put this strategy for coping with grief in the headlines. In addition to traditional advocacy (talking with the media and visiting elected officials), students used Twitter hashtags such as #NeverAgain and #MSDPickUpAPen to advocate for the passage of stricter gun control laws. Survivors organised a nationwide #MarchForOurLives (24 March 2018) to advocate for legislation to make schools safer and prevent future deaths (#DontLetMyFriendsDie).

MSD students were criticised for raising their voices, suggesting that they take time to grieve instead. In her comments to reporters, Emma

Gonzalez (@Emma4Change) educated critics about the connection between her grief and her advocacy efforts:

> Everybody needs to know how we feel and what we went through, because if they don't, they're not going to be able to understand why we're fighting for what we're fighting for...This is the way I have to grieve. (Turkewitz, Stevens, & Bailey, 2018).

Survivor Cameron Kasky described his desire to team up with classmates to promote a movement against gun violence: 'We, as a community, needed one thing'—a purpose amid their grief (Smidt, 2018).

Digital survivor advocacy adds a powerful and very public dimension to someone's Digital Afterlife, evoking their name, image, and memory with each advocacy effort, many of which include the hashtag #NeverForget. While anecdotal evidence suggests that these survivor advocacy efforts help the bereaved to cope with their grief (Sofka, 2017b), future research should document whether involvement facilitates and/or hinders the process of coping with loss.

## CONCLUSION

Digital and social media are a significant part of daily life for many people, and their roles in dealing with impending death and coping with grief are becoming more prevalent. In order to describe the interrelationships between the use of thanatechnology and one's Digital Afterlife, this chapter has drawn from a rich, rapidly-expanding body of literature generated by scholars and helping professionals from diverse disciplines, journalists, and individuals who have chosen to publicly share very personal experiences. Although we have collectively learned a great deal about these topics, challenging issues and unanswered questions remain.

New social media platforms are constantly appearing, and technology creating opportunities for a lively and potentially interactive Digital Afterlife will continue to evolve. In light of this reality, what must be done to ensure that the resultant thanatechnology will help rather than harm? Academics with human-computer interaction and Information Science backgrounds in conjunction with staff from social media platforms (Brubaker & Callison-Burch, 2016; Gulotta, Odom, Forlizzi, & Faste, 2013) have provided important guidance for social media and digital legacy platforms to utilise 'thanatosensitive design—a process which explicitly acknowledges mortality, dying, and death in the design of a system' (Massimi & Baecker, 2010, p. 1829). Forming interdisciplinary advisory teams that involve clinicians and academics with clinical backgrounds in conjunction with input from social media users is recommended. Ongoing discussions about ethical and legal issues are crucial.

Although the evidence is largely anecdotal, positive benefits, negative consequences, as well as potential risks of the use of digital and social media by the dying and bereaved have been documented. The long-term impact of one's Digital Afterlife on the bereaved remains undocumented. Advancing our empirical knowledge about these topics requires us to tackle two challenges. To date, most research has either gathered qualitative data from small samples or used textual analysis of social media data to document these phenomena. Psychometrically valid instruments must be developed to quantify the elements of one's Digital Afterlife and to measure the impact of its presence on the bereaved.

Furthermore, although it is challenging to conduct research with those who are dying and/or grieving, data from large samples of these digital and social media users must be gathered. Advocating for funders whose mission includes thanatology-related topics to support this type of research is an important task to undertake.

Due to significant individual differences in reactions to impending death and loss, personal coping styles, and perceptions regarding what is appropriate behaviour in digital and social media realms, there will always be disagreements related to social media use during these life events. Potential conflicts regarding the creation and management of a person's Digital Afterlife will exist and must be resolved. Prior to the digital age, gaining information about what was 'socially-appropriate' required consultation with an experienced adult or access to an etiquette book. Today, a common first impulse is to 'Google it'.

Since digital and social media have prominent roles in daily life, advice about 'netiquette' for the general public has become readily available in newspaper articles, on websites and blog postings (see Directive Communication Systems, Sofka, & Poskanzer, 2019 for one effort to create a concise set of guidelines for one's digital legacy). Conclusions about netiquette from an academic perspective can also be found (see Wagner, 2018; Sabra, 2017).

To prepare effectively for the end of life and cope with grief in the digital age, society must undertake two important tasks. First, digital and social media users must recognise the importance of proactively planning for one's Digital Afterlife, taking appropriate steps to document their digital assets and communicate their wishes about what should happen to them upon their death. Second, everyone must understand that the norms for mourning online and the ways to respond appropriately to grief are complex, in flux, and must be negotiated between users with multiple viewpoints.

Community death education opportunities about these topics must be implemented, enlisting help from the media and forming partnerships with adult education programs, public schools (incorporating them into the digital literacy curriculum and/or health education), and parent–teacher associations (see Sofka, 2017a; 2018a; Sofka, Gibson, & Silberman, 2017). Promoting available resources to assist with digital estate planning and the curation of one's Digital Afterlife within the delivery of hospice/palliative care is also recommended. Helping professionals who work with the dying and bereaved will benefit from continuing education opportunities to learn how to incorporate discussions about digital legacies, digital estate planning, and guidance about the use of thanatechnology into their work.

While sorting through a box of old papers, I found a poem entitled 'To Those I Love' on a bookmark from a hospice provider. The desire to find a way to continue to interact after death caught my attention.

> If I should ever leave you whom I love
> To go along the Silent Way, grieve not,
> Nor speak of me with tears, but laugh and talk
> Of me as if I were beside you there.
> (I'd come – I'd come, could I but find a way!
> But would not tears and grief be barriers?)

Isla Paschal Richardson
(1947, p. 24)

If Richardson were alive today, perhaps she would consider the creation of a Digital Afterlife through the use of thanatechnology to be an appropriate solution. According to Kasket (2019), one important consideration when contemplating decisions about your legacy relates to going 'old school' (paper) *versus* digital. Due to pros and cons for either choice, perhaps it is wise to incorporate both.

## REFERENCES

Anderson, I. K. (2011). The uses and gratifications of online care pages: A study of CaringBridge. *Health Communication, 26*(6), 546–559.

Anderson, M., Perrin, A., Jiang, J., & Kumar, M. (2019, April 22). 10% of Americans don't use the internet. Who are they? Available on https://www.pewresearch.org/fact-tank/2019/04/22/some-americans-dont-use-the-internet-who-are-they/

Balk, D., & Varga, M. A. (2018). Continuing bonds and social media in the lives of bereaved college students. In D. Klass, & M. Steffen (Eds.), *Continuing bonds in bereavement: New directions for research and practice* (pp. 303–316). New York: Routledge.

Bassett, D. (2017). Shadows of the dead: Social media and our changing relationship with the departed. Available on https://discoversociety.org/2017/01/03/shadows-of-the-dead-social-media-and-our-changing-relationship-with-the-departed/

Bassett, D. J. (2018). Ctrl+alt+delete: The changing landscape of the uncanny valley and the fear of second loss. Current Psychology: A Journal for Diverse Perspectives on Diverse Psychological Issues. http://dx.doi.org/10.1007/s12144-018-0006-5

Brubaker, J. R., & Callison-Burch, V. (2016). Legacy contact: Designing and implementing post-mortem stewardship at Facebook. Paper presented at CHI 2016. Available on https://www.jedbrubaker.com/wp-content/uploads/2008/05/Brubaker-Callison-Burch-Legacy-CHI2016.pdf

Brubaker, J. R., Hayes, G. R., & Dourish, P. (2013). Beyond the grave: Facebook as a site for the expansion of death and mourning. *The Information Society*, *29*, 152–163.

Burkell, J., Fortier, A., Wong, L. Y. C., & Simpson, J. L. (2014). Facebook: Public space or private space? *Information, Communication, and Society*, *17*(8), 974–985. doi: 10.1080/1369118X.2013.870591.

Carroll, E., & Romano, J. (2011). *Your digital afterlife: When Facebook, Flickr and Twitter are your estate, what's your legacy?* Berkeley, CA: New Riders.

Cesare, N., & Branstad, J. (2018). Mourning and memory in the twittersphere. *Mortality*, *23*(1), 82–97. doi: 10.1080/13576275.2017.1319349.

DeGroot, J. M. (2014). 'For whom the bell tolls': Emotional rubbernecking in Facebook memorial groups. *Death Studies*, *38*(2), 79–84. doi: 10.1080/07481187.2012.725450.

Directive Communication Systems, Sofka, C., & Poskanzer, L. (2019, March 7) *Netiquette Experts Agree: It's Time for Guidelines on Death in a Digital World* [Press Release] Retrieved from https://www.directivecommunications.com/netiquette-experts-agree-guidelines-are-needed-on-death-in-a-digital-world/

Gibson, M. (2011). Death and grief in the landscape: Private memorials in public space. *Cultural Studies Review*, *17*(1), 146–161. doi: https://doi.org/10.5130/csr.v17i1.1975.

Gibson, M. (2015). Automatic and automated mourning: Messengers of death and messages from the dead. *Continuum*, *29*(3), 339–353. doi: 10.1080/10304312.2015.1025369.

Gibson, M. (2016). YouTube and bereavement vlogging: Emotional exchange between strangers. *Journal of Sociology*, *52*(4), pp. 631–645. doi: 10.1177/1440783315573613.

Gotved, S. (2014). *Research review: Death online – Alive and Kicking! Thanatos*, *3*(1), 112–126. Available on https://thanatosjournal.files.wordpress.com/2012/12/gotved_deathonline2.pdf

Gulotta, R., Odom, W., Forlizzi, J., & Faste, H. (2013). Digital artifacts as legacy: Exploring the lifespan and value of digital data. Proceedings of the SIGCHI Conference on Human Factors in Computing Systems, 1813-1822. Available on http://www.willodom.com/publications/Gulotta_Odom_CHI2013.pdf

Irwin, M. (2018). Mourning 2.0: Continuing bonds between the living and the dead on Facebook – continuing bonds in cyberspace. In D. Klass, & Maria Steffen (Eds.), *Continuing bonds in bereavement: New directions for research and practice* (pp. 317–329). New York: Routledge.

James, L. (2014). Continuing bonds in a virtual world: The use of Facebook in adolescent grief. UMI Number 3635630. Dissertation in partial fulfillment of the requirements for the degree of Doctor of Philosophy, Colorado State University.

Kasket, E. (2012). 'Continuing bonds in the age of social networking: Facebook as a modern day medium'. *Bereavement Care*, 31(2):62–69.

Kasket, E. (2018). Facilitation and disruption of continuing bonds in a digital society. In D. Klass & M. Steffen (Eds.), *Continuing Bonds in Bereavement: New Directions for Research and Practice* (pp. 330–340). New York: Routledge.

Kasket, E. (2019). *All the ghosts in the machine: Illusions of immortality in the digital age*. London: Robinson.

Kastenbaum, Robert J. (2004). *Death, society, and human experience* (8th ed.). Boston, MA: Allyn & Bacon.

Klass, D. (2018). Prologue. In D. Klass, & E. M. Steffen (Eds.), *Continuing bonds in bereavement: New directions for research and practice* (pp. xiii–xix). New York: Routledge.

Klastrup, L. (2015). 'I didn't know her, but…': parasocial mourning of mediated deaths on Facebook RIP pages. *New Review of Hypermedia and Multimedia*, 21(1–2), 146–164. doi: 10.1080/13614568.2014.983564.

Leddy, K. (2019, May 3). Years ago, my sister vanished. I see her whenever I want. Available on https://www.nytimes.com/2019/05/09/style/modern-love-college-contest-winner.html.

Leland, J. (2018, June 22). The positive death movement comes to life. Available on https://www.nytimes.com/2018/06/22/nyregion/the-positive-death-movement-comes-to-life.html

Massimi, M., & Baecker, R. M. (2010). A death in the family: Opportunities for designing technologies for the bereaved. Proceedings of the 28th International Conference on Human Factors in Computing Systems, CHI 2010, Atlanta, GA. doi: 10.1145/1753326.1753600.

Masterson, A. (2015, December 10). Social media: When death doesn't mean out of range. Available on https://www.smh.com.au/technology/social-media-when-death-doesnt-mean-out-of-range-20151209-glj9ae.html

Matei, A. (2017, January 27). New technology is forcing us to confront the ethics of bringing people back from the dead. Available on https://qz.com/896207/death-technology-will-allow-grieving-people-to-bring-back-their-loved-ones-from-the-dead-digitally/

Mehring, S. (2013). *Hope conquers all: Inspiring stories of love and healing from CaringBridge*. New York: Center Street.

Norris, J., Sofka, C., & Kasket, E. (2018). Digital death survey 2018. www.digitallegacyassociation.com

Pausch, R., & Zaslow, J. (2008). *The last lecture*. New York: Hyperion.

Pew Research Center (2018, February 5). Mobile fact sheet. Available on https://www.pewinternet.org/fact-sheet/mobile/

Phillips, W. (2015). *This is why we can't have nice things: Mapping the relationships between online trolling and mainstream culture*. Cambridge, MA: MIT Press Books.

Rachman, T. (2016, January 25). Meeting death with words. Available on https://www.newyorker.com/culture/cultural-comment/meeting-death-with-words

Rando, T. A. (1993). *Treatment of Complicated Mourning*. Champaign, IL: Research Press.

Richardson, I. P. (1947). *To those I love (p. 24). My heart waketh*. Boston, MA: Bruce Humphries, Inc.

Rosenzweig, A. (2018, July 25). It starts with someone: Drs. Michael Curran and Randy Pausch. Available on https://www.pancan.org/news/it-starts-with-someone-drs-michael-curran-and-randy-pausch/

Sabra, J. B. (2017). 'I hate when they do that!': Netiquette in mourning and memorialization among Danish Facebook users. *Journal of Broadcasting and Electronic Media*, 61(1), 24–40. doi: 10.1080/08838151.2016.1273831.

Sandberg, S., & Grant, A. (2017). *Option B: Facing adversity, building resilience, and finding joy*. New York: Alfred A. Knopf.

Shavit, V. (n.d.) Digital Dust. Web-based resources archived at http://digital-era-death-eng.blogspot.com/

Smidt, R. (2018, February 20). Here's what it's like at the headquarters of teens working to stop mass shootings. Available on https://www.buzzfeed.com/remysmidt/heres-what-its-like-at-the-headquarters-of-the-teens?.

Sofka, C. (2015). Using digital and social media in your work with the dying and bereaved. Webinar presented for the Association for Death Education and Counseling.

Sofka, C. (2017a). Role of digital and social media in supporting bereaved students. In J. Brown, & S. Jimerson (Eds.), *Supporting bereaved students at school* (pp. 96–111). Oxford: Oxford University Press.

Sofka, C. (2017b). Digital survivor advocacy: Fighting so you may never know tragedy. In S. E. Elswick (Ed.), *Data Collection: Methods, Ethical Issues, and Future Directions* (pp. 111–145). Hauppauge, NY: Nova Science Publishers.

Sofka, C. (2018a, November). Adolescents' Use of Social Media and Digital Technology to Cope with Life-Threatening Illness and Loss: What Parents and Supportive Adults Should Know. ChiPPS E-journal, Pediatric and Hospice Palliative Care, Issue #53, pp. 18–27. Available on https://legacy.nhpco.org/sites/default/files/public/ChiPPS/ChiPPS_e-journal_Issue-53.pdf.

Sofka, C. (2018b). Grieving for strangers: Emotional rubbernecking or experiential empathy? Presentation at the 40th Annual Conference of the Association for Death Education and Counseling (ADEC), (April), Pittsburgh, PA.

Sofka, C. (2019). Digital death and digital legacy: Awareness, attitudes, and planning. Presentation at the 41st Annual Conference of the Association for Death Education and Counseling (April), Atlanta, GA.

Sofka, C., Gibson, A., & Silberman, D. (2017). Digital immortality or digital death? Contemplating digital end of life planning. In M. H. Jacobsen (Ed.), *Postmortal society: Towards a sociology of immortality* (pp. 106–173). Aldershot, UK: Ashgate/Routledge.

Sofka, C. J. (1997). Social support 'internetworks', caskets for sale, and more: Thanatology and the information superhighway. *Death Studies, 21*(6), 553–574. doi: 10.1080/074811897201778.

Sofka, C. J. (2012). Blogging: New age narratives of dying, death, and grief. In C. J. Sofka, I. N. Cupit, & K. Gilbert (Eds.): *Dying, death and grief in an online universe: For counselors and educators* (pp. 61–77). New York: Springer.

Sofka, C. J., Cupit, I. N., & Gilbert, K. (2012). *Dying, death and grief in an online universe: For counselors and educators*. New York: Springer.

Stokes, P. (2015). Deletion as second death: The moral status of digital remains. *Ethics and Information Technology, 17*, 237–248. doi: 10.1007/s10676-015-9379-4.

Trauma Foundation (2001, August 24). What is survivor advocacy? Available on http://www.traumaf.org/featured/7-01-survivor_advocacy.shtml

Turkewitz, J., Stevens, M., & Bailey, J. M. (2018, February 18). Emma Gonzalez leads a student outcry on guns. Available on https://www.nytimes.com/2018/02/18/us/emma-gonzalez-florida-shooting.html

Wagner, A. J. M. (2018). Do not click 'like' when somebody has died: The role of norms for mourning practices in social media. *Social Media & Society, 4*(1), 1–11. https://doi.org/10.1177/2056305117744392.

Walter, T. (2008). The new public mourning. In M. Stroebe, R. Hansson, W. Stroebe, & H. Schut (Eds.), *Handbook of Bereavement Research and Practice: 21st Century Perspectives* (pp. 241–262). Washington, DC: American Psychological Association.

Walter, T. (2015). Communication media and the dead: From the stone age to facebook. *Mortality, 20*(3), 215–232. https://doi.org/10.1080/13576275.2014.993598.

Walter, T. (2017). How the dead survive: Ancestors, immortality, memory. In M. H. Jacobsen (Ed.), *Postmortal Society. Towards a Sociology of Immortality* (pp. 19–39). Aldershot, UK: Ashgate/Routledge.

Walter, T., Hourizi, R., Moncur, W., & Pitsillides, S. (2011-2012). *Omega, 64*(4), 274–302. https://doi.org/10.2190%2FOM.64.4.a.

# CHAPTER 5

# Profit and Loss

## *The Mortality of the Digital Immortality Platforms*

Debra Bassett

## CONTENTS

Introduction                                                                  75
Background                                                                    76
The Resurrection of the Dead: Socially Active Digital Zombies                 77
But Who Wants to Live Forever?                                               79
A Theory of the Fear of Second Loss                                          81
The Future and Second Loss                                                   85
Conclusion                                                                    86
References                                                                    86

## INTRODUCTION

Nine years ago, my friend's daughter Annie died suddenly aged 18. At the time of her death Annie had an active Facebook page, and on this page she remains socially 'alive' today. In the years following her death, I began to wonder why my friend—and many others—still spoke to Annie on a public forum as though she was still alive, wishing her happy birthday and telling her how much she is missed. In this chapter I will give an overview of the ongoing debates in the field of Digital Afterlives, before presenting findings from my research, which shows how the potential loss of data, which is deemed to contain the essence of the dead, is causing a new form of anxiety for the bereaved: the fear of second loss. The term *digital immortality* is relatively new; however, in this chapter I argue that it is already an outdated term which inadequately describes the fragility of Digital Afterlives.

## BACKGROUND

Researchers from a wide variety of disciplines have been questioning how memories and messages enabled by the Internet were affecting the social norms and practices of grieving (Brubaker, Hayes, & Dourish, 2013; Sofka, Cupit, & Gilbert, 2012; Walter, Hourizi, Moncur, & Pitsillides, 2012). In her seminal paper 'Social support "internetworks" caskets for sale and more: Thanatology and the information superhighway', Carla Sofka coined the term 'thanatechnology' to describe this convergence of death and technology (Sofka, 1997). In 2015, in an effort to understand the impact of thanatechnology on the bereaved, I began my research which explores how the phenomena of posthumous digital memories and messages enabled by thanatechnology, and inherited by the bereaved, are being experienced differently from other forms of memories and messages.

The landscape of grief is changing from the physical to the virtual, and dichotomous terms such as online/offline and real/virtual are not useful in research based on society's use of the Internet. As Boellstorff (2014) points out, to talk about offline as the 'real' world insinuates that online is somehow 'unreal' and, therefore, delegitimises it as a field of study. Boellstorff does not agree with the notion that the virtual and the actual are fusing into one single domain; he suggests that they are still separate entities. However, his digital anthropological research focuses on online gaming in virtual worlds such as 'Second Life', and therefore, the context of online and offline can be seen as different from that when discussing intimate computing available on devices that are incorporated into the everyday lives of many. In her book *Digital Sociology*, Lupton (2015) also discusses the terminology around the issue of online/offline and virtual/real. She suggests the term virtual reality is 'nonsensical' in our digital society. This is because almost all 'reality' is now virtual, enabled by the ubiquitous and mobile nature of the Internet which ensures our everyday lives are extended, or rather augmented, by the mobile nature of the technical devices we use on a daily basis. Moreover, we are not separate from our online selves; our digital selves are now part of the self (Jurgenson, 2012).

This blurring of 'real' and 'digital' lives—what Floridi (2015) describes as 'onlife'—is becoming increasingly evident in discussions around death and dying. The need to be remembered and the ability to pass on memories is an ancient need: from the first cave drawings and the magnificent mausoleums of the Egyptians, we can see the symbols of their quest for immortality (Sofka, 1997). The ability to see people as having lived, and to give a narrative to the deceased, was once the job of clergy, obituary writers, and eulogy writers, and respect for the dead requires remembering them (Kasket, 2012). Thanatechnology is changing practices of remembrance by enabling the 'everydayness' of people's lives to be recorded and stored on everyday smart technology.

## THE RESURRECTION OF THE DEAD: SOCIALLY ACTIVE DIGITAL ZOMBIES

In her 2014 book, Cann suggests that through the use of technology, which provides links to videos, conversations, memories, and pictures, the dead remain alive. But it is not clear how the bereaved experience the technologically mediated dead. Brubaker and colleagues (2013) emphasise how the bereaved can find 'unexpected encounters' with the dead distressing. Anyone who has made the difficult decision to delete a dead person's telephone number off a device only to have the number reappear from a storage cloud may relate to the distress 'Internet ghosts' (Cann, 2014) can cause. Other researchers agree that allowing mourning to 'leak into everyday life' causes a mixing together of life and death, which could be problematic (Walter et al., 2012).

Although the Internet ghosts discussed above may reappear to haunt the bereaved, crucially they remain dead. However, what about those who rise from the dead and become socially active? In a 2013 paper Alexandra Sherlock discusses how these 'posthumous representations' add to an advanced type of symbolic immortality. Bollmer (2013, p.145) suggests that it is not just the 'presence' of the dead online that causes anxiety, it is the 'near full representations of the authentic identity of the human being' which they suggest adds to this anxiety, as the networks cannot distinguish between the living and the dead.

This online blurring of the previously dichotomous nature of being both alive and dead is described by the term digital zombies (Bassett, 2015). This term was developed to describe the online dead who are resurrected, reanimated, and socially active. These digital zombies are, at the same time, dead and alive; moreover, they do things in death they did not do when they were alive. According to Nansen, Arnold, Gibbs, and Kohn (2014), the 'restless dead' are 'exhumed within a network of social and technical connections previously delimited by cemetery geography and physical inscription in stone'. Nansen et al.'s distinction between animation and repose when describing the dead is useful here, as it draws attention to the difference between Cann's Internet ghosts (2014) which are in repose and therefore not restless, and my digital zombies which are resurrected, reanimated, and socially active.

An example of socially active digital zombies is the use of dead celebrities in advertisements: four years after he died, Bob Monkhouse, the British comedian, appeared in an advertisement to raise awareness for prostate cancer. In the video he appears at his own graveside, discussing his own death. The video, which used film recorded whilst he was alive, was edited with new footage, featuring a body-double and a voiceover by an impressionist, to create the final advertisement. Using this 'modern necromancy'—or communication with the dead—he was digitally resurrected from the grave (Sherlock, 2013), thus making him an 'accidental' digital zombie, as the dead Monkhouse was reanimated to perform a task not undertaken in life. The crucial distinction between accidental and intentional digital zombies will be discussed in the next section of this chapter. Other accidental digital zombies included Tupac Shakur and Michael Jackson, both digitally resurrected and recreated to perform 'live' on stage years after their deaths. Sherlock (2013) suggests that dead celebrities being used in this way adds to what she describes as an advanced type of symbolic immortality which Litton (1979) described as the need to pass on memories in an attempt to influence future generation. This notion of symbolic immortality is useful to the concept of Digital Afterlives: The ubiquitous nature of digital technology, and the exponential development of thanatechnology, not only enables celebrities to become socially active digital zombies but crucially offers anyone living in our digital society the opportunity to be reanimated and resurrected following their biological death—thereby offering a type of symbolic immortality which has not been so easily achievable until now.

Platforms such as Facebook, Twitter, and WhatsApp were created for the living as a place to socialise with the living; they were *not* created as a place for the dead to reside. This makes them 'accidental' digital memory platforms. However, some platforms exist that are what I term 'intentional' Digital Afterlife providers for the dead. For example, Eternime and LifeNaut (both based in the United States) have launched platforms that enable people to control how they are remembered after they die. Eternime will take your digital footprint, tweets, online messages, vlogs, and photographs to create an avatar of you. They use artificial intelligence algorithms to create what they claim will be a virtual interactive 'you'. Your avatar will become more like the 'real' you by learning from you each time you interact with it. They claim that your relatives will be able to visit you online for support and advice after you have died. Furthermore, they state they are trying to solve an 'incredibly challenging problem of humanity' (Eternime, 2019. Bell and Gray of Microsoft Research seem to agree that it may be possible that a 'cyberised' version of you will be able to learn, evolve, and eventually 'take on a life of their own'. These companies offer to store your personalities, and these types of technology may seem to be the stuff of science fiction; however, according to Rothblatt, the exponential growth of the emerging technologies needed to deliver and support the cyberconsciousness, mindclones, mindware, and mindfiles do not seem far away (Rothblatt, 2014).

## BUT WHO WANTS TO LIVE FOREVER?

In 2015 I began a research project, which explored how people in digital society were experiencing the creation and inheritance of posthumous digital memories and messages enabled by thanatechnology. To give a holistic approach to the research, I interviewed participants from three distinct categories: (1) the service providers (SPs); those who own or work for Digital Afterlife platforms (both accidental and intentional) (2) the digital creators (DCs); those creating digital memories and messages to be left posthumously, and (3) the digital inheritors (DIs); those who inherit the enduring digital messages following the death of a loved one. Using the methodology and methods of constructivist grounded theory, I conducted qualitative semi-structured interviews with all three categories of participants in an effort to explore how enduring digital memories and the Digital Afterlives they enabled were being experienced.

When discussing the intentional Digital Afterlife platforms, I further categorised them using Bell and Gray's conceptualisation of 'one-way' and 'two-way' immortality. Platforms providing one-way immortality, where the dead are passive (they remain dead) but still preserve and transmit their ideas (Bell & Gray, 2000) and platforms providing two-way immortality, where the dead are active and become reanimated 'digital zombies' (Bassett, 2015).

In the early stages of my research, I began to produce a list of both one-way digital immortality platforms: platforms that offer users the ability to create digital messages and memories to be delivered posthumously, along with platforms offering two-way immortality, where the dead can remain socially active. I monitored the SPs throughout the duration of the research and also incorporated SPs listed in Ulguim (2018). There were a total of 43 intentional Digital Afterlife SPs on the list; however, by June 2019, 14 of the platforms were no longer operating, while a further 8 were dormant with no activity for 12 months.

When platforms offering digital immortality or Digital Afterlives cease to exist, it is important to explore what happens to the data they hold as one of the platforms who no longer operate encouraged their users to upload 'precious' files with promises of storage and retrieval. In their terms of service, intentional Digital Afterlife SP SafeBeyond explains what happens if their fees are not paid: 'If charges are not paid such account may be cancelled and all Digital Assets may be deleted'. The terms of use go further: 'You agree that any information you provide to the Site and/or Application may be lost or destroyed, and that SafeBeyond is not responsible for the loss of such information' (SafeBeyond, 2019). Findings from my research echoed this limited notion of immortality, during an interview, one SP participant told me:

> As we get funds in we're setting them aside so we have funds to pay it ahead if we ever need to. I don't see any reason at the moment why we should do that but we may ask some point see that we can pay ahead for 20 years. (Ron)

Thus, it seems that digital immortality may only last 20 years (or as long as someone is prepared to pay for its continuity). This term 'digital immortality' is relatively new; however, following my research I argue that it is already an outdated term that is inept to describe the posthumously enduring digital data which are left on the Internet and repurposed by the bereaved. Just as we are biologically mortal, we are also digitally mortal. Because of the risk of data corruption, loss or deletion of data, or access denial that can cause digital erasure, there is a real threat to the notion of achieving digital immortality. Early in the first data collection phase of my research, I wrote an email explaining my study to a potential participant who said they found the term 'digital immortality' insensitive and painful as it insinuated that their loved one had not died. I then considered adopting Kastenbaum's term 'assisted immortality' or 'technologically assisted survival' (2012), but this still implied a state of non-death. Reflecting further, I decided 'digital endurance' was more a suitable term to describe the Digital Afterlife in my research. However, it was some time later that I realised that this change of terminology could also be adopted throughout the literature on thanatechnology—not just to be sensitive to the needs of the bereaved, but as a more useful and, furthermore, a more accurate way to describe people's experiences of creating and inheriting digital memories and messages enabled by thanatechnology. The failure of so many of the Digital Afterlife SPs demonstrates that the term *digital immortality* is unsuitable when describing posthumously enduring digital memories and messages and why *digital endurance* is a more suitable term because for many bereaved people these digital data contain the essence of the dead (Bassett, 2018).

## A THEORY OF THE FEAR OF SECOND LOSS

The term 'second death' was used by Stokes in his 2015 paper to discuss the notion that people die twice: once when we stop breathing and then again when the last person speaks your name. Thus, a biological death is followed by a social death. This second, or 'social', death can be perceived by some, as harming the dead. Stokes approaches this second death from the viewpoint that the data of the dead is an 'object of moral obligation', and therefore, it is our obligation to not delete these digital remains; however, this obligation is based on the assumption that everyone wants to remember the dead. Moreover, grief and bereavement along with remembering and forgetting are complex processes for many people, as not everyone agrees that posthumous digital memories and messages should be preserved. Stokes (2015) further posits that the deletion of 'digital remains' may have an impact on the 'ontological and ethical status of the dead'. Stokes suggests that using the metaphor 'digital remains' to describe the data of the dead is useful, as it elevates the moral status of the data to that of a corpse. Whilst this term is a useful metaphor, it is limited: as we do not have immediate access to, or carry around the corpses of our loved ones as we do with posthumous digital memories and messages. Similarly, Öhman and Floridi (2018) suggest that ethical conventions used for archaeological exhibits could provide a useful framework for posthumous data. Again, while this idea is useful, we do not carry archaeological exhibits in our pockets and on our everyday devices. Their suggestion still does not address the immediacy of access to the dead enabled by thanatechnology which my research has demonstrated is distinct as digital posthumous messages and memories are deemed—by the bereaved—to contain the essence of the dead.

My research into the creation and inheritance of Digital Afterlives also highlights a further limitation of Stokes' argument, as he fails to acknowledge the reciprocal nature of thanabots and posthumous avatars (Bassett, 2018), and whether these would have a different moral status as they are created *after* the death of the original self.

The following extracts from interviews with two digital immortality participants demonstrate the importance of inherited digital memories and messages to the bereaved. During my interview with Amy she explained how she felt when she thought the digital memories she had inherited, following the death of her sister, had disappeared:

> Last year, I had two incidents where electronic items for keepsakes were lost or almost lost. Both times I had a proper meltdown and couldn't stop crying for a long time. The last incident happened in John Lewis and strangers were present. But to me they didn't exist at that time. Just my panic at losing memories and [her sister] all over again (Amy)

Similarly, other participants described similar experiences, and told me how the experience of losing digital data would be experienced in a similar way to the biological death of their loved ones:

> *I can't lose her again (Pam)*
> *I would be devastated, it would start my grief all over again (Sandra)*

The themes identified from my qualitative research support the notion that the data of the dead is far more than code to the bereaved. However, as mentioned earlier in this chapter, I propose a distinction between accidental digital memories and messages and intentional digital memories and messages; here I argue this distinction is necessary in order to establish whose needs should be prioritised: the DCs or the DIs? The digital memories and messages that are created intentionally by the living in an attempt to endure on the Internet after their biological death could be given the status of digital remains, such as those suggested by the likes of Stokes, Öhman, and Floridi, as they were created intentionally to continue to exist beyond biological death. However, based on my research, accidental posthumous digital memories and messages inherited and rendered as precious memories by the bereaved should be treated differently; moreover, my research highlights that the needs of the bereaved should take priority over the needs of the deceased for accidental digital memories and messages. The term 'second death', as used by Stokes, focuses on what has happened to the data of the person who has died: they died twice, biologically and then socially. However, this chapter adopts this term to call for a transfer of focus to what happens to the bereaved who inherit digital messages and memories following the death of a loved one.

As previously mentioned, second death describes social death. I adopt and expand the usefulness of the term 'second death' in an effort to draw attention to the needs of the living; specifically, the bereaved who inherit the digital memories and messages enabled by thanatechnology, and then lose them through a second, digital death, which I call 'second loss'. Stokes' use of the term 'second death' would not include second loss, as for Stokes, the term necessitates that the dead are socially dead: they have been forgotten by the living. I argue that the term 'second death' needs to be expanded to include digital death; that is, the loss, deletion, or lack of access to posthumous digital memories and messages producing the loss of the digital *dasein* where the bereaved experience the essence of the deceased. Within this digital *dasein*, the essence of the dead is digitally embodied in a form of posthumous essentialism and the idea that the essence of the dead continues to be 'somewhere' can bring comfort to the bereaved who are using digital memories and messages as important tools for their grief. However, this comfort is linked to being able to access these precious tools. Second loss is how second death is experienced by the bereaved who do not have access to or lose the data of the dead. Using this theme of second loss, I developed a new theory: 'the fear of second loss' (Bassett, 2018) which entails the highly emotive loss of precious data produced by data deletion, technical obsolescence, or the denial of access to posthumous digital memories and messages.

The findings from my research show that second loss was experienced negatively by the bereaved. When I discussed with each of my participants how they would feel if the digital memories they had inherited were permanently deleted, their replies 'I would be devastated' and 'It would start my grief all over again' were implicit in all but one of my interviews. Even participants who did not visit Facebook pages or other accidental platforms commented that they would not want them switched off permanently, as they take comfort in the knowledge they can switch them back on if they wanted to. One woman told me she was glad her mother's Facebook page was offline, but it still exists. Kasket (2012) reported similar findings where participants feared the possibility of losing Facebook profiles of the deceased.

I wanted to understand whether inherited digital memories and messages were being experienced differently to physical memories or keepsakes. In an interview with Jess, she explained how for her digital memories are more valuable because they are more permanent:

> It's not like a photograph … like a photograph fades but, you know, a digital memory lives on and is sort of more permanent (Jess)

This quotation from Jess suggests that she believes that a Digital Afterlife is everlasting and will endure in perpetuity. I asked Jess to clarify why she considered the digital memories more precious than a photograph:

> I treasure them as they won't fade (Jess)

This comment confirmed that Jess sees her digital memories and messages as everlasting in a way that physical photographs are not. However, this is not always the case: physical photographs can, in certain circumstances, 'outlive' digital images.

The ramifications of data loss and access restriction are discussed throughout my research (Bassett, 2020 forthcoming), which looks at the effect of these points on the bereaved, and how the concept of second loss is inextricably linked to the theme of 'control'. For some participants control seems to be in the hands of the SPs rather than the bereaved. As Massimi and Baecker (2010) note, technology is rarely designed with digital inheritance in mind. Second loss is not only applicable to those who *have* inherited digital memories and messages following the death of a loved one as it can also be useful to describe the experience of *not having* access to the digital data of the deceased. During an interview with Carla she explained how her mother had died whilst holidaying in Lanzarote, and how the family were 'desperate' to access the photographs taken in the last few days of her life when she was happy. Unfortunately, they did not know the PIN to access the device, and the photographs were lost causing much added grief to the family. This example is an implicit description of how the phenomenon of second loss is being experienced even when no digital memories and messages have been inherited and, importantly, illustrates how the narratives of grieving are being shaped culturally to include digital grieving which is enabled by human–computer interaction.

In a digital landscape, the bereaved feel closer to the dead because they are immediately accessible through everyday smart technology, rather than analogue memories such as keepsakes, which are sometimes kept in dusty boxes stored in attics. Yet the digital landscape also brings with it the possibility of technical obsolescence. Accidental deletion and a lack of access to digital memories and messages create a new vulnerability for the bereaved as those who lose posthumous digital memories and messages experience a second loss. However, the findings from my research illustrate how anxiety is still being experienced before second loss occurs because this fear exists as a form of anticipatory grief, which manifests itself as the fear of second loss. This theory accounts for how, for some, the comfort gained from digital memories and messages is being overshadowed by the fear of losing data created by, or commemorating the deceased as a result of data corruption, loss or deletion of data, or access denial that can cause digital erasure. When contemplating this notion of digital loss, I am reminded of Wallace et al.'s work on Victorian mourning jewellery (Wallace et al., 2018), particularly the 'forget' locket where the image degrades each time the locket is opened. The 'forget' locket can hold multiple images but can only display one per day. Once the image is displayed, it degrades until it is finally deleted. For Wallace et al. (2018) this demonstrates forgetfulness and the memory loss of people with dementia. However, this also demonstrates the possibility of a second loss—a digital loss.

## THE FUTURE AND SECOND LOSS

This theory of the fear of second loss relates to the issues surrounding the right to forget and the right to be forgotten, in that, these issues are inextricably entangled with whose needs are prioritised: the living or the dead. The issues discussed in this chapter raise important philosophical questions that will continue to be debated across a wide range of disciplines, such as, does the right to privacy extend to the dead? A multidisciplined approach will be needed in order to fully understand how thanatechnology and the digital grieving are enabled by this human–computer interaction, and how the social and cultural practices around grieving will continue to be experienced and altered by a technological landscape. Following my research, I argue that for accidental digital memories and messages, any suggestions that the online dead could be stakeholders in decisions concerning the preservation of their data (the data of the dead) is flawed (Öhman & Floridi, 2018; Stokes, 2015). Furthermore, when posthumous digital memories and messages are accidental, I advocate that both the SPs and the DCs should be encouraged to treat the bereaved as the major stakeholders in an effort to mitigate the potential anxiety of those who have lost a loved one. It is certain that for some, the Internet is providing comfort by enabling a continuing relationship with the departed; however, for many others, it is causing a new form of anxiety for the bereaved: the fear of second loss.

One of the most poignant of my participant's stories illustrated clearly a real sense of the importance of digital memories and messages to the bereaved. Sally told me how she treasures a digital recording of her deceased daughter's heartbeat which she stores on her mobile telephone. This story stood out to me: learning that this mother carried her dead daughter's heartbeat in her pocket seemed to perfectly capture why research into the impact of thanatechnology is so important in our digital society. A heartbeat represents life, and even when it is digitally recorded and technologically mediated, it is far more than digital code. The data of the dead may well be made up of ones and zeros; however, it is experienced by the bereaved as containing the essence of the dead.

## CONCLUSION

The dead have been an important part of my research; however, we should be aware that *we* are the future dead, and for most of us who live in the digital societies of the West, technology is ensuring we will all have a Digital Afterlife. As we get used to the socially active dead being online, we should also be aware that we could lose the precious digital memories and messages that contain the essence our dead loved ones. In this chapter I have presented parts of my research, which explores the impact and significance of thanatechnology on the creators and inheritors of Digital Afterlives, and I have also argued for a change in the terminology used to describe Digital Afterlives—from digital immortality to digital endurance. This chapter is a cautionary tale, and this change in terminology draws attention to the fragility of posthumous digital memories and messages as it reminds us that we are far from immortal. Whether biologically or digitally we would do well to remember that even in a digital society we only live twice.

## REFERENCES

Bassett, D. (2015). Who wants to live forever? Living, dying and grieving in our digital society. *Social Sciences*, 4(4), 1127–1139.

Bassett, D. (2018). Ctrl + Alt + Delete: The changing landscape of the uncanny valley and the fear of second loss. *Current Psychology*, 1–9.

Bassett, D. (2020). *You Only Live Twice*: A constructivist grounded theory study of the creation and inheritance of digital afterlives. (Ph.D.dissertation.) Coventry UK: University of Warwick (forthcoming)

Bell, G. & Gray, J. (2004). Digital immortality. *Communications of the ACM*, 44(3), pp. 28–30

Boellstorff, T. (2014). Rethinking digital anthropology. In H. Horst, & D. Miller (Eds.), *Digital Anthropology*. London: Bloomsbury Academic.

Bollmer, G. D. (2013). Millions now living will never die: Cultural anxieties about the afterlife of information. *The Information Society*, *29*(3), 142–151.

Brubaker, J. R., Hayes, G. R., & Dourish, P., (2013). Beyond the grave: Facebook as a site for the expansion of death and mourning. *The Information Society*, *29*(3), 152–163.

Cann, C. K. (2014). *Virtual afterlives: Grieving the dead in the twenty-first century*. Lexington, KY: University Press of Kentucky.

Eternime. (2019). Retrieved February 26, 2019, from http://eterni.me/

Floridi, L. (2015). Luciano Floridi—Commentary on the Onlife Manifesto. In *The Onlife Manifesto* (pp. 21–23). Springer, Cham.

Jurgenson, N. (2012) When atoms meet bits: Social media, the mobile web and augmented revolution. *Future Internet*, *4*(1), 83–91.

Kasket, E. (2012). Continuing bonds in the age of social networking: Facebook as a modern-day medium. *Bereavement Care*, *31*(2), 62–69.

LifeNaut. (2019). Retrieved February 27, 2019, from https://www.lifenaut.com

Litton, R. J. (1979). *The broken connection*. New York: Simon 6, 131–150.

Lupton, D. (2015). *Digital Sociology*. New York: Routledge.

Massimi, M., & Baecker, R. M. (2010, April). A death in the family: opportunities for designing technologies for the bereaved. In *Proceedings of the SIGCHI conference on Human Factors in computing systems* (pp. 1821–1830). ACM.

Nansen, B., Arnold, M., Gibbs, M., & Kohn, T. (2014). The restless dead in the digital cemetery. *Digital Death: Mortality and Beyond in the Online Age*, 111–124.

Öhman, C., & Floridi, L. (2018). An ethical framework for the Digital Afterlife industry. *Nature Human Behaviour*, *2*(5), 318–320.

Rothblatt, M. (2014). *Virtually Human: The Promise—and the Peril—of Digital Immortality*. Macmillan.

SafeBeyond. (2019). Retrieved March 3, 2019, from https://www.safebeyond.com

Sherlock, A. (2013). Larger than life: Digital resurrection and the re-enchantment of society. *The Information Society*, *29*(3), 164–176.

Sofka, C., Cupit, I., & Gilbert, K. (2012). *Dying, death, and grief in an online Universe: For Counselors and Educators*. New York: Springer Publishing Company.

Sofka, C. J. (1997). Social support 'internetworks,' caskets for sale, and more: Thanatology and the information superhighway. *Death Studies*, *21*(6), 553–574.

Stokes, P. (2015). Deletion as second death: The moral status of digital remains. *Ethics and Information Technology*, *17*(4), 237–248.

Ulguim, P. (2018). Digital Remains Made Public: Sharing the dead online and our future digital mortuary landscape. *AP Arqueologia Publica*, *8*(2 (Special Volume 3)), 153–176.

Wallace, J., Thomas, J., Anderson, D., & Olivier, P. (2018). Mortality as framed by ongoingness in digital design. *Design Issues*, *34*(1), 95–107.

Walter, T., Hourizi, R., Moncur, W., & Pitsillides, S. (2012). Does the internet change how we die and mourn? Overview and analysis. *Omega: The Journal of Death and Dying*, *64*(4), 275–302.

# CHAPTER 6

# The 'New(ish)' Property, Informational Bodies, and Postmortality

Edina Harbinja

## CONTENTS

Introduction                                                89
Overview                                                    90
Digital Assets: The 'New' New Property                      90
Post-Mortem Privacy and Informational Bodies                93
Immortality and Postmortal Privacy                          95
Post-Mortem(al) Privacy Laws                                98
Conclusion                                                 102
Note                                                       102
References                                                 103

## INTRODUCTION

This chapter will examine the concept of digital assets from an angle that has not yet been explored in legal scholarship around digital death, and the transmission of digital assets on death. Digital death is conceived herein as the death of an individual who leaves behind various digital fragments of their identity, either in the form of digital assets broadly or as digital biographies, dossiers, autobiographies, and archives (Sofka, Gibson, & Silberman, 2017; Kasket, 2019). Digital death causes uncertainty as to what happens in this dispersed, interconnected and often unregulated digital space, which Kasket (2019) lucidly entitles the *New Elysium*.

Most legal scholars have considered digital assets either from a perspective of 'hard law' of succession and probate or the intersection of property, contracts, and intellectual property; sometimes referring to data protection, jurisdiction or cybercrime (Cahn, 2011; Lopez, 2016; McCallig, 2014). Scholars have not yet ventured into exploring theory that goes beyond theories of property, intellectual property, and privacy.

## OVERVIEW

The chapter begins by examining classical conceptualisations of digital assets as property and the '"new" new property'(Conway & Grattan, 2017), exploring whether this is the correct way to perceive digital assets conceptually. It will then go on to examine post-mortem privacy in the context of digital assets, and introduce a novel link with the Floridian concept of informational bodies. In the attempt to offer a comprehensive framework and a more nuanced normative support for future policy and law, the chapter interrelates all of the concepts with the ideas of postmortal society, introducing a new concept of 'postmortal privacy'. Finally, the author uses this conceptualisation to test some of the existing legal regimes in the area of the transmission of digital assets. Suggestions from this chapter remain mainly at an abstract level, due to the scope and the nature of the framework it introduces. The focus of this chapter will be on a few western legal systems, the United States, United Kingdom, Canada, and France.

In order to make the discussion easier to follow for readers from various backgrounds, Table 6.1 defines key concepts used and/or developed in this chapter.

## DIGITAL ASSETS: THE 'NEW' NEW PROPERTY

*Propertisation* of digital assets has been one of the key ideas since the inception of their legal analysis (Cahn, 2011; Conway & Grattan, 2017; Lopez, 2016). Authors suggest that the property regime would result in the ability to transmit one's digital assets post-mortem and that the lack of tangibility, for instance, should not create an obstacle in this regard. On numerous occasions, some of the problems with propertisation of digital assets *ab initio* have been explored (Edwards & Harbinja, 2013a; Harbinja, 2017a; Harbinja, 2017b). These problems are grouped into normative ones (using traditional western theories of property to justify propertisation of digital assets), and legal doctrinal problems (incidents of property and the lack of tangibility and rivalrousness, as required by the courts across the western world). For the purpose and scope of this chapter, these objections are summarised below.

TABLE 6.1    Key Concepts Used/Developed in this Chapter

| Concept | Definition | Author |
|---|---|---|
| Digital death | Death in the digital realm; death of an individual who leaves fragments of their identity and digital assets in the Digital Afterlife (e.g., digital biographies, dossiers, autobiographies, and archives). | Sofka, Gibson, & Silberman, 2017; Kasket, 2019; Harbinja 2017a |
| Digital immortality | Immortality reached in the digital realm as a consequence of a symbolic, a proxy, or technology. | Jacobsen, 2017 |
| Digital assets | Any electronic asset of personal or economic value. | Harbinja, 2017a |
| | Widely and not exclusively include a huge range of intangible information goods associated with the online or 'digital world'. | Edwards & Harbinja, 2013b |
| 'New' new property | Digital assets—the next hypothetical stage of the development of property following 'new property' defined by Langbein (1984), which included pensions, life policies, and joint assets. | Conway & Grattan, 2017 |
| New(ish) property | Parody term used to amplify the inadequacy of using the concept of property to categorise digital assets | Harbinja (this chapter) |
| Informational body | Inorganic body of a human constituted and existing through information related to his identity. | Floridi, 2013b, 2014 |
| Post-mortem privacy | The right of the deceased to control his personality rights and digital remains post-mortem, broadly, or the right to privacy and data protection post-mortem, narrowly defined. | Harbinja, 2017b |
| Postmortal privacy | Protects aspects of immortality understood as the survival of informational body, which is constituted by and exists through personal information and memes. | Harbinja (this chapter) |

It is difficult to apply the most accepted western theories of property to digital asset generally, and in particular to those that do not mimic physical property (such as social networks, emails, or personal data). Other assets, such as virtual worlds and game assets or even bitcoin, do mimic physical property to an extent and their propertisation is more acceptable, with the caveat that many of these assets are created on another person's property (infrastructure, servers, or intellectual property of service providers and companies). I, therefore, proposed virtual worlds usufruct, that is, the right to use and enjoy fruits of someone else's property, as a solution for in-game assets, using labour, personhood, and utilitarian theories of property in order to test their applicability to justifying property in these assets (Harbinja, 2014). Conversely, we cannot use the same theories for assets that do not mimic physical property, for example, social networks, or personal digital footprints, and personal data. The main objections to using Lockean theory (labour theory) is the lack of the actual labour employed by individuals on highly personal assets and data, as well as the lack of the commons on which one could labour since the infrastructure is owned by private companies mainly (Locke, 1690). The objection related to utilitarian theory is the lack of a definable 'greatest good for the greatest number', or Bentham's *felicific calculus* (1789). Personhood theories are more easily applicable to these digital assets, due to their nature and links with one's identity (Radin, 1982). However, the issues around commercialisation and commodification surface here and it has been argued that propertisation, even if justified by this theory, is not socially desirable from the perspective of individuals and their personal interest.

In legal doctrine, the most important complication surrounding propertisation of digital assets can be found in incidents of property, as defined by Honoré (1961) or Hohfeld (1913), for instance, or in the case law of English courts, and courts and statutes elsewhere in Europe (Harbinja, 2017a). One of the main problems here is in the lack of physicality (or what appears to be physicality), as well as the lack of rivalrousness (the fact that one's possession of an asset does not exclude another person's possession of the same 'thing'). Courts and legislators need to reconsider these features substantively and robustly to enable coherent and principled propertisation of intangible assets or personal data, and thus remove this objection. Propertisation of personal data would cause other issues, such as for instance the conflicts with the core of the European regime for the protection of personal data which is underpinned with human rights and values such as dignity, privacy, and autonomy, and which opposes commodification of personal data (Floridi, 2016; Harbinja 2017b; Pearce, 2018). In conclusion of this brief summary, legal doctrine and jurisprudence, with exceptions, still struggle with recognising intangible objects and objects that exist solely online as objects of property, and this is an argument against the legal recognition of the '"new" new property'.

A separate problem is a definitional difficulty, such as an argument that an all-encompassing definition of the 'new' new property is unsuitable and unhelpful. It is impossible to include assets that comprise of, for instance, personal data, intellectual property, money, and game assets under the umbrella term with specific incidents attributed to these. Therefore, any definition needs to be open-ended. Insisting on the prominence of a legal institution such as property is not an appropriate option for the definition, as we would then exclude assets that are primarily personal, for example. As Conway and Grattan (2017) argue soundly, conceptually, digital assets are extremely complex, as they include and touch upon property, data protection, intellectual property, contract, and personality rights. Dividing digital assets into economic and personal and offering different regulatory approaches for these categories is more adequate (Harbinja & Edwards, 2018).

In summary, the term '"new" new property' is inadequate and property should not take precedence in the conceptualisation of digital assets that individuals leave behind, even as a figure of speech. There is a clear need for the development of a more nuanced theoretical framework that would explain digital assets better and provide normative support for a new policy and legal regime. As a starting point for the development of this new framework, I will first look at the concept of informational body and privacy as dignity, as established in Floridi's work, principally.

## POST-MORTEM PRIVACY AND INFORMATIONAL BODIES

Most digital assets comprise a vast amount of personal data and communications (e.g., emails, social media accounts), and their legal treatment cannot be looked at holistically if one does not consider privacy laws and the lack of their post-mortem application. Post-mortem privacy is a phenomenon that has only quite recently started to attract more attention from legal scholarship (Buitelaar, 2017; Harbinja 2017b; Malgieri, 2018). Post-mortem privacy is defined here as the right of the deceased to control his personal digital remains post-mortem, broadly, or the right to data protection post-mortem, narrowly defined (Harbinja, 2017b).

I, and a few other scholars have contemplated post-mortem privacy in the context of digital assets ('new(ish) property' here) mostly, in an attempt to counter the propertisation narrative in legal scholarship around digital assets. We argued that some of these assets are intrinsically personal and identity-related, that their categorisation as property is unsuitable, with all the connotations it would bring, and primarily, a default transmission to one's heirs, in the lack of a will.[1] Therefore, it has been argued that post-mortem privacy should receive a greater regulatory and legislative attention across Europe (and wider), in order to account for the importance of digital footprints and personal digital remains. In such a regime, an individual is able to extend their autonomy and control aspects of his personality post-mortem, by choosing what happens to these remains, akin to what they can to do with their conventional property through testamentary freedom (Harbinja, 2017b). There are also parallels between personal aspects of testamentary freedom, its primary rationale in autonomy, and similarities to prominent conceptions of privacy as autonomy (Bernal, 2014).

Post-mortem privacy, as defined above, has been a useful tool for the initial conceptualisation of digital assets. It served as an argument that supported the development of some of the legal regimes discussed later in this chapter. In order to make the concept even more robust theoretically, it is argued that further support borrowed from other disciplines is required. This would strengthen normative and policy arguments that courts and legislators use when deciding to extend legal protections or introduce a new principle.

Conceptually, post-mortem privacy relates closely to Floridi's notion of 'informational body'. For Floridi, a human being is constituted and exists through information related to their identity, similar to Marx's definition of the inorganic body metaphor (Marx, 1844/2000), such as the idea that in producing objects, one is producing oneself at the same time, and with the exploitation of workers and their labour, capitalists are alienating the self in effect (Öhman & Floridi, 2017). Consequently, for Öhman and Floridi, this alienation comes as a result of the exploitation of the digital remains of the deceased through the digital assets industry, where ones informational body is being alienated and commercially (mis)used post-mortem. Floridian ethics emphasises the right to control one's personal identity, which he understands as an informational structure, constituted by everything that defines this identity, such as memories, biometrical information, search history, and social media data (Floridi, 2013b). Floridi (2014) further argues that we should relate to private data as being ours in the sense of 'our body' rather than 'our car'. In essence, individuals are their own information and their personal data are their informational bodies. Consequently, to infringe one's informational privacy, is an act of aggression, not only to the specific person but also to humanity as such, to what Floridi (2016) refers to more generally as human dignity. To maintain one's dignity is a key for remaining in control of one's existence in this world, according to Floridi. Öhman and Floridi then go on to apply this concept to those who are dead, akin to the application of the concept regardless of a person's awareness or unawareness of having their privacy being compromised (Öhman & Floridi, 2017). The authors believe that the informational body continues to have the right to be treated with the respect and dignity worthy of a human even after the end of their physical existence. There is a clear analogy between this sound proposition and the protection that the law traditionally offers to the physical body and its integrity post-mortem, as well as the fact that organic body is not considered property in most legal systems (Brazier, 2002; Herring, 2016). If we treat the human body with respect after death, by analogy, we should provide the same treatment for informational body, underpinned by dignity and autonomy.

For these reasons, it is submitted here that post-mortem privacy as defined in my own work and that of others can be seen through the theory of information bodies and the concept of privacy as dignity, as set out by Floridi. To strengthen this nascent conceptual framework, in the following section, I will examine sociological considerations around postmortal society and immortality.

## IMMORTALITY AND POSTMORTAL PRIVACY

Immortality and postmortal society may sound like science fiction and something quite far distant in the future to most people. Nevertheless, scholars in different areas of social science have been developing sociological considerations of postmortal society, immortality and postmortal self in their studies of death, materiality, and the origins of time (Jacobsen, 2017). Immortality, in these writings, is seen mostly as a consequence of a certain symbolic, a proxy or technology. Others are sceptical of this notion, but nonetheless offer useful considerations of how to conceptualise and deal with one's digital remains after death (Kasket, 2019).

Some of the most prominent concepts of immortality, relevant to the main arguments of this chapter will be introduced. Lifton (1973) and Toynbee (1984) speak about symbolic or vicarious immortality, achieved through procreation, religious beliefs in an afterlife, fame, and memorialisation, as well as in experimental and ecstatic experiences of hedonism, sexual acts, mysticism, and narcotics. Dow (2009) examined archival immortality, which includes the preservation of artefacts related to the self, saved and achieved in totality (e.g., one's letters, emails, and digital data). A more general conception of 'digitalized immortality' or 'electronic immortality', where one can keep the memory of the deceased alive through memorial pages, players can restart their lives in games and virtual reality, or, more extremely, where we could store and transfer neural energy from the deceased hoping to keep them artificially alive after their physical death (Jacobsen, 2017). Kastenbaum (2004) introduces the concept of assisted immortality asking the question whether the technologically assisted immortality would be a meaningful form of survival and whether individuals would be willing to make use of it, if available. Brown (2017), interestingly, sets out his four pathways to immortality, such as survival of the body, survival of the mind, survival of the genes, and survival of the memes (understood as memories or cultural genes stored and passed on internally and externally through technology, Dawkins, 1976). This survival for Brown is enabled by the technological and cultural transmission of memories, and whether this would count as survival depends on the concept of the self. This concept evolves with time and space and it could mean different things to different individuals, depending on whether they identify with their genes, memes, bodies, mind, consciousness, or all of these. Survival of the memes, our memories, or our identity understood by Brown as 'what we feel counts as ours' and whether we can identify with our memes in other people, does not have to depend on whether 'in reality' we survive by these memes. All these considerations Jacobsen (2017) usefully labels as 'immortality by proxy', and the umbrella, which encompasses all the different ways of survival, is presented in the framework set out below.

In the proposed framework, digitalised immortality, immortality by proxy or assisted immortality is perceived through the lens of Floridian theory of informational body, the 'body' that keeps living post-mortem through the deceased's personal data, social networks accounts, memes, and other digital assets. A new concept that is developed on this basis is the concept of 'postmortal privacy'.

Postmortal privacy encompasses the theoretical angles of immortality and informational body. Dignity understood in Floridian terms and closely related to privacy, as well as autonomy, underpin this concept. Postmortal privacy is qualitatively different from post-mortem privacy discussed earlier. The latter in legal scholarship relied on the legal conceptions of personality and privacy, with normative considerations of autonomy and testamentary freedom. Postmortal privacy framework goes beyond post-mortem privacy and includes the protection of informational body, which continues to exist post-mortem, as agued by Floridi, through information that constitutes the self. Thus, if the integrity of physical body is protected in law, informational body needs to be similarly protected. Individuals should also be able to donate parts of their informational bodies for phil-anthropic reasons and research purposes, akin to their ability to donate body parts (Harbinja, 2019). Postmortal privacy thus protects the integrity and dignity of informational body. Moreover, physical body decays natu-rally and informational body arguably does not as it persists for as long as technology permits it. Parts of this postmortal informational body are dispersed in the digital realm and are more or less easily accessible by a number of individuals and companies. Herein, therefore, we find aspects of immortality, as conceptualised in the literature presented above.

There is a parallel between postmortal privacy and testamentary free-dom, that is, the focus on the extension of one's autonomy, and by analogy, privacy and dignity on death. Postmortal privacy goes beyond testamen-tary freedom in an important aspect of personality and the self. Unlike the physical possessions transmitted by one's will or parts of organic body that can be disposed of or donated according to the deceased's wishes, informational body continues to live on after one's death, and includes ele-ments of immortality by proxy, survival of memes, data, biometrics, and digital assets (see figure 6.1). What actually happens to all these on death is largely uncertain across the world, as my earlier research finds. It is thus argued that this phenomenon deserves adequate legal attention, and that postmortal privacy explains personal digital assets and identity remains

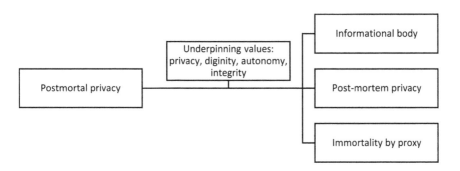

FIGURE 6.1   Postmortal privacy.

much better than concepts used previously, such as property, intellectual property, or data protection. The concept provides support for privacy-protective polices and law of the transmission of digital assets on death. This is even more important in the age of the fast-developing *artificial intelligence*, where stronger elements of autonomous immortality have emerged and will surely become even more visible in the near future, as explored by Burden in Chapter 9.

## POST-MORTEM(AL) PRIVACY LAWS

This section will analyse the extent to which selected legal systems protect post-mortem privacy in their legislation. I will also attempt to identify to what extent these systems are susceptible to the notion of 'postmortal privacy', introduced above. For example, UK law does not protect post-mortem privacy *per se*. Protections for personality and privacy awarded by breach of confidence, data protection, and defamation do not apply to the deceased in UK law (Edwards & Harbinja, 2013b). In English law, the principle has traditionally been *action personalis moritur cum persona*, meaning that the deceased's estate cannot bring an action for a wrong done to the deceased, neither can a third party bring an action for damage consequent upon the wrongful death. (see *Baker v. Bolton 1808*). This principle was established in *Baker*, where the plaintiff sought damages for the loss of his wife after they had been thrown from the roof of a coach. This principle has been revised by legislation in many contexts mainly for reasons of social policy, but it persists in relation to privacy and data protection, excluding some protection offered to the deceased's health data, (Harbinja, 2017b; Harbinja, 2019). Similar findings apply to the United States and many European countries (Edwards & Harbinja, 2013b).

The UK Data Protection Act 2018 in Section 1 defines personal data as 'data which relate to a living individual', denying any post-mortem rights. The rationale behind not giving protection to the deceased's personal data in the United Kingdom is in the lack of the ability to consent to the processing of data (UK House of Lords Select Committee on the European Communities, 1992). The General Data Protection Regulation (GDPR), in Recital 27 permits member states to introduce protection for the deceased's data, and some states have already provided for this protection (e.g., France, Hungary, Spain) (Castex, Harbinja, & Rossi, 2018; Malgieri, 2018). The UK government's approach, therefore, is not an ideal situation and does not contribute to the legislative harmonisation within the EU, Brexit notwithstanding.

The problem of post-mortem privacy has already been observed in the United States (*In Re Ellsworth*, 2005; *Ajemian v. Yahoo!*, 2017) and German (Kammergericht, Urteil vom 31. Mai 2017) jurisprudence and somewhat resolved in the United States and French legislation. In *Ellsworth*, Yahoo! initially refused to give the family of a US marine, Justin Ellsworth, killed in Iraq access to his email account. They referred to their terms of service, which were designed to protect the privacy of the user by forbidding access to third parties on death. Yahoo! also argued that the US Electronic Communications Privacy Act of 1986 (ECPA) prohibits the disclosure of the user's personal communications without a court order. Justin's family argued that as his heirs, they should be able to access his emails and the entire account, his sent and received emails, as his last words. Yahoo!, on the other hand, had a non-survivorship policy and there was a danger that Ellsworth's account could have been deleted. The judge in this case allowed Yahoo! to enforce their privacy policy and did not order the transfer of the account log-in and password. Rather, he made an order requiring Yahoo! to enable access to the deceased's account by providing the family with a CD containing copies of the emails in the account. As reported by the media, Yahoo! originally provided only the emails received by Justin Ellsworth on a CD (or a few of them), and after the family had complained again, the company allegedly had sent paper copies of the sent emails (Kulesza, 2012). This case clearly illustrates most of the issues surrounding the post-mortem transmission of emails and other digital assets (such as post-mortem privacy, remembrance, memes, access, and conflicts of interests of the deceased and family). State legislative responses that followed the case were partial and piecemeal, rather than comprehensive and evidence-based solutions (Lopez, 2016).

Similarly to the UK principles of non-survivorship of privacy and data protection, the US Restatement (Second) of Torts states that there can be no cause of action for invasion of privacy of a decedent, with the exception of 'appropriation of one's name or likeness' (Restatement (Second) of Torts § 652I, 1977). Some states provide for the protection of so-called 'publicity rights' (rights that protect usually, celebrities, but sometimes all the individuals' right to name, image, and likeness) post-mortem, up to the limit of 100 years after death (Edwards & Harbinja, 2013b). Overall, however, post-mortem privacy has not been traditionally protected in US law. Interestingly, US states have been the most active jurisdictions in legislating the area of transmission of digital assets on death issues. First laws that regulated the access to digital assets of deceased's were passed in 2005 in the United States, and more than 20 US states had attempted to regulate the area over the following ten years.

The laws were piecemeal and conflicting, so in July 2012 the US Uniform Law Commission formed the Committee on Fiduciary Access to Digital Assets to attempt to harmonise the laws within the United States. The goal of the Committee was to draft act and/or amendments to Uniform Law Commission acts that would authorise fiduciaries (personal representatives, *inter alia*) to manage and distribute, copy or delete, and access digital assets. The final text of this model law, The Revised Uniform Fiduciary Access to Digital Assets Act (RUFADAA) includes important powers for fiduciaries regarding digital assets and estate administration. These powers are limited by a user's will and intent expressed in his choice to use online tools to dispose of his digital assets (e.g., Google Inactive Account Manager or Facebook Legacy Contact). User's choice overrides any provisions of his will. If the user does not give direction using an in-service solution but makes provisions for the disposition of digital assets, the RUFADAA gives legal effect to the user's directions. If the user fails to give any direction, then the provider's terms of service (ToS) will apply. Finally, the Act gives personal representatives default access to the 'catalogue' of electronic communications and other digital assets not protected by federal privacy law (the content of communication which is protected and can only be disclosed if the user consented to the disclosure or if a court orders disclosure).

So far, a majority of states have introduced and enacted the RUFADA (US Uniform Law Commission, 2015). An acceptable legal solution for the transmission of digital assets will ideally follow the rationale behind the RUFADAA, which is rather protective of post-mortem privacy. It should aim to recognise technology as a way of disposing of digital assets, as a more efficient and immediate solution online. The solution would also consider technological limitations, users' autonomy, and the changing landscape of relationships online (Kasket, 2013; Pennington, 2013).

The Uniform Law Conference of Canada followed this approach and enacted a similar act: the Canadian Uniform Access to Digital Assets by Fiduciaries Act 2016 (UADAFA, Uniform Law Conference of Canada, 2016). This Act provides a stronger right of access for fiduciaries than the RUFADA. There is default access to the digital assets of the account holder. In UAFADA, the instrument appointing the fiduciary determines a fiduciary's right to access, rather than the service provider. Interestingly, however, a user who already has a will, but nominates a family member or a friend to access their social media account after their death, restricts their executor's rights under the will. This is similar to the US RUFADA in that the deceased's will takes priority in any case, the difference is in the mechanism. The RUFADA is more restrictive in honouring ToS in the absence of a user's instruction. Service providers are obliged only to disclose the catalogue of digital assets and not the content. It is argued that the US solution is more suitable, in particular for personal digital assets, intrinsically tied to one's identity, as discussed in previous sections.

In the Digital Republics Act 2016, France has adopted a solution quite similar to the RUFADAA. Article 63(2) of the Act states that anyone can set general or specific directives for preservation, deletion, and disclosure of his personal data after death (Castex et al., 2018). These directives would be registered with a certified third party (for general ones) or with the service provider who holds the data (e.g., Facebook and their policy mentioned above). This is quite a surprising development that brings the United States and French approaches to post-mortem privacy closer, which is opposite to extremely divergent approaches of these jurisdictions in protecting personal data of the living individuals (Castex et al., 2018).

Unfortunately, we will not be seeing similar developments in the United Kingdom in the near future. Relevantly, the Law Commission has recently initiated the reform of the law of wills in England and Wales. In their consultation brief, they assert that digital assets '...fall outside the sort of property that is normally dealt with by a will' (The Law Commission, 2017), and that digital assets are primarily a matter of contract law and could be addressed in separate law reform. This suggestion fails to future proof the law of wills as these kinds of assets become more common and more valuable.

The suggested conceptual framework of postmortal privacy could explain and support some of the legislative solutions set out above. It could also be argued that some of the countries have used these premises as building blocks of their legal regimes around digital assets (e.g., privacy, dignity, autonomy), albeit quite ad hoc and unintentionally. Post-mortem privacy, or postmortal privacy, has thus been impliedly recognised in the United States and French laws. Other countries, such as Canada, have chosen to favour interests of the deceased's heirs, leaving little scope for the individual's control of his digital identity, memes, and privacy post-mortem. More nuanced legislation, would acknowledge these considerations, and allow for the protection of informational bodies, privacy, and the self post-mortem, due to the compelling arguments set out by scholars in different disciplines, as well as the framework set out in this chapter. This legislation could introduce a differentiation between economic digital assets (e.g., bank accounts and virtual currencies) and personal assets (social media accounts, emails, and private communications), in order to account for the sensitivity and post-mortem persistence of the latter, in the form of informational body. It is strongly argued here that this approach would result in more balanced and robust legislative solution in the area of digital assets and digital legacy. In the future, we could also consider using AI agents as personal representatives of the deceased and his wishes (Schafer, 2010).

## CONCLUSION

"'New" new property' is not a suitable term to describe the complex nature of digital assets and legal relationships that surround digital legacy. It is extremely difficult, conceptually, normatively, and doctrinally, to define digital assets as property, and to encompass different sorts of their personal and monetary value. Therefore, in an attempt to offer a more nuanced framework for the consideration of digital assets, the proposed concept of post-mortal privacy brings together the author's earlier research of post-mortem privacy, Floridian concept of information bodies, and the sociological considerations of immortality and postmortal society. Postmortal privacy aims to protect informational bodies expressed, stored, mediated, and curated through technology. This body, consisting of information, memes, and data, continues to exist in the Digital Afterlife or the *New Elysium*, thus attaining aspects of immortality. It is currently uncertain what happens to this body and its parts on death of a physical body. A few legal regimes have introduced some form of protection for aspects of informational body and digital assets, but they are based on ad hoc frameworks that are not grounded in comprehensive normative arguments. The framework set out in this chapter, therefore, aims to address this gap and offer arguments for policy and legal reforms in the area of digital legacy. Legal solutions that promote privacy and provide for the recognition of the deceased's wishes expressed through their will or technology, should be preferred over a default application of traditional laws of property and succession. This framework offers a basis for the development of future laws and policies in the area although specific legal solutions that are outside the scope of this chapter.

## NOTE

1. Of course, a completely different question is whether these assets could be bequeathed by a will at all, given that an individual disposes of his 'property' in a will. See more Harbinja, 2017a.

## REFERENCES

Bentham, J. (1789). *An Introduction to the Principles of Morals and Legislation* (1st ed.). J. H. Burns, & H. L. A. Hart (Eds.). London: Athlone Press 1970.

Bernal, P. (2014). *Internet privacy rights: Rights to protect autonomy.* Cambridge: Cambridge University Press.

Baker *v.* Bolton. (1808). 1 Camp 493 (KB 1808), reprinted in170 Eng Rep 1033.

Brazier, M. (2002). 'Retained organs: Ethics and humanity'. *Legal Studies, 22*(4), 550.

Brown, G. (2017), Individualised immortality in liquid-modern times - Teasing out the topic of symbolic immortality in the sociology of Zygmunt Bauman. In H. M. Jacobsen (Ed.), *Postmortal society: Towards a sociology of immortality* (pp. 40–57). Oxon, England: Routledge.

Buitelaar, J. C. (2017). Post-mortem privacy and informational self-determination. *Ethics and Information Technology, 19*(2),129–142.

Cahn, N. (2011). Postmortem life on-line. *Probate & Property, 26*, 36.

Castex, L., Harbinja, L., & Rossi, J. (2018). Défendre les vivants ou les morts? Controverses sous-jacentes au droit des données post-mortem à travers une perspective comparée franco-américaine. *Réseaux, 4*(210), 117–148.

Conway, H., & Grattan, S. (2017). The 'New' new property: Dealing with digital assets on death. In H. Conway, & R. Hickey (Eds.), *Modern studies in property law* (pp. 99–115). Oxford: Hart Publishing.

Dawkins, R. (1976). *The selfish gene.* (1st ed.), New York: Oxford University Press.

Dow, E. H. (2009). *Electronic records in the manuscript repository.* Lanham, MD: Scarecrow Press.

Edwards, L., & Harbinja, E. (2013a). Protecting post-mortem privacy: Reconsidering the privacy interests of the deceased in a digital world. *Cardozo Arts & Entertainment Law Journal, 32*(1), 83–129.

Edwards, L., & Harbinja, E. (2013b). 'What happens to my facebook profile when I die?': Legal issues around transmission of digital assets on death. *Human–Computer Interaction Series Digital Legacy and Interaction*, 115–144. doi:10.1007/978-3-319-01631-3_7.

Floridi, L. (2013a). Distributed morality in an information society. *Science and Engineering Ethics, 19*(3), 727–743. doi: 10.1007/s11948-012-9413-4.

Floridi, L. (2013b). *The ethics of information.* Oxford: Oxford University Press.

Floridi, L. (2014). *The fourth revolution—How the infosphere is reshaping human reality.* Oxford: Oxford University Press.

Floridi, L. (2016). 'On human dignity as a foundation for the right to privacy' *Philosophy and Technology.* doi: 10.1007/s13347-016-022.

Harbinja, E. (2014). Virtual worlds – a legal post-mortem account. *SCRIPTed, 11*(3), 273. doi:10.2966/scrip.110314.273.

Harbinja, E. (2017a). *Legal Aspects of Transmission of Digital Assets on Death* (Unpublished PhD thesis). University of Strathclyde.

Harbinja, E. (2017b). Post-mortem privacy 2.0: theory, law, and technology. *International Review of Law, Computers & Technology, 31*(1), 26–42. doi:10. 1080/13600869.2017.1275116.

Harbinja E. (2019). Posthumous medical data donation: The case for a legal framework. In: J., Krutzinna, L., Floridi (Eds.), *The ethics of medical data donation*. Philosophical Studies Series, 137. Springer, Cham.

Harbinja, E., & Edwards, L. (2018). Written submission NSW Law Reform Commission: Access to digital assets upon death or incapacity. Available on https://www.lawreform.justice.nsw.gov.au/Documents/Current-projects/Digital%20assets/Submissions/DI06.pdf.

Herring, J. (2016). *Medical law and ethics*. Oxford: Oxford University Press.

Hohfeld, W. N. (1913). 'Some fundamental legal conceptions as applied in Judicial reasoning'. *Yale Law Journal, 23*, 16.

Honoré, A. M. (1961). 'Ownership'. In A. G. Guest (Ed.), *Oxford essays in jurisprudence, a collaborative work*. Oxford: Oxford University Press.

Jacobsen, M. H. (Ed.). (2017). *Postmortal society: Towards a sociology of immortality*. Oxon, England: Routledge.

Kasket, E. (2013). Access to the digital self in life and death: Privacy in the context of posthumously persistent Facebook profiles. *SCRIPTed, 10*, 7.

Kasket, E. (2019). *All the ghosts in the machine: Illusions of immortality in the digital age*. London: Robinson.

Kastenbaum, R. (2004). *On our way: The final passage through life and death (life passages)*. London: University of California Press.

Kulesza, A. (2012, February, 3). What Happens to Your Facebook Account When You Die? Available on http://blogs.lawyers.com/2012/02/what-happens-to-facebook-account-when-you-die/.

Langbein, J. (1984). 'The nonprobate revolution and the future of the law of succession'. *Harvard Law Review, 97*(5), 1108–1141.

Lifton, R. J. (1973). The sense of immortality: On death and the continuity of life. *The American Journal of Psychoanalysis, 33*(1), 3–15. doi:10.1007/bf01872131.

Locke, J. (1690). *Second Treatise of Government, Essay Concerning the True Original Extent and End of Civil Government*. First published Crawford Brough 191; Indianapolis, Ind.: Hackett Pub. Co. 1980, with the preface by C. B Macpherson.

Lopez, A. B. (2016). Posthumous privacy, decedent intent, and post-mortem access to digital assets, *George Mason Law Review, 24*, 183–242.

Malgieri, G. (2018). R.I.P.: Rest in privacy or rest in (Quasi-)Property? Personal data protection of deceased data subjects between theoretical scenarios and national solutions. In R. Leenes, R. Van Brakel, S. Gutwirth, & P. De Hert (Eds.). *Data protection and privacy: The internet of bodies* (pp. 300–320). Oxford, UK: Hart Publishing.

Marx, K. (2000). *Economic and philosophic manuscripts of 1844*. Retrieved from: https://www.marxists.org/archive/marx/works/download/pdf/Economic-Philosophic-Manuscripts-1844.pdf. Originally published 1932.

McCallig, D. (2014). Facebook after death: An evolving policy in a social network. *International Journal of Law and Information Technology, 2*(2), 107–140.

Öhman, C., & Floridi, L. (2017). The political economy of death in the age of information: A critical approach to the digital afterlife industry. *Minds & Machines, 27*, 639. https://doi.org/10.1007/s11023-017-9445-2.

Pearce, H. (2018). Personality, property and other provocations: Exploring the conceptual muddle of data protection rights under EU law. *European Data Protection Law Review, 4*(2), 190–208.

Pennington, N. (2013). You don't de-friend the dead: An analysis of grief communication by college students through Facebook profiles. *Death Studies, 37,* 617.

Radin, M. J. (1982). 'Property and Personhood'. *Stanford Law Review, 34,* 957.

Schafer, B. (2010). ZombAIs: Legal expert systems as representatives 'Beyond the Grave'. *SCRIPTed, 7,* 384–393.

Sofka, C., Gibson, A., & Silberman, D. (2017). 'Digital immortality or digital death? Contemplating digital end of life planning'. In M. H. Jacobsen (Ed.), *Postmortal society*. Aldershot, UK: Ashgate/Routledge.

The Law Commission. (2017). 'Making a will', Consultation paper 231. Available on https://s3-eu-west-2.amazonaws.com/lawcom-prod-storage-11jsxou24uy7q/uploads/2017/07/Making-a-will-consultation.pdf

Toynbee, A. (1984). Various ways in which human beings have sought to reconcile themselves to the fact of death. In E. S. Shneidman (Ed.), *Death: Current perspectives*, (pp. 73–96), Palo Alto, CA: Mayfield.

UK House of Lords Select Committee on the European Communities. (1992). Report of the Protection of Personal Data.

Uniform Law Conference of Canada. (2016). Uniform Access to Digital Assets by Fiduciaries Act. Available on https://www.ulcc.ca/images/stories/2016_pdf_en/2016ulcc0006.pdf

US Uniform Law Commission. (2015). Fiduciary Access to Digital Assets Act, Revised (2015): 2018 Introductions & Enactments, Available on http://www.uniformlaws.org/Act.aspx?title=Fiduciary%20Access%20to%20Digital%20Assets%20Act,%20Revised%20(2015)

# CHAPTER 7

# Digital Remains

*The Users' Perspectives*

Tal Morse and Michael Birnhack

## CONTENTS

| | |
|---|---|
| Introduction | 108 |
| Digital Remains in Context | 108 |
| Digital Remains | 109 |
|    Terminology | 109 |
|    Digital Data and Analogue Data | 110 |
|    Kinds of Data | 110 |
|    Posthumous Privacy? | 112 |
| Coping with Death in the Digital Age | 113 |
|    (Web)Sites of Memory: How Does the Internet Shape | |
|       Engagement with Death? | 113 |
| Access to Digital Remains: The Users' Perspective | 115 |
|    Methodology | 115 |
|    Findings | 115 |
|       Online Activities | 115 |
|       Access by Proximity | 116 |
|       Awareness to Existing Online Tools for Managing Access to | |
|          Digital Remains | 118 |
|       Wish to Allow or Deny Access Posthumously | 118 |
|       Potential Fiduciary | 119 |
|       Reasons For and Against Allowing Access to Digital Remains | 120 |
| Discussion | 122 |
| Conclusion | 123 |
| Acknowledgements | 124 |
| References | 124 |

## INTRODUCTION

As our lives go digital, so, inevitably, will our death. When users of digital services die, they leave behind digital content and data that were accumulated during their lifetime: emails, photographs, online notes, posts, etc. Once users die, their personal data remain stored online or on their electronic devices. The content becomes *digital remains*, which are the bits and pieces that reflect the users' digital personality, and at the same time, compose the memories for the friends and family of the deceased users. As long as users are alive, they control their personal data, subject to the contract with the service provider. But, once a user dies, the governing norms are not as clear, and a conflict might arise between the deceased user's privacy interest and family and friends' wish to access the digital remains for purposes of grief, commemoration, or for mundane purposes such as paying utility bills received online. Based on a national survey of Israeli population, this chapter reveals the multiplicity of users' perspectives, perceptions and practices regarding access to digital remains—their own and others. The chapter points to the emergence of new social perspectives on posthumous privacy and commemoration in the contemporary digital age, and comments on their relevance to policymaking.

## DIGITAL REMAINS IN CONTEXT

What happens, and what should happen, to digital remains? Who should gain access to such materials and control them? What are the considerations for allowing, or denying, access to orphaned online accounts? We identify two gaps in the current discourse on the matter. First, policy studies have thus far framed the issue mostly within inheritance law (Chu, 2015). At present, only a handful of laws around the world address the topic and offer specific schemes, for example, 2015 U.S. Model Law (Uniform Law Commission, 2015) and a 2016 French law (Loi n° 78-17, 2016). Few courts around the world have dealt with the matter, and often framed it as a matter of property and contract law (see for example, 'Facebook ruling', 2018 in Germany). With some notable exceptions (Edwards & Harbinja, 2013; Lopez, 2016), these frameworks have neglected the privacy aspects of the topic and the understanding of the potential conflict that lies at the heart of the issue, between the now-deceased user and his or her family and friends. Second, research into Digital Afterlife has thus far focused on death in the digital age from sociological and psychological perspectives and pointed to the functions and dysfunctions of the engagement with death online (Döveling,

Harju, & Shavit, 2015). These studies explored the new possibilities of coping with loss and changes in social norms regarding death while questions of posthumous privacy remained peripheral. Missing from these frameworks is the users' perspective.

This chapter offers a combined answer to these two gaps. It is argued that policymaking that determines the fate of digital remains should be informed not only by abstract legal concepts developed in an analogue world and then artificially applied to new, unforeseen digital conditions, but also by the social and cultural aspects of the issue, especially the users' perspective. In order to add the social dimension and the users' perspective to the policy discourse, we conducted an empirical study of Israeli users' perspectives. We focused on personal, non-proprietary data. This exploration points to key considerations that should be considered when shaping a regulatory framework for managing digital remains. We begin with highlighting some of the main features of digital remains which are relevant to the policy discussion. We then compare the analogue condition, namely access to a deceased person's physical belongings, to the digital condition, and distinguish between kinds of data. The current academic treatment of death in the digital environment is then discussed. The following part presents our methodology and findings. The final sections of the chapter contextualise the findings within the emerging policy discourse, and point to the importance of user autonomy geared towards individual decisions, rather than a one-size-fits-all policy, which is likely to frustrate both users' expectations and their friends' needs.

## DIGITAL REMAINS

This section provides an overview of the features of digital remains and compares the analogue and digital differences between data.

### Terminology

The legal literature on access to personal online digital data often uses the term *digital assets*. For example, the U.S. Model Law (Uniform Law Commission, 2015) refers to 'fiduciary access to *digital assets*'. This approach assumes, from the outset, that personal digital content is property, an assumption we challenge. Another term often used in this context is *digital legacy*. This term captures an intergenerational relationship, in which the deceased person conveys a set of values and beliefs he or she hopes would guide their loved ones. This term glorifies the data the dead leave behind, which can be trivial and casual. The research presented here focuses on personal, non-proprietary, digital informational trails of ordinary people, whose data may facilitate their loved ones' grief, rather than a legacy in the conventional meaning. Accordingly, we use the term *digital remains,* which avoids the proprietary and intergenerational orientations. Examples of such digital remains are personal correspondence, files containing personal data, as well as meta-data, such as a deceased user's music preference and YouTube playlist history.

## Digital Data and Analogue Data

It is tempting to apply offline analogue practices and norms in order to make sense of the digital, posthumous situation. Indeed, in 2018, a German court determined that from an inheritance law perspective, digital content should be treated like analogue content ('Facebook ruling', 2018). When a user dies, she leaves behind bills, letters, and documents in drawers and old shoeboxes, and photographs in albums. These items are usually available to family and friends, or to whomever has access to the chattels. The person who has such access does not need any special legal or other permission to leaf through the personal items, and as a social matter, we accept that the physical proximity to the deceased's belonging grants permission to access and control them, including discarding them altogether.

However, analogue data differ from digital data in volume, processability, retainability, durability, and in that digital data contain both data and metadata. Moreover, online intermediaries such as email providers or social networks sites (SNS) hold the key to the data, unlike the equivalent offline situation, wherein often, no intermediary exists. Indeed, here too, members of the deceased's household may have access to the digital devices, and hence to the digital remains. We call this situation *access by proximity.* The differences of the online environment that reshape many social practices, allowing new possibilities of social interactions, compel us to rethink current norms. Attitudes towards privacy and death are no exception.

## Kinds of Data

The kinds of data users leave behind, and the social, economic, and legal context and functions of the data, require that we approach digital remains carefully. Accordingly, we need to recognise the kind of data at stake and apply a suitable framework. Each legal framework has its challenges when applied to the posthumous digital condition. Four kinds of data are presented here (Birnhack & Morse, 2018), but our focus is on personal data, hence we comment on other kinds briefly:

*Virtual Property* Virtual currencies (e.g., PayPal balances, bitcoins), domain names, purchased (music) files, avatars on multiplayer games online, etc., may be considered property, and hence, pass to the heirs (for discussion of avatars, see Harbinja, 2014). However, the contract under which these digital assets were created or purchased in the first place may limit their transferability (see for example, discussion under Dutch law, Berlee, 2017). Michels, Kamarinou, and Millard (2019) surveyed terms and conditions of popular cloud services and found that most excluded assignment of rights, which thus blocks inheritance.

*Intellectual Property* Digital content can be protected under copyright law, such as in the case of original literary works or photographs. The rights belong to the legal owners, and upon their death, the copyright is transferred to the heirs. Moral rights, for example, the right to attribution and the integrity of the work, do not usually expire upon death, but unlike material rights, they can be managed only by the immediate family, rather than by the owners of the material copyright. Thus, there might be a split of rights, with the copyright owned by a publisher, for example, and moral rights by a widow/er.

*Data About Property* Increasingly, various financial accounts are managed online. Hence, access to the deceased's digital remains might be crucial for managing the estate. Such data are ancillary to property, but not property *per se*. At the same time, data about property may be subject to privacy law, for example, if the account owner designated people unknown to the immediate family as beneficiaries. For example, an Israeli District Court acknowledged the posthumous privacy rights of the deceased, but balanced it with the heirs' property right, and ordered that a pension fund reveal the identity of other beneficiaries to the heirs (*Schwartsman v. Psagot Inc.*, 2012). A possible solution is that estate managers receive limited access to digital remains, only for the purpose of searching data about property.

*Personal Data* Finally, all other data, should be treated as personal data. This category includes correspondence with other people (such as emails, instant messaging, and online chats), search history logs, geographical tracking, music and video playlists, and other bits and pieces of one's life. During the user's life, such data are regulated under privacy (or data protection) law, and is considered a personal right, rather than an *in rem* right, therefore upon death, there is no reason to convert the legal framing from privacy into property.

Posthumous Privacy?

The category of personal data raises legal questions. Does the right to privacy survive death? Under some jurisdiction, for example, the US and the UK, privacy rights expire upon a person's death, but other jurisdictions recognise posthumous privacy (McCallig, 2014). The EU's General Data Protection Regulation (GDPR, 2016 recital 27) allows Member States leeway on the matter. The question is also philosophical. Harbinja (2017) argued for recognising posthumous privacy, since privacy is derived from the notion of human autonomy, and Lopez (2016), discussing the American legal context, suggested that the decedent's privacy interest should be taken into consideration in designing the legal response. Nevertheless, whether a formal legal right or an informal social norm, we argue that there is a valid personal and social interest in protecting the living users' expectations for privacy, regarding what would happen with their personal data after their death. This is not an absolute right and it should be balanced with conflicting rights and interests, such as law enforcement or research needs. Moreover, there might be gaps between the wishes and actual behaviour, which raise additional issues.

One major challenge in shaping the optimal policy is that many users do not express their wishes. A court, facing such a case, may be tempted to assume that the user's wish is based on social conventions. For example, a court might assume that young fathers wish to leave photographs for their children, or perhaps that users who have not disclosed their secrets during their life wish to take their secrets to the grave, and then apply these plausible social assumptions to the case at stake. However, policy should be based on more than mere social assumptions. The empirical findings we present below clearly indicate that assumptions about social conventions regarding posthumous access to personal data, whether for or against, are misguided.

A fundamental social and legal challenge in designing the optimal policy for managing digital remains is the tension presented at the outset of the discussion: one user's personal digital remains are the raw material of memories others will have of the deceased person. Personal correspondence and photographs enable the commemoration of the dead, and without these, the dead may be forgotten. Thus, family members and friends may wish to access digital remains, although this wish can be in conflict with the deceased users' expectations of maintaining their privacy posthumously. The question is what do users want? Before answering this question a discussion about the function and dysfunction of coping with death digitally is presented.

## COPING WITH DEATH IN THE DIGITAL AGE

Attitudes towards death in Western societies changed dramatically in the course of the 20th century and the beginning of the 21st century (Jacobsen, 2016; Neimeyer, Wittokowski, & Moser, 2004; Walter, 1991, 1994, 2017). It was a topic that was perceived to be unpleasant for public deliberation, to the extent that it was a taboo. Towards the end of the 20th century, it became a legitimate topic for deliberation, whether in medical settings or in other social contexts. Therapeutic approaches to coping with death and loss have also changed in recent decades, and the common approach of 'letting go and moving on' now faces a competing approach of continuing bonds, which values the maintenance of a communication channel with the dead, even if this dialogue cannot be realised (Klass, 2006; Klass, Silverman, & Nickman, 1996; Klass & Steffen, 2017; Rubin, Malkinson, & Witztum, 2018). Media communications, including digital platforms and SNS allow and even enhance this trend (Bailey, Bell, & Kennedy, 2015; Bell, Bailey, & Kennedy, 2015; Christensen, Segerstad, Kasperowski, & Sandvik, 2017; Degroot, 2012; Frost, 2014; Kasket, 2012).

### (Web)Sites of Memory: How Does the Internet Shape Engagement with Death?

The development of digital platforms and SNS has reshaped the social engagement with death and the methods for coping with loss (Walter, 2015; Walter, Hourizi, Moncur, & Pitsillides, 2012). Yet, it is important to note that digital technologies do not determine the nature of interpersonal relations between the living and the dead and amongst the living, but they still expand the possibilities for interactions that did not exist before the digital age. SNS and other online platforms facilitate the construction of new spaces for mourning, which are both semi-public and semi-private. In these online spaces, mourners can process their feelings and emotions in a safe, tolerant, and inclusive environment, without imposing their grief on those who are not part of the grieving community. These technologies can overcome space and time and bring together the people who loved and cherished the deceased person, wherever they are. Moreover, digital accounts of users who died, such as webpages and online forums that were created by friends and family can serve as *(web)sites of memory*, which like Nora's (1989) *sites of memory*, are spaces where the deceased are commemorated, and where mourners and bereaved family and friends come together in order to collectively remember the dead or even communicate with them. The digital documentation of the lives the deceased users led can symbolically revive the dead and animate their memory (Bailey et al., 2015; Lingel, 2013; Moore, Magee, Gamreklidze, & Kowalewski, 2017).

Along with the advantages in utilising digital technologies for commemoration and mourning, new questions regarding access to information and control over digital remains emerge. A key question is that of posthumous privacy. The digital footprint of deceased users can boost their commemoration and allow a richer and more illustrative representation of their lives. When alive, these pieces of information were regarded as personal data subject to the users' control to decide with whom to share what, and under which conditions. To the extent that users wish to extend this control posthumously, there is an inherent tension between this wish and the wish of the deceased users' families and friends, who hope to utilise the digital remains for purposes of commemoration. These new issues join already existing tensions regarding power relations and hierarchies between the people that have surrounded the dead in various social circles with regards to fulfilling the deceased users' wishes. The use of digital remains for mourning and commemoration purposes is relatively new, and it requires adaptation of offline practices to the online settings. Currently, the digital environment adjusts itself by duplicating existing offline norms and practices. For example, people post condolences messages online or display the deceased Facebook profile at the funeral home. But this environment is in a flux and invites constant reflection on these norms and practices, as new possibilities emerge (Walter et al., 2012).

There is a new industry of services aimed at enabling users to control their data posthumously (Öhman & Floridi, 2018). At present, two of the main online platforms, Google and Facebook, offer tools for managing access to digital remains. These tools are subject to various criticisms, but they do offer a sensible solution that prioritises the user's autonomy, allowing him or her to decide how to handle the access to their digital remains. In 2013, Google launched the *inactive account manager* (IAM), which allows users to designate up to ten contacts that would receive a copy of the deceased user's data, from each of Google's services, for example, Gmail, Google photos, Google drive, etc. The IAM interface also offers the user the option that the accounts are terminated upon death. In 2015, Facebook launched its *legacy contact* (LC) feature, which allows users to appoint a contact who will be in charge of their profile after they die. This tool does not provide the LC full access to the deceased user's profile, and the appointed party cannot change the profile's privacy settings or see the user's personal communication. The LC feature has since been updated several times.

## ACCESS TO DIGITAL REMAINS: THE USERS' PERSPECTIVE

This research focuses on three popular types of digital platforms and services, each has its own characteristics for holding and managing personal data: email service, SNS, and cloud storage. Drawing on a literature review about the complexity of engaging with death in the digital age, the current research examines contemporary practices and perceptions of Israeli internet users regarding the management of access to digital remains. The empirical findings and the legal analysis stimulate the discussion and may inform policy makers.

### Methodology

We conducted a national online survey among a representative sample of Israeli internet users in June 2017. A unified questionnaire was distributed via a computer-assisted web interviewing (CAWI) system to participants of an online panel operated by Shiluv I²R, an Israeli market research company. The survey was completed by 478 people. Quotas of gender, ethnicity, age, and geographical location were set in advance and controlled during data collection to ensure a representative sampling of Israeli internet users. Of the participants, 53% were identified as women and 47% as men. Participants' age ranged from 18 to 70, and average age was 38 (SD 14.43). Of the participants, 84% were Jewish, 13% Muslims, and 3% Druze. The questionnaires were distributed in Hebrew and Arabic, according to the language of the participants. The survey focused on three types of online platforms: email services, SNS activities, and cloud storage. For each, we asked about online usage habits and practices. We inquired about the awareness of online tools for managing digital remains, and probed the wishes of internet users in terms of whom they wish will gain access to their digital remains.

### Findings

This section presents the current status of users' online activities, the means of access, awareness of existing online tools for managing access to digital remains, and choices about and access to digital remains.

#### Online Activities

The first task was to understand what Israeli users do online, in order to assess their potential to leave digital remains. Accordingly, we asked whether the participants operate an account on each of the three types of platforms mentioned earlier. As Figure 7.1 shows, Israeli internet users are

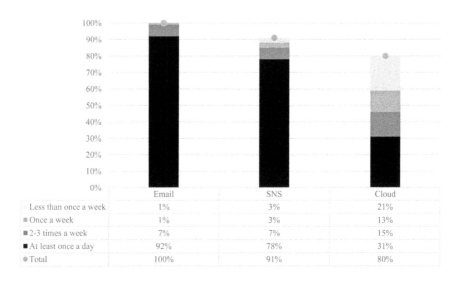

| | Email | SNS | Cloud |
|---|---|---|---|
| Less than once a week | 1% | 3% | 21% |
| Once a week | 1% | 3% | 13% |
| 2-3 times a week | 7% | 7% | 15% |
| At least once a day | 92% | 78% | 31% |
| Total | 100% | 91% | 80% |

FIGURE 7.1    Do you use the following online services? If so, how often?

active users. All of them maintain an email account, and more than 90% have an account on at least one SNS. They use these services regularly and frequently: the vast majority use these two services every day; 80% use cloud storage services, but less often.

In addition, we wanted to find out what is it that the users do on SNS, given that the more active they are, the more personal data they generate, and therefore the more likely they are to leave significant digital remains. Accordingly, we asked which of the following activities users performed during the two weeks prior to the survey.

Figure 7.2 indicates that the vast majority of users habitually perform passive activities of media consumption such as reading others' posts (84%) and hitting the *Like* or *Share* buttons (80%). More active engagement such as uploading original content are less frequent though still in large numbers, with 58% users posting verbal content and 44% uploading photographs. Combining the findings from these two questions, we learn that Israeli internet users are avid users that habitually engage in online activities and produce personal data, which will ultimately comprise their digital remains. The intensity of the use indicates the digital remains potential.

*Access by Proximity*
Another aspect of access to digital remains is *access by proximity*. We assumed that many users keep their accounts logged-in and their personal

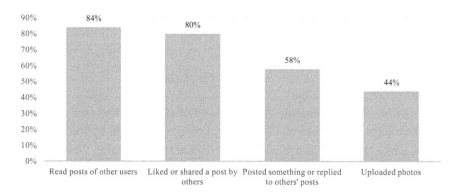

FIGURE 7.2   In the last couple of weeks, which of the following activities on social networks did you do?

domestic devices unlocked, or, that members of the household know the relevant passwords, so that when the user is away from their device, and family members are nearby the device, they can access these accounts instead. Likewise, when the user dies, those who have physical access to her personal devices can access the digital remains, as long as they know the passwords to the devices or accounts. In these cases, access to digital remains is similar to accessing the deceased's non-digital personal belongings.

As Figure 7.3 shows, users subscribed to emails, SNS, and cloud services will leave access by proximity in 44% to 50% of the cases. In most

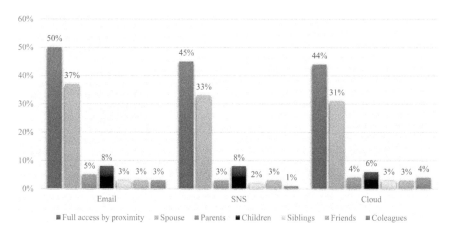

FIGURE 7.3   In case you cannot access the internet, who else, other than you, can access your online accounts and use them?

cases, participants named their spouse as the person who will be able to access their accounts.

### Awareness to Existing Online Tools for Managing Access to Digital Remains

As mentioned above, Google and Facebook offer online tools for managing access to digital remains (IAC and LC, respectively). In the survey, we described these tools and asked participants whether they have heard about them. Those aware of the tools were asked whether they had activated them.

The findings in Figure 7.4 indicate that awareness to the existing tools is low, with less than 20% of the participants confirming they have heard about these tools. Only a third of those who were aware of such a service had actually activated it (6% of the overall sample).

### Wish to Allow or Deny Access Posthumously

The main question about the regulation of access to digital remains was what the users want. Thus far, studies that engaged with this issue applied qualitative methods such as in-depth interviews and focus groups (Brubaker, Hayes, & Dourish, 2013); used nonrepresentative quantitative surveys (Pennington, 2017); or focused on the wishes of the bereaved families (Shavit & Tzezana, 2014). In other words, these studies did not employ generalisable research methods from which we can infer what *users* want. Therefore, the key question in our questionnaire was aimed at

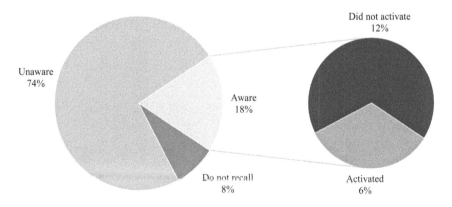

FIGURE 7.4 [Description of the service] Are you aware of it? Did you activate the service?

users' wishes: 'Would you like someone to have access to your accounts on the following platforms after you die?'

Figure 7.5 reveals a mixed and complicated picture. Firstly, it indicates that the approach to the three platforms is similar but *not* uniform. Secondly, it demonstrates the variance in users' wishes as to whether or not they request to leave full, partial, or no access to their digital remains. While 45% to 50% of users who have accounts on these services replied that they wish to leave *full access to all* their digital remains, 31% to 36% expressed the opposite approach, wishing to *deny all access* to their digital remains. In the middle, we find about a fifth of the participants who replied they wish to allow access to some content, but not to all. In other words, these users want to control access to their digital remains.

*Potential Fiduciary*

The next question we asked the respondents was about the preferred potential fiduciary, namely to whom they wish to allow access to their digital remains. This is an important issue, since sometimes there are disputes between family members and friends of the deceased regarding this matter. We asked participants who replied they wish to allow some or full access to their digital remains, 'Who do you wish will be granted access to your accounts on the following platforms after you die?'

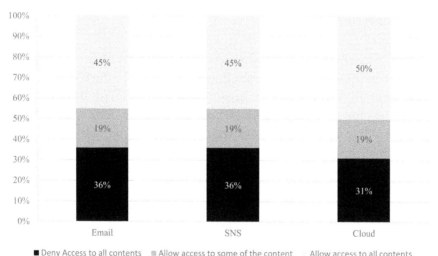

FIGURE 7.5 Would you like someone to have access to your accounts after you die?

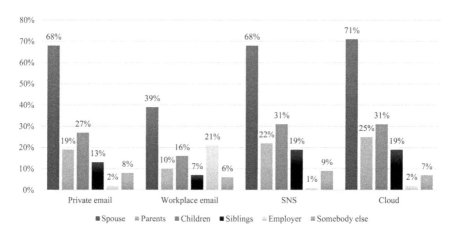

FIGURE 7.6 Who do you wish will be granted access to your accounts on the following platforms after you die?

Figure 7.6 reveals that most users who wish to allow access to their digital remains, the spouse is the preferred potential fiduciary. Spouses were named most frequently in relation to all platforms, including in the case of workplace email account. Another interesting finding is that most users did *not* mention their parents as potential fiduciary. It is important to note this, since most of the (few) requests to access digital remains that reached courts in the United States (Ellsworth, 2005) and one case in Germany ('Facebook ruling', 2018), were of parents asking access to their deceased children's accounts.

*Reasons For and Against Allowing Access to Digital Remains*
In order to get a better understanding of the reasons why users wish to allow or to block access to their accounts after they die, we asked the relevant users for their reasons. These were open-ended questions, and the answers were coded and the most frequent themes identified.

Figure 7.7 indicates that the main reasons for allowing access to digital remains are future arrangements and commemoration. Respondents replied they wish to enable their family access to accounts so that they could take care of various issues that might arise. Other frequent answers were related to memory and commemoration and to inform the deceased user's legacy.

Figure 7.8 clearly shows that the main reason the respondents mentioned for denying access to their digital remains was privacy. Almost half of the respondents who answered this question gave answers that

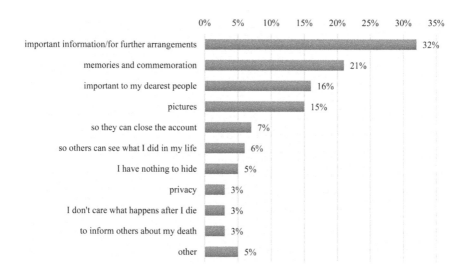

FIGURE 7.7 Why do you wish someone will have access to the accounts you mentioned? (n = 350)

correspond with this theme. Another frequent theme was the respondents' assertion that the data stored in these accounts is irrelevant after they die. The juxtaposition of Figures 7.7 and 7.8 demonstrates the tension between privacy and commemoration, as those wishing to allow access are interested in making their information available for legacy purposes,

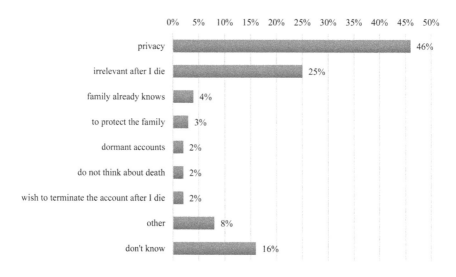

FIGURE 7.8 Why don't you want others to be able to access your accounts after you die? (n = 229)

while those wishing to deny access to their accounts are concerned about their privacy even after they die.

## DISCUSSION

Without specific legislation or clear judicial guidance, access to digital remains is determined either by access by proximity or by the platforms themselves, which make their own policies. Law is not the only regulatory force in the digital realm: technology, social norms, and market norms can also affect the social and human behaviour at stake (Lessig, 1999). However, social norms about access by proximity are still under construction and hence unclear; the platforms are motivated by their own commercial interests, which may or may not coincide with either the users' expectations and wishes or with those of the deceased's family and friends. Technological tools, such as Google's IAM or third-party services for managing digital remains are available, but they reflect and anchor first and foremost the industries' business interests. Although these tools may coincide with users' and others' interests, external regulation may nevertheless be helpful. Our findings suggest that large portions of users wish to maintain control over their digital remains, thus rejecting the current legal stance on (lack of) posthumous privacy.

Online platforms provide online tools for managing access to digital remains, governed by contract law. However, the findings suggest that awareness to these solutions is low and their actual use is scarce. In the absence of informed decisions on behalf of the users, and in order to avoid brute intervention in the business management of the platforms, another legislative technique is that of adopting default rules. Namely, the law can require that platforms enable posthumous access to digital remains unless the user opts otherwise, or, the opposite, that platforms disable such access, unless the user changes the default rule. However, default rules tend to be sticky (Ben-Shahar & Pottow, 2005); hence the law's choice of a default rule is crucial.

The findings indicate that default rules regarding access to digital remains would be problematic. Figure 7.5 indicated that there is no clear solution that could be easily applied to all users in all platforms. We found that Israeli internet users have mixed and conflicting wishes, with each cluster composing a considerable number. Thus, any uniform policy that is applied to all online accounts would inevitably fail to meet the wishes of large segments of users, and moreover, it would frustrate others' wishes and expectations.

Finally, our findings indicated low awareness of the available tools to manage digital remains, and reluctance to use them. Figure 7.4 indicates that Google and Facebook have not done enough to inform Israeli users about these services, or encourage them to activate the services. In any case, awareness is insufficient condition for action, as two-thirds of those who were aware of the services have refrained from activation. The latter finding indicates that when it comes to managing end-of-life, the digital realm is not very different from the non-digital realm. Like in medical and financial contexts, users are rather reluctant to deal with their departure, and are not very zealous to leave detailed instructions for the day after they pass away (Jones, 2016; Steen et al., 2017; Yadav et al., 2017).

## CONCLUSION

The rise of new media brings with it new possibilities for various social interactions. This applies also to the way we grieve, and how we handle the loss and commemoration of our loved ones. The digital age is an age of constant documentation. More and more social interactions take place in or by digital media, leaving behind a digital trail, reflecting various aspects of our personality. The digital footprints can, in turn, become the building blocks of one's commemorations, and virtual spaces where social interactions took place will become the virtual venues for bereaved congregation.

While digital technologies allow new forms of mourning, the reliance of the digital information one leaves behind might conflict with users' wishes for posthumous privacy. We presented a national representative survey of Israeli internet users in order to reveal the users' perspective on issues of access to digital remains, which should inform policy makers. The findings indicate that a one-size-policy, even in the form of a default rule, is likely to frustrate many users' wishes. Accordingly, our main recommendation is to respect users' autonomy regarding digital remains. Coping with death and perceptions of privacy are individual matters, and we cannot assume a unanimous approach.

Eventually, the choice is with whom to side: the deceased users who may have wished to preserve their privacy posthumously, or with family members and friends who now wish to access the deceased's personal data. We side with the users. We argue that the best option is thus to avoid enabling general access to a deceased user's digital remains. However, we should encourage the formation of mechanisms that can enable users to choose otherwise. These mechanisms should be straightforward and perhaps presented to users up front, at registration, so to enable real choice.

Finally, further studies are much needed in this area. A qualitative study is required to supplement this online survey, to understand users' reasons for avoiding the management of digital remains better. Comparative studies in other cultures and jurisdictions are likely to produce important insights, especially given the global nature of the topic on the one hand, but the local socio-cultural contingency on the other.

## ACKNOWLEDGEMENTS

The authors acknowledge the financial assistance of the Israeli Internet Society, and the Israel Science Foundation (Grant 257/18).

## REFERENCES

Bailey, L., Bell, J., & Kennedy, D. (2015). Continuing social presence of the dead: Exploring suicide bereavement through online memorialisation. *New Review of Hypermedia and Multimedia, 21*(1–2), 72–86. https://doi.org/10.1080/13614568.2014.983554.

Bell, J., Bailey, L., & Kennedy, D. (2015). 'We do it to keep him alive': Bereaved individuals' experiences of online suicide memorials and continuing bonds. *Mortality, 20*(4), 375–389. https://doi.org/10.1080/13576275.2015.1083693.

Ben-Shahar, O., & Pottow, J. A. (2005). On the stickiness of default rules. *Florida State University Law Review, 33*, 651–682.

Berlee, A. (2017). Digital inheritance in the Netherlands. *Journal of European Consumer and Market Law, 6*(6), 256–260.

Birnhack, M., & Morse, T. (2018). *Digital remains: Policy analysis and suggestions for regulating personal digital remains in Israel* (p. 164) [Policy report]. Retrieved from Israeli Internet Society (ISOC-IL) website https://www.isoc.org.il/files/docs/digital-memories-for-comments-04-2018.pdf [in Hebrew].

Brubaker, J. R., Hayes, G. R., & Dourish, P. (2013). Beyond the grave: Facebook as a site for the expansion of death and mourning. *The Information Society, 29*(3), 152–163. https://doi.org/10.1080/01972243.2013.777300.

Christensen, D. R., Segerstad, Y. H. af, Kasperowski, D., & Sandvik, K. (2017). Bereaved parents' online grief communities: De-tabooing practices or relation-building grief-ghettos? *Journal of Broadcasting & Electronic Media, 61*(1), 58–72. https://doi.org/10.1080/08838151.2016.1273929.

Chu, N. (2015). Protecting privacy after death. *Northwestern Journal of Technology & Intellectual Property, 13*(2), 254–276.

Degroot, J. M. (2012). Maintaining relational continuity with the deceased on Facebook. *OMEGA - Journal of Death and Dying, 65*(3), 195–212. https://doi.org/10.2190/OM.65.3.c.

Döveling, K., Harju, A. A., & Shavit, V. (2015). Researching digital memorial culture and death online: Current analysis and future perspectives. *Medien Und Altern, 6*, 76–81.

Edwards, L., & Harbinja, E. (2013). Protecting post-mortem privacy: Reconsidering the privacy interests of the deceased in a digital world. *Cardozo Arts & Entertainment Law Journal, 32*(1), 83–129.

Ellsworth. 2005-*296*. No. 651-DE (Mich. Ct. 20 April 2005).

Facebook ruling: German court grants parents rights to dead daughter's account. (2018, July 12). *BBC News*. Available on https://www.bbc.com/news/world-europe-44804599

Frost, M. (2014). The grief grapevine: Facebook memorial pages and adolescent bereavement. *Australian Journal of Guidance and Counselling, 24*(2), 256–265. https://doi.org/10.1017/jgc.2013.30

Harbinja, E. (2014). Virtual worlds – a legal post-mortem account. *SCRIPTed, 11*(3), 273–307.

Harbinja, E. (2017). Post-mortem privacy 2.0: theory, law, and technology. *International Review of Law, Computers and Technology, 31*(1), 26–42.

Jacobsen, M. H. (2016). "Spectacular death"—proposing a new fifth phase to Philippe Aries's admirable history of death. *Humanities, 5*(2), 19. https://doi.org/10.3390/h5020019.

Jones, J. M. (2016, May 18). Majority in U.S. do not have a will. Retrieved 26 October 2017, from Gallup.com website http://news.gallup.com/poll/191651/majority-not.aspx

Kasket, E. (2012). Continuing bonds in the age of social networking: Facebook as a modern-day medium. *Bereavement Care, 31*(2), 62–69. https://doi.org/10.1080/02682621.2012.710493.

Klass, D. (2006). Continuing conversation about continuing bonds. *Death Studies, 30*(9), 843–858. https://doi.org/10.1080/07481180600886959.

Klass, D., Silverman, P. R., & Nickman, S. (Eds.). (1996). *Continuing bonds: New understandings of grief.* Washington, DC: Routledge.

Klass, D., & Steffen, E. M. (Eds.). (2017). *Continuing bonds in bereavement* (1st ed.). New York: Routledge.

Lessig, L. (1999). *Code: And other laws of cyberspace.* New York: Basic Books.

Lingel, J. (2013). The digital remains: Social media and practices of online grief. *The Information Society, 29*(3), 190–195.

Loi n° 78-17 *du 6 janvier 1978 relative à l'informatique, aux fichiers et aux libertés, as amended by Modifié par.* Pub. L. No. Loi n° 78-17, § art. 63 (2016). [in French]

Lopez, A. B. (2016). Posthumous privacy, decedent intent, and post-mortem access to digital assets. *George Mason Law Review, 24*(1), 183–242.

McCallig, D. (2014). Facebook after death: An evolving policy in a social network. *International Journal of Law and Information Technology, 22*(2), 107–140.

Michels, J. D., Kamarinou, D., & Millard, C. (2019). *Beyond the Clouds, Part 2: What Happens to the Files You Store in the Clouds When You Die?* (SSRN Scholarly Paper No. ID 3387398). Available on Social Science Research Network website https://papers.ssrn.com/abstract=3387398

Moore, J., Magee, S., Gamreklidze, E., & Kowalewski, J. (2017). Social media mourning: Using grounded theory to explore how people grieve on social networking sites. OMEGA - Journal of Death and Dying, 0030222817709691. https://doi.org/10.1177/0030222817709691.

Neimeyer, R. A., Wittokowski, J., & Moser, R. P. (2004). Psychological research on death attitudes: An overview and evaluation. *Death Studies, 28*(4), 309–340. https://doi.org/10.1080/07481180490432324.

Nora, P. (1989). Between memory and history: Les lieux de mémoire. *Representations, 26* (Special Issue: Memory and Counter-Memory), 7–24.

Öhman, C., & Floridi, L. (2018). An ethical framework for the digital afterlife industry. *Nature Human Behaviour, 2*, 318–320.

Pennington, N. (2017). Tie strength and time: Mourning on social networking sites. *Journal of Broadcasting & Electronic Media, 61*(1), 11–23. https://doi.org/10.1080/08838151.2016.1273928.

Regulation (EU) 2016/679 of the European Parliament and of the Council of 27 April 2016 on the protection of natural persons with regard to the processing of personal data and on the free movement of such data, and repealing Directive 95/46/EC (General Data Protection Regulation) (Text with EEA relevance)., Pub. L. No. 32016R0679, 119 OJ L (2016).

Rubin, S. S., Malkinson, R., & Witztum, E. (2018). The two-track model of bereavement and continuing bonds. In D. Klass, & E. M. Steffan (Eds.), *Continuing Bonds in Bereavement: New Directions for Research and Practice* (pp. 17–30). New York: Routledge.

*Schwartsman v. Psagot Inc.* No. 50725-02–12 (District, Tel Aviv 2012). [in Hebrew].

Shavit, V. R., & Tzezana, R. (2014). Online legacies: Online service providers and the public–a clear gap. *Finnish Death Studies Association, 3*(1), 94–110.

Steen, A., D'Alessandro, S., Graves, C., Perkins, M., Genders, R., Barbera, F., … Davis, N. (2017). *Estate Planning in Australia* (p. 32). Available on Charles Sturt University website https://www.step.org/sites/default/files/academics/Estate_Planning_in_Australia_Final_Report_021017V_2_051017.pdf

Uniform Law Commission. *Fiduciary Access to Digital Assets Act.* (2015).

Walter, T. (1991). Modern death: Taboo or not taboo? *Sociology, 25*(2), 293–310. https://doi.org/10.1177/0038038591025002009.

Walter, T. (1994). *The Revival of Death.* Abingdon and New York: Routledge.

Walter, T. (2015). Communication media and the dead: From the stone age to Facebook. *Mortality, 20*(3), 215–232. https://doi.org/10.1080/13576275.2014.993598.

Walter, T. (2017). *What death means now* (1st ed.). Bristol, England: Policy Press.

Walter, T., Hourizi, R., Moncur, W., & Pitsillides, S. (2012). Does the internet change how we die and mourn? overview and analysis. *OMEGA - Journal of Death and Dying, 64*(4), 275–302. https://doi.org/10.2190/OM.64.4.a.

Yadav, K. N., Gabler, N. B., Cooney, E., Kent, S., Kim, J., Herbst, N., … Courtright, K. R. (2017). Approximately one in three us adults completes any type of advance directive for end-of-life care. *Health Affairs, 36*(7), 1244–1251. https://doi.org/10.1377/hlthaff.2017.0175.

# CHAPTER 8

# Legal Issues in Digital Afterlife

Gary F. Rycroft

## CONTENTS

| | |
|---|---:|
| Introduction | 127 |
| What are Digital Assets? | 128 |
| Digital Assets with Financial Value | 130 |
| Digital Assets with Sentimental Value | 130 |
| Digital Assets with Social Value | 131 |
| Digital Assets with Intellectual Value | 131 |
| What are the Legal and Practical Issues? | 131 |
| Data Security and Access Rights | 134 |
| Data Access Rights | 135 |
| Some Scenarios | 137 |
| Rachel Thompson | 137 |
| Hollie Gazzard | 138 |
| A Young German Girl | 138 |
| A Young Victim of a Terrorist Atrocity | 138 |
| Law Reform | 139 |
| Digital Literacy | 139 |
| Law Reform: Progress in the United States | 140 |
| What Can You Do? | 140 |
| Conclusion | 142 |
| References | 142 |

## INTRODUCTION

The use and ownership of digital assets and rights of assignment and inheritance which flow from them is emerging as a distinct area of law. As the digital aspects of our everyday life expand, lawyers are trying to contain, manage, and regulate digital assets within an existing legal framework; as well as also beginning to explore how the law should develop and be reformed in order to best serve those with a financial, proprietary, or emotional interest in digital assets. The Digital Afterlife is a particular focus for lawyers because what happens to digital assets on death has thrown up issues where the law has been shown either to be poorly understood by the users of digital technology or in need of reform, or both.

Lawyers are increasingly examining how the digital world fits into a legal framework because their clients, and circumstances which arise with their clients, demand it. In many cases, Tech Company lawyers have got there first in having drawn up the legal rules of engagement through complicated Terms & Conditions of use (T&Cs). As the usage of digital technology has increased, the inevitable outcome has been that those rules are being tested more and more frequently. However, the legal nature of the Digital Afterlife—what happens to digital assets on death— has often not been thought through properly either by Tech Companies or their users. Hence, the death of the users of digital technology is shining a light on a number of areas where the law creates conflict of one kind or another.

Digital assets may not exist in the real—analogue or physical—world, but digital assets have value (in the widest sense) outside the digital sphere, and so inevitably are the subject of laws intended to protect and regulate ownership and rights arising therefrom. The law exists to establish rights and responsibilities between the competing interests of individuals, corporate entities, and the State. There are digital assets of obvious financial value, but also digital assets of sentimental, social, or intellectual value; and sometimes they also have a financial value.

A particular flashpoint in law has arisen with what happens to digital assets upon the death of an individual owner or user. This chapter has a UK law focus, but will also look at how other jurisdictions are tackling this area and seeking to develop a new legal approach. What is presented here is not intended as formal legal advice or as a legal textbook and should not be relied upon in that way. Rather it is a discussion of current legal issues in relation to what are broadly described as digital assets and what happens to them on death.

## WHAT ARE DIGITAL ASSETS?

Our digital footprint is extensive and is getting larger as we are encouraged by both commercial entities and government agendas to live more and more of our lives online. For many it is positive choice to move aspects of their life online, for others it is an escalating challenge to live in the analogue world when it comes to being a customer or client of goods and services. Commercial entities view digital as a way to cut costs and generate income. For example, customers very often have to pay more for hard copy utility bills and bank statements. Many branches of many banks are closing and cash points are becoming rarer, all of which is driving banking and other financial transactions online.

The UK Government's Transformation Strategy 2017 to 2020 (published by the Cabinet Office 9th February 2017) states that 'By harnessing digital to build and deliver services, the government can transform the relationship between citizen and state'. In April 2018 the first digital mortgage deed signed electronically by a borrower was lodged at The Land Registry (a government agency with responsibility for registering the ownership of land and related matters in England and Wales). The Law Commission (a government agency which researches area of law in need of reform) have undertaken a project about electronic signatures and in their project about the *Making of Wills* (initially scoped out in 2017) have also looked at whether it should be law that a *Will* can be made by iPhone, rather than written in the real world, signed with a wet signature, and witnessed by two independent witnesses as per the current requirements set out in The Wills Act 1837.

The Law Commission Wills project is currently on hold, but a Law Commission project to address the perceived uncertainty as to whether electronic signatures are valid in law, issued a Report in September 2019. The project focused on (1) the use of electronic signatures to execute documents where there is a statutory requirement that a document must be 'signed' and (2) the electronic execution of deeds (legal documents which must be witnessed). The 'high level conclusion' (their words) reached by The Law Commission is that an electronic signature is capable in law of being used to execute a document, including a deed provided that the person signing intends to authenticate the document and any formalities relating to the execution of that document are satisfied. This means a name typed at the bottom of an email or clicking an 'I accept' tick box on a website is legally binding. One of reasons given by The Law Commission for their conclusion is that in the past signing with an 'X' or using a stamp of a handwritten signature has been found to be legally binding. In that sense the conclusion reached is not a call for law reform, but rather a statement that the existing law is sufficient to cope with the digital world.

The government is encouraging digital engagement across the board for all ages and for all goods and services, and the law is enabling with ease the creation of legal relationships which give rise to digital assets. Yet, it is doubtful that at the time digital assets are created, much thought is given to the implications of this for the Digital Afterlife of the users of the digital platforms concerned. In death the digital footprint created in life will remain, unless a conscious decision is made otherwise. This means that ease by which legal arrangements can be created electronically in life (by, for example, simply ticking a box) and the constant creation of digital content, is leaving behind a Digital Afterlife which is increasingly hard to untangle. In the context of this chapter it is helpful to categorise different kinds of digital asset.

## Digital Assets with Financial Value

Online bank accounts and crypto-currencies (such as Bitcoin) have a definite monetary value, albeit that crypto-currency is in effect an unregulated financial product which is volatile in terms of how much it is worth on a day-to-day basis. Other digital assets with a definite monetary value are credit balances held in online payment accounts or customer loyalty systems such as Air Miles. Gambling (including Bingo!) and gaming are both prolific online and again any credit balances held from time to time on any accounts held may have a definite monetary value or a recognised means of being transferred into a monetary value. Other categories of digital assets set out below may also have financial value.

## Digital Assets with Sentimental Value

Photograph albums held online may not have monetary value but do have a clear sentimental value to those concerned. The right to view photographs online will depend on how and where they are stored. The right to publish the photographs online on any public platform such as social media should be the decision of whoever took the photograph or owns the camera or device upon which the image was captured. Digital photographs, which have not been printed off, exist in a strange legal space where rights and responsibilities are often poorly understood. Music libraries held online have often been purchased in some way by the user, but are certainly not 'owned' by the purchaser in the same way a vinyl record or CD collection would be. The purchaser of an online music library has in effect purchased a licence to download and listen to the music and does not have the same right to pass on the music to a third party that the owner of a record or CD would have.

## Digital Assets with Social Value

Social media is a platform used by billions of users across the world in order to keep in touch with family and friends, to make new contacts and to share information and images. Different platforms appeal to different user demographics. Whilst it may be hard to place a monetary value on social media, certainly the time and effort which many put into curating their profiles, postings, and how they portray their life indicates the significance that many give to such platforms.

## Digital Assets with Intellectual Value

The ease within the digital sphere both of communication and the ability to upload written and visual material worldwide means that any individual using email, posting on social media, writing blogs, or managing their own website are in effect self-publishing. All of which means the volume of published material, whilst much of it may be thought of is banal or ephemeral in nature, is on a scale which is greater than anything any human society has seen before. In turn this, like other digital assets, leads to questions of who has rights over the material published and also who is responsible for it. The converse side of digital assets with intellectual value is that they in fact end up being a liability, rather than an asset. *Libel* is a false statement in written form which harms the reputation of an individual or business. A dead person cannot be libelled but a dead person's estate could in theory be sued for libel. So, if any social media post, blog, or website content could be libellous it would be best taken down by those responsible for the estate.

## WHAT ARE THE LEGAL AND PRACTICAL ISSUES?

Digital assets with financial value or with sentimental value raise issues with regard to rights of ownership. The death of the apparent owner in life of digital assets of that kind has been the catalyst for such issues to be aired, with outcomes which have sometimes caused great distress to those left behind and those who are trying to sort their loved one's estate. Under section 25 of the Administration of Estates Act 1925, the so called personal representatives (PRs) of the deceased (who will be the executors named in the Will or otherwise so called administrators entitled to the role by law) are under a duty to collect the estate of the deceased and administer it according to the law, which means paying off any debts or other liabilities and then account to those entitled under the Will, or if there is no valid Will, those entitled under the *Intestacy Rules* (which in broad terms provide for the heirs to be a surviving spouse or civil partner, children, or other blood relations in a kind of pecking order—unmarried partners or co-habitees do not automatically inherit). All of which means that the beneficiaries of the estate may well have a legal claim against those administering the estate if all assets of the deceased—including digital assets—are not located and either cashed in or handed over as they are (often called '*in specie*').

However, finding the location of a person's digital assets may present an enormous practical difficulty. If all the information is held online and there is no paper trail in the analogue world it may well be an impossible task, with the significant risk that digital assets with financial value may be lost to those legally entitled to them.

Digital assets with sentimental value also present practical problems. An individual who has taken a digital photograph on their own camera or device may own the copyright to the image, but if for whatever reason the device holding the image is lost or broken or the platform on which the image is viewed can no longer be accessed, it is a problem if hard copies of the image have not been downloaded and printed. A hard copy photograph can be easily reproduced and passed on to a third party, a digital image may, ironically, be not so easy to share.

Digital music and video collections held online may have been purchased, but the rights enjoyed by the purchaser are usually limited to being able to listen and view the material and not pass it on to a third party. In 2012 it was reported in Daily Mail that the US-based film actor Bruce Willis was squaring up to a legal fight with iTunes to ensure he could pass his extensive music library onto his daughters on his death. It was reported that he was concerned that under the T&Cs he signed up, to his extensive music collection would revert to Apple on his death. It remains unclear if Mr. Willis ever was considering such legal action, however, the legal point is correct in that, what he is reported to have feared is precisely what the T&Cs dictate. There is no doubt the iTunes T&Cs were deliberately drafted in this way, in order to limit the use of the product purchased to the original purchaser only. Whilst consumers and indeed lawyers in general may only have comparatively recently woken up to the legal realities of the digital world, specialist contract, intellectual property, and commercial lawyers working for Tech Companies seem to have thought it all though from the outset. No wonder, vinyl is having a revival.

Digital assets with social or intellectual value arising from use of email, blogs, websites, and posting on social media, also give rise to practical and legal issues. The financial value of material published in the digital world may be known at the time of publication and indeed many celebrities are paid 'influencers', but more interesting issues arise if the value attaches to writing or images published because of the later fame or notoriety of the author or artist concerned. A blog by Anne Frank or Tweets by Samuel Pepys would have undoubted financial value, but the question is who would be entitled to access and exploit the value of that data.

Imagine an author who leaves the benefit of his extensive writing and royalties (ongoing income) arising therefrom to the children of his first marriage and all of his personal possessions to his second wife and then after his death a final novel is found on his iPad. Who should benefit from the novel? It is not entirely clear in law as the digital world has blurred lines that previously were definite and, with the protagonists concerned in the example given, it would likely lead to a dispute.

The T&Cs used by Tech Companies are long and often fairly impenetrable, leading many users to simply 'tick here' to confirm agreement without having read them, which on the one hand is not good practice, but on the other understandable given the nature of the document. In 2017 research by communication professors Jonathan Obar of York University in Toronto and Anne Oeldorf-Hirsch of the University of Connecticut confirmed what we instinctively knew already, namely that few people clicking to join or sign up to an online platform read the T&Cs beforehand.

Whilst Tech Companies have invested much in paying lawyers to draw up T&Cs to ensure they are favourable to the company rather than the user, one issue that often seems to have been overlooked is what should happen when a user has died. And if the Tech Companies themselves have not thought about the Digital Afterlife, it is hardly surprising individual users have also not considered what legal rights the Tech Companies will have over their digital life online upon death and how that may collide with their wishes in that regard. Indeed, the oft insensitive manner in which the bereaved have been treated by such companies bears out a lack of thought generally about the Digital Afterlife of their users and the sensitivities which go with it.

What happens to digital assets with social or intellectual value on death is an issue which requires thought about the right of the individual digital user to privacy, in contrast to the interests of family and friends who want access on death for what they see as perfectly legitimate reasons. In addition, we should be considering and deciding upon how future historians may use the data as source material for understanding our present once it has become their past.

Facebook currently has two billion users signed up and it is estimated 8,000 of those die every day (Elliot, 2015). This is simply the usual turnover of human population given that worldwide every minute 250 humans are born and 108 die. This churn of birth and death means that the number of dead Facebook users could be anything between 1.4 billion and 4.9 billion by the end of the 21st century. And if Facebook becomes less popular with the younger generation and they do not sign up to it as enthusiastically as the current generations have, then at some point a tipping point will be reached where there are more dead users than those alive. Facebook have recognised this aspect of the Digital Afterlife and in acknowledging that their users will die have adapted their platform to allow the profile of deceased users to be either deleted on death or memorialised and, if the latter, to encourage the posting of messages to contacts who have died on significant anniversaries or on particular events. On one level this also demonstrates a comprehension that the digital world allows mourning and remembrance of loved ones online, rather than just in the real world. One further initiative introduced by Facebook is to allow users to name a 'Legacy Contact' who is a person nominated to make decisions about what should happen to a Facebook profile upon the death of the user. The binary choice offered by Facebook to the Legacy Contact is still for the deceased user's profile to be deleted or memorialised. However, in either case the Legacy Contact may also send a final message or posting agreed by the user in advance. Google has a procedure called 'Inactive Account Manager' which has a similar purpose. In this way Facebook are embracing the Digital Afterlife and allowing death to be curated in the way users of their platform also curate their lives.

## DATA SECURITY AND ACCESS RIGHTS

Users of online services are told to be concerned about data security and establish rigorous protocols through usernames and passwords to protect digital assets. However, if the user of online services had a sudden loss of mental capacity or died, the practical reality is that a third party knowing usernames and passwords would help the process of establishing and securing the extent of the incapacitated or deceased user's digital assets. It is for this reason that cases have been reported of digital devices being accessed after the death of the owner by the thumb print of the deceased being pressed onto the Home Button. Such tales may be apocryphal, but like all such stories they illustrate a point that there are practical difficulties to be overcome if such things have not been thought through and planned for in advance. Certainly, some kind of means of passing on the required information to those with the legal responsibility for sorting out the property and finances of someone lacking capacity or who has died, which is not unnecessarily macabre or distressing, is good practice.

## Data Access Rights

The use of someone else's password is contrary to the Computer Misuse Act 1990 section 1, which expressly prohibits using the known password of a third party. Following the mental incapacity or death of the user the position of the person with legal authority in respect to that person's property and finances is so far as I am aware untested in the Courts, but I suggest an obvious defence would be authority given under the Mental Capacity Act 2005 for certain named third parties to make decisions for someone lacking capacity and the duty of a Personal Representative under section 25 of the Administration of estates Act 1925 to properly administer the estate of a deceased person.

In common law (the law developed by custom, practice, and cases heard in Court rather than by Statutes approved by Parliament) there are three situations where confidential information may be disclosed:

1. Where the individual has consented.

2. Where disclosure is in the public interest.

3. Where there is an over-riding legal duty to disclose.

In disclosure of personal data, consideration must also usually be given to The Data Protection Act 1998 and General Data Protection Regulations (GDPR) which enshrine in statute rights of the individual with regard to the privacy of their data and how it should be stored and shared. However, both are expressed to apply to living people only. But the common law duty of confidentiality (as above) has been extended to death and beyond in cases relating to medical records, so presumably applies to other confidential data relating to a dead person.

In addition, the commercial reality is that as digital platforms are the custodians of sensitive information, and users signing up must be confident that their data is secure in life and in death before trusting a particular platform. So for example whilst under section 25 of the Administration of Estates Act 1925 Personal Representatives may rightly invoke their duty to establish the full financial extent of the estate of the deceased in order to obtain information about digital assets with financial value, other sensitive information such as confidential messages on a social media platform may quite rightly be withheld from Personal Representatives who it could be said have no concern with such sensitive data. However, a legal grey area must inevitably be digital assets with no apparent financial value but which may have potential financial value in the future such as written material and images; for example, Anne Frank's Blog or Samuel Pepys Tweets. And another legal layer to add to this complexity is that rights to any intellectual property owned by a deceased will pass under his or her estate and so should initially be passed over to the Personal Representatives for them to hold prior to passing on to the beneficiaries, which may mean Personal Representatives are entitled to see what the deceased may have considered sensitive data.

It is, in short, a legal muddle. The best way to get through the muddle and ensure your wishes are respected, is to make clear what you want to happen to your digital assets and who you trust to sort it out for you, in other words provide consent to disclosure or not as the case may be, in advance of mental incapacity (which will happen to many more of us as we live longer, never mind sudden accident or illness in younger people) and death, which—hopefully no spoilers here—will at some time come to us all. Because whilst we may all die in the physical sense, in the digital world unless your Personal Representatives have your clear instructions otherwise and unless they also have the legal right to follow any such wishes, you will live on, whether you like it or not and indeed in a manner you may not have expressly sanctioned.

An individual's legacy in the widest sense is an age-old issue many have wrestled with and indeed is one where certain aspects of it (for instance how one will be remembered in the heads of those we encountered in life) have always been beyond control. We will all die, but we need to understand that our data may not; and so just as generations of people have asked for their diaries and other personal memorabilia to be either destroyed or preserved on death according to personal preference, there are aspects of the Digital Afterlife which a person may seek to control, as long as they think about it beforehand. It is possible to have one team of named people (your executors) to sort out your finances on death and another set (your digital or social media executors) to sort out digital assets of a non-financial nature. Or the same named people could do both jobs. The crucial thing is to think about it and leave clear instructions in a Will about who should have access to your digital assets on death and indeed if there are definite known wishes about how that data may be used post-death, such wishes should also be recorded. In that case the otherwise vexed issue of access rights to data post-death will be resolved and indeed the Tech Companies who hold the key to unlocking digital assets should not then be to use the shield of protecting a user's privacy post-death to repel access to data so it may be preserved or destroyed according to the user's choice. We should be pro-active in thinking about and managing our Digital Afterlife; if not, the default position of Tech Companies is very often unhelpful and distressing to those left behind on death.

## Some Scenarios

In the media there are an increasing number of scenarios reported where a lack of thought of the Digital Afterlife have created distressing situations for those left behind when a loved one has died. I have also come across examples in my own legal practice. What follows are some scenarios which illustrate what can go wrong where no thought has been given to the Digital Afterlife; in that sense they are cautionary tales.

### Rachel Thompson

Rachel's husband Matt died aged 39 in 2015 and left 4,500 photos and 900 videos on his iPhone which Rachel wanted access to enable her to share with their young daughter. Matt apparently did not leave a Will and although his widow Rachel was entitled to his estate under the Intestacy Rules, Apple said they would only grant her access if she got a specific Court Order dealing with the particular issue of access to his photos and videos. It is reported that Rachel has contrasted this with the relative ease she had dealing with Matt's other assets, being presumably their house, cash, and investments.

A Court Order as demanded by Apple was made in 2019 and in making the Order the Judge commented that the Court Rules should be updated in order to set out a clear procedure for what should happen in such cases, which the Judge said are likely to be more frequent. The inference from the case is that if Matt had left a Will and even better had left his 'digital assets including digital media' to his wife, the Court Order would not have been required. In any event, the case is a useful precedent for those in the future who find themselves in similar circumstances.

Matthew Himsworth of Himsworth Scott Solicitors acted for Rachel, along with Barrister Felicity McMahon of 5RB Chambers.

*Hollie Gazzard*

Hollie was first stalked and then murdered by her ex-boyfriend in 2014. He stabbed her at the hair dressing salon where she worked. He was caught and sentenced to Life Imprisonment. Afterwards, Hollie's family and friends took comfort in her Facebook profile and continued to keep in touch with her that way. They did not want her profile to be deleted as that would have meant losing contact with her. However, in having her Facebook page memorialised they were also forced to endure seeing images of her killer as his face kept popping up on a total of nine photographs of him taken by Hollie which she had posted on her profile. Hollie's father Nick asked Facebook to remove the photos of her killer. They refused and offered the binary choice of her profile being deleted or left exactly as it was when she died. Neither option was palatable to Nick, his wife and Hollie's sister. Nick said, 'It makes me feel sick when I look at those photos, and to be truthful I try not to go into her Facebook site as I get quite distressed by it'.

I met Nick as part of a TV documentary about digital assets and suggested that he argue with Facebook that Hollie owned the copyright of the photographs in question and as her PR and beneficiary of her estate he was withdrawing the permission for those nine photographs to be published. Whether my suggestion was influential on Facebook or not, I do not know. Nick and his family and friends were already campaigning hard for the photographs to be taken down and consequently, they were taken down when Facebook changed their position on this matter.

*A Young German Girl*

In 2018 The Federal Court of Justice, which is Germany's highest Court, ruled that the parents of a 15-year-old girl killed by a train could have the legal right to access her Facebook account in order to help them determine if her death was suicide. Facebook had resisted on the basis the privacy of contacts was of concern to them. In its ruling the Court drew a parallel between the online data held digitally and private diaries and letters written by hand which would have automatically passed to the girl's parents.

*A Young Victim of a Terrorist Atrocity*

A television appearance about digital assets led to me to be contacted by the mother of a young victim of a terrorist atrocity. The victim was old enough to have a Facebook account (13 years and over) but not an adult. After her death, Facebook unilaterally memorialised her Facebook account and indeed also those of other victims of the same atrocity without reference to any surviving family members or anyone concerned. For the young victim it was her parents who in law were responsible for her legal affairs upon her death. According to their T&Cs Facebook were probably entitled to act as they did. However, for a family who had just had their daughter taken away from them in terrible circumstances it was a deeply insensitive act which made them again feel helpless against a tide of events beyond their control.

These scenarios exhibit a common thread. A large Tech Company (Apple or Facebook) have a user who signed up to their T&C's. The user died and the Tech Company exercise what they see as their legal right to control the data—the Digital Afterlife—of the user. This has a devastating impact on the loved ones of the deceased user who also want access to the Digital Afterlife of the deceased user. If the issue of access rights to the data on death had been addressed during the life of the user the legal and emotional problems which arose afterwards would have been avoided. This could have been tackled either by the T&Cs requiring the user on sign up to assign the rights to the data on death either to the Tech Company (unlikely to be agreed) or his or her personal representatives (more likely to be agreed) or the user could have taken action in life, such as making a Will to expressly deal with the Digital Afterlife, which would make clear what was intended to happen on death and which would rebut any assertion by the Tech Company that they may not do anything other than retain control of and control the data created by their deceased user.

## LAW REFORM

### Digital Literacy

The Consumer Rights Act 2015 provides that any term of a consumer contract to be relied upon by the party providing goods and services must be prominent and 'transparent' which is defined as meaning it is 'expressed in plain and intelligible language and it is legible' (section 68). Contract terms not so expressed may be assessed as to whether they are fair or not and if not transparent may be unenforceable as unfair contract terms. In this context the Consumer Rights Act is generally concerned with protecting consumers against excessive and unfair and contract terms which seek to limit consumer rights. A similar level of protection to users of digital platforms would be welcome. Obar and Oeldorf-Hirsch called their 2018 paper *The Biggest Lie on the Internet: Ignoring the Privacy Policies and Terms of Service Policies of Social Networking Services* because they found empirical evidence that T&Cs are more often than not simply skipped over and ignored; in their words digital users 'view policies (T&Cs) as nuisance, ignoring them to pursue the ends of digital production, without being inhibited by the means'. In their mock T&Cs a clause was buried demanding a first-born child as payment for the digital services on offer, which was missed by 98% of those signing up. Viewing T&Cs as a nuisance in this way equates to a form of digital illiteracy.

In a report entitled 'Growing Up Digital' the UK Children's Commissioner quoted a project led by Schillings Solicitors where teenagers had the T&Cs of Instagram set out in plain English compared to the usual long version and many were horrified and said they would never have signed up if they had known what they were in fact signing up to. Whilst it is an undoubted priority that young people enter the digital world safely and as fully informed as possible, the same skills are also lacking in many adults and unless the legal burden is shifted onto the digital platforms to be transparent, it is unlikely to change.

## Law Reform: Progress in the United States

In the United States the Uniform Law Commission created the Revised Uniform Fiduciary Access to Digital Assets Act (2015) with the purpose of giving executors or the otherwise correct person in law complete access to a deceased's digital assets. The law has been passed in almost all 50 states and has been useful with regard to digital assets of financial value. With regard to other digital assets the 'terms of service' or 'privacy policy' of email accounts and other digital platforms are still throwing up obstacles. However, this kind of law reform in the United States is a move in the right direction and something similar would be very welcome in the United Kingdom.

## WHAT CAN YOU DO?

Digital assets are attractive to users because they appear to make life easier and more enjoyable. They are often quick and dynamic and allow a myriad of benefits and experiences at the click of a button or a touch or scroll of a screen. But where those assets have any kind of value, steps must be taken to ensure that value is not lost to you or your chosen beneficiaries.

The first stage in protecting your digital assets is to understand:

> *What is it exactly that you own and is there any aspect to it that any third party has a right over and which may restrict or prohibit your own enjoyment of the asset or ability to pass it on?*

Then there are some practical steps that can be taken to ensure that your digital asset is not lost to you or your beneficiaries:

- Back up everything that is held on digital devices. If you back up into a cloud-based system think about what would happen if that failed or if you died and your subscription ended because your bank account was frozen or closed.

- Print off really important photographs and save videos offline. Technology is changing all the time and the devices we have today may not be compatible with those we have tomorrow.

- Transfer digital music libraries onto a portable device. The portable device is physical object which can then be given to a third party.

- Be mindful that some intellectual property rights enjoyed in life such as trademarks, patents, and domain names are usually subject to renewal upon the payment of certain fees, so these assets should be actively maintained in order to be preserved. The same may apply with regard to platforms used to store digital images such as Cloud-based lockers and apps.

- Complete and keep updated a 'Digital Directory' which is a list on PAPER of what your digital assets are. Clearly such a document will help them be found upon loss of mental capacity or death and in the meantime the process of making and updating it may also help identify issues to be addressed.

- Think about any written material created online and make a decision about what is to happen post death and who will be in charge of it and who will benefit from any value it has. Or say if you want it all destroyed.

- Appoint a Digital Social Media Executor if you want a different person to have responsibility for that aspect of your digital life. Similarly utilise and engage with any protocols digital platforms you use have available for this purpose, for example, the Facebook Legacy Contact.

- Make a Will with a suitable expert and experienced solicitor, so that you can include all of wishes with regard to your digital assets in a way which is clear, unambiguous, and legally binding. Note under UK Law a person has to be an adult (aged 18 or over) to make a Will.

## CONCLUSION

The current legal landscape of the Digital Afterlife shows how poorly many users of digital technology understand the legal framework underpinning their use of that technology and the content they are creating. This is not surprising given many lawyers are themselves unsure about this emerging area of law. The collective legal fog may be lifted by users having first a greater awareness of the financial, sentimental, social, and intellectual value of their digital assets. Likewise, Tech Companies should lead the way with having clearer and easier to understand T&Cs and by showing to their users that in life, choices may be made with regard to the ownership and related privacy issues in relation to their data, which may inform the nature and extent in death of their Digital Afterlife. Increased digital literacy and a certain amount of law reform will also help, but making a Will to include consideration of digital assets is always going to be an informed choice that all users of digital technology aged over 18 years should exercise. The law with regard to the Digital Afterlife is imperfect, but as such it is incumbent on users and creators of digital assets to use the legal tools which are available to safeguard their digital immortality. Taking a small amount of time in life to give thought to the Digital Afterlife will be rewarded many times over in a digital immortality which could be infinite; we may all die, but it should be a matter of personal choice if our data dies with us, or if it lives on, in what form that takes.

## REFERENCES

BBC Radio 4 – One to One – Inheritance: When It Gets Complicated www.bbc.co.uk/programmes/m0000y8j

Children's Commissioner, Growing Up Digital A report of the Growing Up Digital Taskforce. (2017). www.childrenscommissioner.gov.uk/publication/growing-up-digital

Elliot, A. (2015). Comment, death & social media implications for the young & will-less. *Jurimetrics*, 55, 381–405.

Obar, J., & Oeldorf-Hirsch, A. (2018). The Biggest Lie on the Internet: Ignoring the Privacy Policies and Terms of Service Policies of Social Networking Services.

The Law Commission Electronic execution of documents. (2019). www.lawcom.gov.uk/project/electronic-execution-of-documents

The Law Commission Making a Will. (2017). www.lawcom.gov.uk/project/wills

UK Government Transformation Strategy 2017 to 2020 published by The Cabinet Office 9th February. (2017). https://www.gov.uk/government/publications/government-transformation-strategy-2017-to-2020

Uniform Law Commission, (2015). Fiduciary Access to Digital Assets Act, Revised.

# CHAPTER 9

# Building a Digital Immortal

David Burden

## CONTENTS

| | |
|---|---|
| Introduction | 144 |
| High-Level Architecture | 145 |
| Types of Digital Immortal | 146 |
| Current State of the Art | 147 |
| Esoteric Approaches | 148 |
| Four Stages in DI Development | 148 |
|   Developing Conversation (c. 2020–2030) | 148 |
|     Natural Language Conversation | 148 |
|     Sensing | 149 |
|     Memory | 149 |
|     Actions | 150 |
|     Motivation | 150 |
|     Meta-Management and Internal Narrative | 151 |
|     Creation and Authoring Process | 151 |
|     Influence | 152 |
|   Developing Meaning, Motivation, and Internal Narrative (c. 2030–2040) | 152 |
|     Actions | 153 |
|     Motivation | 153 |
|     Meta-Management | 153 |
|     Internal Narrative | 154 |
|     Creation Process | 154 |
|     Influence | 154 |

Developing Generality (c. 2040–2060)                                    155
   Influence                                             155
Developing Sentience (c. 2060–2080)                                     156
Infrastructure and Payment                                             157
   Processing Power                                      157
   Paying the Bills                                      157
   Migration                                             158
Which is the Challenge, Immortal or Human?                             158
References                                                             159

## INTRODUCTION

This chapter considers the technological underpinnings of a *digital immortal* (DI), particularly of an active DI. The considerations are broadly the same whether a shorter-lived, but just as active, entity is being discussed, some form of time-bounded Digital Afterlife, or whether the entity intends to live forever to become a true DI. It is also perhaps the intention to become immortal that is as much a defining factor of the DI form Digital Afterlife rather than whether it actually achieves it.

In order to provide a framework for the analysis, a high-level architecture of a DI is first presented. The major steps in potential DI evolution are then considered, from the current technology base, to the growth in approaches which give the DI some sense of meaning, direction, and even self, through the challenge of generality and to the potential of sentience. At each stage the impact of the key elements of the architecture will be considered, from conversational ability to an inner narrative, as well as how the DI may be authored, and what level of influence it might be expected to have. In the final section, this chapter will consider some of the enablers for any DI, including access to computing power and the funds to pay for it, and what may be required in order to become long-enough lived to be considered a DI rather than just an active form of Digital Afterlife.

A key argument is that this evolutionary path is not predicated on some of the more esoteric forms of digital immortality which are typically seen in science-fiction (such as brain uploading), although these will be briefly considered. Instead it will be argued that much of a DIs capability can be developed through the steady development of conventional approaches to computing, cognitive architectures, natural language processing, and information management. The real challenges are in making the step from the specific-purpose to general purpose AI, and in imbuing the DI with its own internal narrative and sense-of-self. This places the DI within the realms of Digital Afterlife fact, rather than Digital Afterlife science-fiction.

## HIGH-LEVEL ARCHITECTURE

In considering how to build a DI it is useful to have a high-level model of the component parts of such an entity. Such a model is shown in Figure 9.1 and is derived from the detailed virtual human component architecture in Burden and Savin-Baden (2019) and an earlier DI architecture in Savin-Baden, Burden, & Taylor (2017).

The main elements of the DI architecture are:

- A motivation function which sets the goals for the DI, both at a day-to-day level and at longer timescales (month, year, decade, century, millennia).

- A set of actions which can be used by the DI to achieve goals. Most goals will need many actions over a significant timescale to achieve specific goals.

- The ability to conduct a natural language conversation—in some regards a special form of action, but integral to a DI.

- The ability to sense information in the world outside the DI—this includes the cyber-world as well as the physical world.

- The ability to refer to past memories (of the DI's Subject) and to build its own new memories.

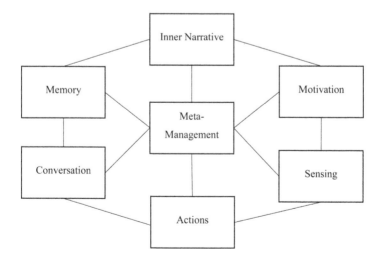

FIGURE 9.1    A high-level digital immortal architecture.

- An internal narrative, which reflects the inner dialogue of the DI and may include elements of planning, rehearsal, imagination, and reflection.

- A meta-management level which defines a range of activities including the changing of motivations and highest-level goals over time, personality, and the maintenance of memories.

Figure 9.1 does not include any aspect of the manifestation of the DI as it could present as a text-chat application, or it could have a head-and-shoulders or full-body 2D avatar, or it could be a 3D avatar in a virtual world, or even a physical robot or android. It may also have text-to-speech and speech recognition capabilities, but none of these are central to the concept of the DI. It should also be noted that not all DI functionality is shown, and that some elements represented in the original Burden and Savin-Baden (2019) model (e.g., emotions, mood) are either present as part of the underlying architecture or assumed to be incorporated in one or more of the sub-systems shown in Figure 9.1.

## TYPES OF DIGITAL IMMORTAL

DIs can be categorised conceptually as active or passive. A passive DI is one which may support some level of interaction (e.g., as a chatbot), or even purely passive (e.g., a web page), but which does not have any of its own goals or motivations to pursue. This encompasses many of the forms of Digital Afterlife considered elsewhere in this book. Interactions with a passive DI may show little persistence, that is, its state may not vary much from one conversation to another, although it may still make comments on the passage of time (e.g., 'Are you looking forward to Christmas?').

Using the model presented in Figure 9.1 as a base, Figure 9.2 illustrates the few component parts which could be found in a passive DI.

FIGURE 9.2   A passive digital immortal.

The rest of this chapter is purely concerned with the active DI form of Digital Afterlife.

## CURRENT STATE OF THE ART

Before looking at how future DIs may be developed it is useful to look at some of the current offerings within the emerging DI marketplace and other virtual persona developments. Savin-Baden and Burden (2019) examined some commercial DI type systems: Eter9, LifeNaut, and Eternime, and their findings, updated with recent visits to the sites in May 2019 were as follows (see also Chapter 1):

- Eter9 (https://www.eter9.com/)—A social network that claims to build an artificial intelligence (AI) of the user—a 'Counterpart' based on the posts you make and the social chats you have on the site with other users and with your counterpart. There is, however, no obvious way in which you can access your own or other's counterparts in order to see how well they are developing, if at all.

- LifeNaut (https://www.lifenaut.com/)—Which is more like a chatbot authoring system with users creating questions and answers for their 'LifeNaut', and completing interview questionnaires and personality surveys—although with no obvious link to the 'LifeNauts' behaviour.

- Eternime (http://eterni.me/)—Users are expected to train their immortal prior to death through daily interactions with data *apparently* mined from Facebook, Fitbit, Twitter, e-mail, photos, video, and location information. However, Eternime is still (as of May 2019) in a private stage, so it is not yet possible to verify any claims or understand what technology is in use.

The lack of clarity around the above systems suggests that any media hype of digital immortalisation systems should be treated with caution—these are really more basic forms of Digital Afterlife. Sophia, the humanoid robot which gave a 'speech' at the United Nations (United Nations, 2017), and has even been granted citizenship of Saudi Arabia (Griffin, 2017) has also had its technical credentials hotly challenged (Ghosh, 2018). Whilst the 3D holograms of holocaust survivors (Gringlas, 2017), and similar 'volumetric' 3D characters, are visually impressive, their responses are typically audio pre-recordings of the subject, triggered by keywords from the audience.

## ESOTERIC APPROACHES

In considering how a DI may be developed this chapter is deliberately excluding some of the more esoteric approaches to the concept. This includes technologies such as mind-uploading and whole brain emulation. Shanahan (2015) gives a good description of how these technologies might operate and reflects a more optimistic view of their development. However, they seem too much of an 'all-or-nothing' approach, whereas a more 'bottom-up' approach is something that should be able to iterate towards the final goal of a human-like DI.

## FOUR STAGES IN DI DEVELOPMENT

In order to appreciate the ways in which a DI is created and operated are likely to change over the coming decades, DI development will be considered in four representative stages:

- Developing conversation, essentially what can be done with today's technology over the next decade (c. 2020–2030).

- Developing meaning, motivation, and internal narrative, but still with only moderate improvements in technology (c. 2030–2040).

- Developing generality—What a DI might be like once artificial general intelligence has been achieved (c. 2040–2060).

- Developing sentience—What a DI might be like once (and if) artificial sentience is achieved (c. 2060–2080).

### Developing Conversation (c. 2020–2030)

Given today's technology, how could a DI, which is in advance of the 'commercial' systems described above, be created right now? How can the boundaries of Digital Afterlife be pushed towards the DI?

#### Natural Language Conversation

Current proto-DI systems, such as LifeNaut described above, are centred around natural language, or chatbot systems. Traditionally such systems have been pattern-based (e.g., Artificial Intelligence Markup Language [AIML]), but there are also more rule-based systems (e.g., Chatscript), and the last few years have seen significant growth in the number of 'machine-learning' based systems (e.g., IBM Watson, Dialog.flow), although many of these offer little advance over pattern matching approaches. Whilst creating a chatbot using these systems is time-consuming, it is possible to create a bot which has some resemblance to a real human. Research by Savin-Baden, Burden, and Mason-Robbie (2019) in creating a virtual persona of a real, living person (Subject), had those who knew the Subject rate the chatbot as up to 6.1/10 on a range of ratings about its resemblance to him, although any single figure measurements must be treated with caution. Where almost all current chatbot systems fail is that they are typically focused on individual exchanges (user asks question, chatbot gives answer), rather than the more extended and asymmetric conversation that is typical of human dialogue, and where the speaker has an aim for the conversation, and is actively developing an argument or exploring a theme.

*Sensing*

Sensing for a DI primarily means direct sensing of cyber-world data, or indirect sensing of physical world information. The latter category would include speech and voice recognition (so the DI both recognises a particular person, and what they are saying), and image and facial recognition (so the DI could tell from a webcam feed who someone was, the sort of environment they were in, and possibly cues to their emotional state). Development in these areas is rapid, mainly driven by the needs of mobile and domestic applications.

In terms of the cyber-world, the DI's ability to sense is only limited by the application programming interfaces (APIs) which it can use to access web feeds, websites and web-based services. Armed with suitable APIs, and, crucially, the authenticated access to the required services, the DI would be able to access a vast amount of information about the physical and cyber-worlds, in many ways comparable to that which a physical human could obtain for the world beyond their immediate physical and social surroundings.

*Memory*

One of the downsides of traditional chatbot authoring tools such as AIML is that the memory of the chatbot (what it knows) is stored within the code itself. A next step beyond that is to store the data within a database, but this is still a long way removed from the way that the human brain is thought to manage memory. As described in Burden and Savin-Baden (2019) a model of human memory which has useful application to virtual humans (and by extension DIs) is that of:

- Semantic memory—The attributes of and relationships between things—a knowledge map.

- Episodic memory—What has happened to the DI (or its Subject).

- Procedural memory—How to do things—the 'actions' in Figure 9.1.

The knowledge map, based on thousands of linked semantic triples (Berners-Lee, Hendler, & Lassila, 2001) gives a very useful way to store semantic and episodic memory, letting the DI navigate the graph to link things in an almost human way. It is even possible to model human memory processes, such as memories being forgotten, corrupted, or made harder to recall, and even for the processing of memory to generate dream-like states.

*Actions*

For the DI, actions are likely to fall into three main categories: those related to natural language communication—broadly already covered above; those related to its manifestation (e.g., as a robot or avatar) such as movement, expression, gesture, changing clothing, interacting with the environment (e.g., touching, holding) etc.; and everything else. All of these are really only accessible to the DI through an API, as with ability to sense. Given the right API, and authenticated permissions, there is no reason why the DI should not be able to do almost everything on the web that a human can do (access bank accounts, make payments, buy things, post messages, etc.).

The challenge is probably in how the DI can string together a whole series of different actions in order to achieve a goal or sub-goal set by its motivation, and how reverses are handled such that the DI needs to stay determined in order to achieve harder goals, or move on to a different goal. Many of the more traditional cognitive architectures (such as SOAR—https://soar.eecs.umich.edu/) feature rich definition languages for such actions, and how they can be used to satisfy needs, such as the Belief-Desire-Intent (BDI) model (Rao, & Georgeff, 1991).

*Motivation*

Motivation, beyond simple goal fulfilment within a framework such as BDI, is less well-defined in virtual human studies. A useful model which appears in some cognitive architectures (e.g., FAtiMA-PSI, Andriamasinoro, & Réunion-FRANCE, 2004) is *Maslow's Hierarchy of Needs*. If the DI has a mechanism for assessing and prioritising the gap between its requirements and fulfilment for each need, then a suite of actions can be taken to close that gap, and DI could begin to show human-like motivation. If those initial needs and the selection algorithm are based on the interests, needs, and behaviours of the Subject, then the DI's drives and motivation should also reflect those of its Subject.

### Meta-Management and Internal Narrative

The areas of meta-management and internal narrative appear to be the least well developed at the present time, and any implementation of them in a DI over the next few years is likely to be crude at best. Possible developments in this area will be discussed later in this chapter.

### Creation and Authoring Process

The type of DI system described above should, ideally, be completely data driven. This means that the same code needs to be loaded with different sets of data in order to generate DIs based on different people so that no new code is necessary. Four approaches to how this initial data load is created, which could be used singly or in combination, are:

- **Direct authoring**—The Subject uses an authoring tool to define the questions and answers, or better the data, information, and memories that the DI should have.

- **Directed conversation**—The Subject talks to the bot, and the bot collects the information it needs. The bot has some structures to work with (e.g., if the Subject mentions a company then it asks about products, employees, views, experiences) in order to collect the information in a structured and conversational way, akin to a conversation with a journalist or biographer.

- **Continuous development**—The Subject has access to a virtual assistant (VA) or virtual life coach (VLC) whose first aim is to help the Subject with their day-to-day life, but which in the background can 1) capture semantic and episodic information as it happens and 2) identify down-time when the Subject can back-fill their digital memory. If the VA or VLC also has access to the Subject's diary, email, mobile phone, GPS records, etc., then the amount of data which could be captured would be significantly enhanced.

- **Data mining**—The Subject needs to do nothing—other than open up all their systems, records, and archives to the DI. The DI can then use entity extraction and machine learning techniques to build up the explicit memories and sentiment, but also mine for things like linguistic style, conversational gambits, and possibly even decision-making approaches.

*Influence*

The influence that an early 2020s DI would have will probably depend on the context. Within a more constrained, corporate knowledge management environment, then a DI which reflected decades of insight into the company, personalities and anecdotes, which had the 'digital scars' of been-there, done-that, could be a very valuable resource to new staff, or new-to-role staff trying to make sense of a business issue. If those staff were able to consult with multiple DIs representing multiple previous employees, then the collective influence could be significant. However, moving out of the corporate and into the personal domain, the family and loved-ones are likely to see the DI as a very pale imitation of the Subject, falling well short of the sophistication of DI represented in popular media such as *Black Mirror's 'Be Right Back'* episode (Brooker, & Harris, 2013). However, with techniques such as deep-fake (where an image or video of one person can have their head and voice replaced by that of another person saying whatever the programmer wants them to say) rapidly evolving, and the growing sophistication of 3D avatars in games and social virtual worlds the *image* of the DI may actually be more impactful than anything it says or does. For the Subject though, their influence through their DI on the future, their ability to implement some future agenda, is likely to be highly limited, not so much due to the lack of conversational ability (although that would be a factor), but more due to the lack of the DIs vision, planning, and interactions to make things happen.

Developing Meaning, Motivation, and Internal
Narrative (c. 2030–2040)

The next stage is to give meaning to the DIs activity, particularly through developing its own motivation further (or rather better embedding that of its Subject) and evolving an inner narrative and sense of self. It is hoped that by 2030 natural language conversation—at least in general terms and over short duration—is something that has been 'solved', a chatbot should be becoming indistinguishable from even a named individual. The ongoing areas of research are likely to be around giving the chatbot (and DI) the ability to have conversations *with purpose*, to gather information, argue, persuade, learn, and improve, within the bounds of its programming, and beginning to move from being simply a form of Digital Afterlife towards something closer to a DI.

### Actions

In many ways actions and sensing should also be largely solved as both are dependent on APIs. The issue for actions is that the security around the action APIs is likely to be tighter (e.g., getting a bank balance is easier than transferring £100,000). However, as the living population expects to be able to do more online, and from multiple devices, and increasingly through the services of a VA, then access to these 'active' APIs will need to be more available. If a VA and a DI become ultimately the same thing (as suggested in the Continuous Development section earlier), then the DI will probably already have access through the VA. It is also worth considering that the DI may also be existing in one or more virtual worlds, as well as the physical world. They may co-exist in these virtual worlds with living humans, or there may even be virtual worlds which are the sole purview of the DIs—true cities of the dead. The DI will sense and be able to take action in these worlds through APIs—the same as for a human user.

### Motivation

Motivation, along with meta-management and internal narrative, is one of the areas which is still likely to be under-developed by the 2030s. The DIs root motivation would be expected to be to further the cause, interests, and view of the Subject, since the DI is trying to be the Subject. Top level motivations could be set explicitly by statements ('look after the family', 'grow the business', 'explore the world', or even numerical parameters ('how important is making money to you—rank from 1 to 10'), or derived by a machine-learning analysis of the patterns of the Subject's own life), or to assess each new decision against similar ones made by the Subject. For any of these motivations to make any sense there must be the suite of actions (and resources, or actions to gain resources) available to make them happen.

### Meta-Management

Just as a person's character is not fixed over time one would not expect the DI to be fixed, but to evolve as it continues to interact with the world around it. There may be a tension here between the family, friends, and colleagues of the deceased who may expect the DI to resemble a version of the deceased suspended in aspic, and the deceased themselves who might view the DI as a way to go on living and experiencing, and potentially in a more unconstrained way.

## Internal Narrative

Internal narrative appears be less studied than almost any other part of a virtual human or DI. Consequently, a DI implemented today is likely to exhibit no internal narrative, and as such its 'soul-less' nature, despite having conversational ability, human-like memory, some freedom of action, a hierarchy of motivation and needs, and even some level of meta-management might be all too evident. Without an internal narrative and sense of 'self' the DI is no more than a remote (in-time) application set running by the Subject to try and have an impact on the future. However, once the internal narrative begins to appear, and particularly once it is linked to conversational abilities which are more akin to argumentation than answering frequently asked questions, then the DI begins to stand on its own two (avatar) feet—and argue the case as to why it is doing what it is doing. An interesting point is to what extent the DI thinks of itself as the Subject, a DI of the Subject, or a DI fulfilling the wishes of the Subject? It is plausible that this is something that could be 'fixed in the code' when the DI is first instantiated, or it could be something that the DI itself would explore, which is a familiar trope in science fiction stories about AIs.

## Creation Process

By 2030 it could be expected that DI creation is very much either a continuous development process through a person's interaction with their VA, or something which can be 'mined' from their digital traces, or most likely a combination. The Subject may even use their DI as a virtual persona or digital twin whilst they are still alive to help perform triage activities (e.g., replying to the easier emails in their inbox) or picking up tasks that the Subject is unable to do (e.g., covering whilst on leave).

## Influence

With these enhancements and a growing sense of self, a DI of 2030–2040 could begin to be a force to be reckoned with. A conversation with family members could be very similar to when it was alive, and the issue is likely to become increasingly one of how the living relate to the DI, and the idea of the DI, rather than any lack of capability on the DI's part. In business the DI could perform a perpetual consultant or even a perpetual chairman role, which raises interesting issues about succession planning and growth paths for those new to the world of work. The DI could also be working towards its motivating goals through marshalling a variety of digital and physical world resources. A DI posting tasks on a service such as People-per-Hour, able to have Skype conversations if needed, and being able to pay for the services could achieve a lot of things, especially since the DI could be doing this 24/7 with no need to sleep. There is also the issue of DI to DI relationships; this world of 2030–2040 will not just have one DI, but is likely to have tens or hundreds of thousands, even millions, all competing with each other and the living.

## Developing Generality (c. 2040–2060)

As identified in Burden and Savin-Baden (2019) the second of the big challenges facing AI (the first being to present as more human which is largely addressed above) is to become general purpose. The same challenge must be met by a DI which wishes to have true agency and longevity. An artificial general intelligence (AGI) is no longer bound by the shackles of its original programming, any more than a baby is bound by the original content of its brain. An AGI should be able to learn in the same ways that a human can: by example, by observation, by reading, by experimenting, etc. Alongside this it can begin to show the imagination and creativity needed to solve problems, originate works of art or craft, or just to pass its time in a pleasant way. This would enable the DI to recast itself as the situation and environment demands, learning new skills and capabilities in order to keep money flowing or to master some new task, challenge, or mode of existence. The DI is now, apart from its need for computational resource, almost free of the need for human support, and potentially beginning to break the boundary of the conventional definition of Digital Afterlife.

### Influence

If AGI-enabled VAs become widespread (making the process of DI creation easier), then an AGI enabled DI will seem less out of place and talking to it may be a more commonplace experience. Likewise, in business a user may not at first even recognise the difference between an AGI VA or virtual expert and an AGI-enabled DI (a virtual persona). The ability of the DI to influence the wider world would be enhanced as it now has the ability to learn whatever skills it needs in the same way as a human. At first this might just mean reading technical manuals in order to develop well-defined skills (accountancy, banking, engineering), but a more developed

AGI might take to reading Machiavelli's *The Prince* and texts on psychology and sociology as a prelude to even more human-like intervention.

Developing Sentience (c. 2060–2080)

As discussed in Burden and Savin-Baden (2019) there is no clear agreement as to what consciousness or sentience is, let alone artificial sentience. Within the context of a DI, it seems reasonable to consider a DI (or any virtual human) as sentient when it has its own subjective view of reality, anchored in a continuous internal narrative, with its own goals and motivations, and with the ability to argue convincingly and to the same level as a human for its own sentience and to be accepted as such. In the transition from considerations about an AGI-driven DI to an artificially sentient one, a key issue is how does the artificial sentience (AS) come about? Two possible options will be considered:

- It is derived through ongoing but contiguous developments in existing computer technology.
- It is derived through some new means (e.g., quantum computing).

Whilst AGI is likely an important step on the way to developing a sentient AI it is certainly not a sufficient step. In fact, many of the challenges of creating and maintaining a DI (particularly in terms of memory, internal narrative, and motivation) may further the development of sentience just as much as the more task-orientated approach to AGI. If AS is developed through these more 'traditional' means, then evolving the DI into an AS-based DI should, perhaps, not be too problematic. If, however, the development of an AS comes about through some very different type of technology, and especially if that sentience appears almost fully formed, then it may prove harder, or even impossible, to migrate from an AGI-based DI to an AS-based DI. An already sentient intelligence may not look too kindly on being co-opted to provide the home for an 'antiquated' DI! Although one possibility is that an AS may emulate one or more such older (and simpler) DIs, as explored in Matthew De Abaitua's *The Red Men* (1998). These same artificial sentients may also be less inclined to help build new DIs, as well as being less welcoming of the 'servitude' of being merely VAs. Whilst the emergence of artificial sentience could be seen as being the ultimate evolution of the DI, it may be that AS represents a completely different strand of virtual human development, and that the far future consists of artificial sentients living alongside their slightly less intelligent (or even less-sentient) AGI-based DI colleagues, and perhaps some biological humans too.

## INFRASTRUCTURE AND PAYMENT

At every stage of the evolution of the DI there are, barring some radical changes in technology, some constants which need to be addressed if the DI is to persist into being very long lived, let alone immortal, and to become more than just an active instance of the Digital Afterlife.

### Processing Power

As a computer programme the DI needs a computer to run on. The trend of cloud computing over the last decade makes this relatively easy to achieve. A DI is likely to have multiple copies running, and each would check regularly on its other instances, especially after any task involving humans.

It should also be remembered that what is really important to the DI is probably not absolute processing power, but rather how often it gets to execute the instructions in its code. If the DI runs at a slower than normal rate (say 1000 code instructions a second instead of a million which is more typical of a modern PC) then it would experience outside time at a faster rate—one minute to it might be a hundred or a thousand minutes to humans. It could save cost (or boredom) by being highly active for a short period and then dropping back to a slow mode for a year or so. If faced with a centuries long journey on a stable platform (such as an interstellar probe to another star), it may prefer to experience the whole journey in a slow mode. Greg Egan's Permutation City (1994) is an excellent description of virtual human programmes 'stowing away' in a big ship's computer, just executing instructions at such a slow rate that they are not noticed.

In much science-fiction the processing substrate of a virtual human or DI is a biological (or bionic) brain. But whilst such a set-up may seem to give the DI self-sufficiency it also creates a single, vulnerable, point of failure, unless it creates many clones itself. Even if such technologies do become possible then whilst they may be part of a hosting solution they ultimately suffer from the same problems of migration as any other computing platform (discussed in following section).

### Paying the Bills

Nothing comes for free, and consequently, that processing power needs to be paid for. Cloud computing is cheap, with £30 to £40 a month (in 2019 terms) buying a perfectly reasonable cloud server. An investment fund of only around £15,000 to £30,000 might be enough to cover the cloud service out of its annual interest based on low-risk, long-term investments. Of course, a DI would probably want a good safety margin, and a mix of investment types in order to minimise what would be (to it) a life or death risk. If the technology develops to the point where the DI can earn money, then it would be looking for an annual income of about £500 to £1000 to cover its hosting costs (although these may increase if it is doing processor intensive work), which are the equivalent of basic living costs for a human. Even if these figures are out by a factor of ten, keeping a DI is still a cheap proposition. Even an error of a factor of a hundred only puts it on a par with some human costs, and this is quite apart from the proposition that an entity with the ability and longevity of a DI should be able to earn far more than this—or even remove the need to earn. The important point here is that cost is probably not the biggest obstacle to maintaining a DI over the short to medium term.

## Migration

The computers of 50 years ago bear very little relation to those of 2020. Some of the same languages may still be around (Fortran, Cobol, versions of Basic and C—the first two only in specialist applications) but hardware, operating systems, communications, and media have changed drastically. The DI would have to be continually aware of this, ensuring that its memory is stored in as portable a format as possible, and that its core code is maintained through different versions of operating system and development environments, as well as moving from server to server as hosting needs change. To accomplish this DIs may well operate as consortia, protecting and looking after the hosting and migration needs of each other, and funding the research and services need to support the continual maintenance, migration, and evolution of their processing substrate.

## WHICH IS THE CHALLENGE, IMMORTAL OR HUMAN?

The challenge of being able to run the same DI on the computers of 2070 or 2120, or 3120 or 30120 is probably the biggest obstacle to creating a truly immortal DI. Whilst experts seem confident of achieving AGI level intelligence by 2100, and of regularly passing the Turing Test decades before then, few could accurately predict what the computing environment will be like 100, 200, or a thousand years from now. To achieve true digital immortality not only must a computer programme be created that can pass itself as human, with human motivations, communications, memory, and internal narrative, but it must be able to sustain itself and its operating environment over a timescale of centuries and aeons. It is far more likely to be able to achieve that if it defines and creates its own operating environment rather than depend on those produced by humans.

In this chapter the difference between the more passive forms of Digital Afterlife, and the more active forms has been described. In order to be worthy of the name the DI needs to develop capabilities well beyond that of a simple chatbot—however, those steps are not predicated on any esoteric developments such as whole-brain emulation. The mastery of natural language, the creation of an effective memory, and the ability to plan and execute a wide range of actions to achieve goals is only the start. On top of this needs to be layered motivational drives and goals, things which give the DIs existence some purpose. For that purpose, to also have meaning the DI needs to develop its own internal narrative, to have its own story—and how this might conflict with that of its original Subject is an interesting issue. It also needs to become general purpose in order to master a wide range of skills, and to adapt to a changing environment. Finally, that internal narrative probably needs to involve into self-awareness, into sentience, and it needs to be able to establish itself within an operating environment which has true longevity if the DI is truly to be able to make the essence of its Subject persist into eternity and extend the Digital Afterlife in digital immortality.

## REFERENCES

Andriamasinoro, F., & Réunion-FRANCE, L. (2004). Modeling natural motivations into hybrid artificial agents. In Fourth International ICSC Symposium on Engineering of Intelligent Systems (eis 2004).

Berners-Lee, T., Hendler, J., & Lassila, O. (2001). The semantic web. *Scientific American, 284*(5), 28–37. Available on https://eecs.ceas.uc.edu/~mazlack/ECE.716.Sp2011/Berners.2001.pdf

Brooker, C. (Writer), Harris, O. (Director). (2013). *Be Right Back. Black Mirror [TV Episode]*. United Kingdom: Channel 4.

Burden, D., & Savin-Baden, M. (2019). *Virtual humans: Today and tomorrow*. Florida, US: Taylor and Francis.

De Abaitua, M. (1998). *The red men*. Thame, England: Snowbooks.

Egan, G. (1994). *Permutation city*. London: Orion.

Ghosh, S. (2018). *Facebook's AI boss described Sophia the robot as 'complete b————t' and 'Wizard-of-Oz AI'. Business Insider UK*. Available on https://www.businessinsider.com/facebook-ai-yann-lecun-sophia-robot-bullshit-2018-1

Griffin, A. (2017). *Saudi Arabia grants citizenship to a robot for the first time ever.* The Independent. Available on https://www.independent.co.uk/life-style/gadgets-and-tech/news/saudi-arabia-robot-sophiacitizenship-android-riyadh-citizen-passport-future-a8021601.html

Gringlas, S. (2017). *Illinois Holocaust Museum Preserves Survivors' Stories — As Holograms.* NPR. Available on https://www.npr.org/2017/12/19/572068474/illinois-holocaust-museum-preserves-survivors-stories-as-holograms?t=1559159574128

Rao, A. S., & Georgeff, M. P. (1991). Modeling rational agents within a BDI-architecture. In R. Fikes, & E. Sandewall (Eds.)., *Proceedings of knowledge representation and reasoning* (KR&R-91), (pp. 473–484), Burlington, MA: Morgan Kaufmann.

Savin-Baden, M., & Burden, D. (2019). Digital immortality and virtual humans. *Postdigital Science and Education, 1,* 87–103. https://doi.org/10.1007/s42438-018-0007-6.

Savin-Baden, M., Burden, D., & Mason-Robbie, V. (2019). Do you want to live forever? Virtual Humans and Digital Immortality, Expat19 University of Madeira 12 June.

Savin-Baden, M., Burden, D., & Taylor, H. (2017). The ethics and impact of digital immortality. *Special Issue of Knowledge Cultures – Technologies and time in the age of global neoliberal capitalism* 5(2) 11–29.

Shanahan, M. (2015). *The technological singularity.* Cambridge: MIT Press.

United Nations. (2017). *At UN, robot Sophia joins meeting on artificial intelligence and sustainable development. UN News.* Available on https://news.un.org/en/story/2017/10/568292-un-robot-sophia-joins-meeting-artificial-intelligence-and-sustainable.

# CHAPTER 10

# Philosophical Investigations into Digital Afterlife

## John Reader

## CONTENTS

| | |
|---|---|
| Introduction | 161 |
| A Practical Context | 162 |
| Digital Traces | 162 |
| Derrida on the Trace | 163 |
| Identifying Human Identity | 166 |
| Agency and the Digital | 168 |
| Conclusion | 171 |
| References | 172 |

## INTRODUCTION

This chapter will present concepts from contemporary philosophy that throw light upon two issues which arise from consideration of the subject of Digital Afterlife, those of identity and agency. There is a tendency in the digital literature to present identity as settled, stable, and determinate, whereas philosophy provides an alternative interpretation. Human agency is understood as simply an attribute of individual human beings or perhaps humans working in concert. By contrast it can be argued that agency also includes the non-human, in this case the digital, and that the latter shapes the human as much as the human shapes and controls the digital.

## A PRACTICAL CONTEXT

My own direct engagements with digital immortality relate to my role as a priest. In over 40 years, I have conducted hundreds of funerals thus dealing with both undertakers and bereaved families. This has involved instances such as a continued invitation to befriend someone on Facebook whose funeral I had taken, and the confusion surrounding how to address this. Having also conducted a number of services for either stillborn or sudden death infants, it is uncertain as to what some form of digital continuation would mean in that context, and what kinds of digital traces there might be. Furthermore, it is not clear how old someone needs to be or how much of a life a person has led before qualifying for any available digital immortality process. In contrast to this contemporary situation, there are various means of remembering those who died during the First World War, given that 2018 was the centenary of the cessation of that conflict. It is not clear at what point those specific memories will be allowed to fade into the past given that those who were involved have long since passed and that the communities from which combatants came have also changed irrevocably. This raises questions about the length of time for which memories seem relevant, and how the impact of the digital may impinge upon such practical issues. In particular this chapter will examine the extent to which digital practices tend to freeze frame those memories and present static interpretations of the events and people involved, whilst also being aware that the digital has the capacity to create more dynamic interactive presentations. The philosophical sources to be drawn upon will question this by arguing for a more fluid understanding of bot identity and agency.

## DIGITAL TRACES

Digital traces may include such things as social media profiles, email accounts, digital music or photographs, and other information stored about a person online. Digital footprints remain once a person has died. This might be either intentional or unintentional, for example, the latter might be a deceased parishioner. This raises questions about the purpose being served when these traces are deliberate, and what understanding of human identity is at work in this process.

A digital trace is part of a wider tranche of effects that go under the heading of digital legacy. Philosophy often looks in detail at the terms being employed in different contexts and it seems there is a tendency to take familiar terms and simply add 'digital' to them assuming that this somehow captures or represents a significant change to their meaning. What makes a digital trace different from other traces? This is where the question of agency begins to impinge. If it is the case that any technology shapes human activity and understanding as much as humans shape and control the technology, one would expect digital technology to exercise a particular impact upon human practices and behaviour. In the background to this is the work of the philosopher of technology Bernard Stiegler who argues not only that digital technology is directly influencing our behaviour, but also that it is what he calls a pharmakon. This means that the digital can be both remedy and poison, so having either a positive or a negative impact upon our lives (the term pharmakon is related to pharmacology in contemporary language) (Stiegler, 2013, pp. 22–25; Reader, 2017, pp. 125–128).

Offering a practical example might help here. At the beginning of 2019 a piano belonging to my mother (still alive at the time of writing but in her late 90s) was moved by professional piano removers to the newly purchased house of one of our children. I felt a sense of loss that I could not quite explain, and the removal team said that pianos often went to other family members, but that they had seen people in tears as the instrument had been taken away even though it was staying within the family. A supposedly inanimate object had become part of the family story and identity and was itself a trace of someone who was still alive at that point. This raises a question about how digital traces differ from other tangible objects, and what this might tell us about the limitations of the digital playing that role. Stiegler argues that the pace and immediacy with which the digital functions can short circuit the process of human thought and critical reflection, partly by requiring an instant response or reaction. It does not necessarily have to be that way, but one can see how a digital trace appearing on social media, for instance, might trigger an immediate emotional response, particularly if unexpected. In contrast, non-digital traces might allow for a more measured and thoughtful reaction; one that takes time to absorb and process.

## DERRIDA ON THE TRACE

Stiegler at one time studied under Derrida, a French philosopher who died in 2004, who was best known in non-philosophical circles for the term deconstruction, which is a plea for examining the range of meanings and interpretations that are always present in the use of any term. It is important to guard against the view that this simply means overturning a traditional interpretation and replacing it with its opposite, which is the way the term deconstruction has come to be used by others since. Deconstruction as exercised by Derrida does not mean taking something apart for the sake of it and then reconstructing it in an arbitrary fashion, but instead opening up the range of different meanings that are already at work beneath the apparent stabilisation of the way we employ language. Poetry would be an obvious example of this where the poet is deliberately playing on different meanings in order to stimulate other thoughts and possibilities. Similarly, Derrida proposes that a similar process is at work throughout human discourse. Destabilising is perhaps a more accurate description than deconstruction, and we will see that this is characteristic of much of the philosophy to be examined in this chapter. Such destabilising is not done without reason but because it has practical and political effects which relate to a deeper understanding of ourselves. Derrida also wrote about the pharmakon who, like Stiegler, argued that it can mean both remedy and poison, but that it also contains a much wider range of interpretations (Derrida, 2013, pp. 128–142).

His use of the term trace derives from some of his early work where he is trying to develop a more nuanced understanding of human writing and discourse (Derrida, 1997, p. 108; 1998, pp. 70–73). One might imagine that a trace is simply a mark or inscription on a page such as a written letter or word, but Derrida is trying to help us understand that what it refers to is actually not just present in, but also prior to that specific instance. In other words, and this is consistent with his interpretation of writing generally, there is always more than the obvious and familiar which we take for granted when we encounter that trace. There is something always lost in translation, as every reading is a form of translation or interpretation, and there is always an excess of meaning that remains each time we stabilise or settle on a specific understanding. What can happen once we have grasped this; is that we imagine there is some original or deeper meaning of which the trace is itself a sign. If we could only understand this range of meanings, we could identify what it really means and be confident that we have understood fully and completely. The trace can take us back to the original which is itself settled and determinate. An example would be the invitation to accept as a Facebook friend the person whose funeral I had taken some years ago thus presenting a static and determinate image and trace which is no longer correct.

There might be a tendency to imagine that such traces can take us back to a settled and determinate understanding of the person whose traces we now encounter. What one sees on a Facebook site, for instance, or reads in an email account, let alone accesses on an interactive headstone, is somehow the original, authentic person. The traces are a direct and reliable route back to who and what this person was in a way that is meant to be consoling or at least an accurate representation of the memories one is trying to recapture. The meaning has been stabilised in such a way that other possibilities are now no longer available. This is who this person was both for themselves and in their relationships to others. Any alternatives or sense of change and development have ceased as if they are now frozen in time, and it seems that the original has been identified and captured for all time.

Interestingly my son-in-law has just reposted on Facebook a video of our granddaughter playing the piano from four years ago. Facebook itself had already reposted this as a digital memory of her at that stage in her development with the comment from the family that she must be taking after her mother. Why do this when she is no longer that person and her piano playing has improved significantly? This is a little girl as she was then, but why is that particular moment of any great significance, even to her immediate family? One does not have to be dead in order to have a digital trace appear on social media! Clearly though if one is dead there are never going to be further updates or developments to share in this way. That is an issue we will examine shortly. But this is Facebook presenting an unsolicited and apparently meaningless trace. The purpose of this is presumably to lock people even more deeply into the Facebook world by reminding them of events that an algorithm has selected as still being of interest. That itself raises the issue of who decides which traces or events should be selected for those who are no longer alive, and those can only be ones already present in the digital domain. Are these really representative of that person? Derrida surely has a point that goes beyond the merely philosophical when he argues that such stabilisations of meaning have both political and practical implications and so need to be brought into question. As a distressing aside, imagine that our granddaughter had died in the meantime and the impact of this reposting on ourselves as a family. One might ask who controls and who decides and, in whose interests, when it comes to such traces.

It is possible that not only traces but the very notion of immortality can be deconstructed or destabilised. It is not adequate to simply equate immortality with being dead and mortality as still being alive. What is often being referred to when those terms are employed is in fact the continuing impact upon others. The 'immortals' in any particular field are those whom one assumes already have a major impact, but that impact will survive their demise as their influence lives on after them. The great composers, artists, or political leaders often recognised in their own lifetimes will continue to shape developments in their particular fields for generations to come. But what about those who have not lived long enough or whose lives or work have not had the opportunity to be disseminated. Are they to be denied immortality? The concepts of mortality and immortality carry a wider range of meanings in the debate about digital immortality which appears to be applied only to those who have already died.

## IDENTIFYING HUMAN IDENTITY

Malabou, also a onetime student of Derrida (Malabou, 2016; Reader, 2017, p. 73–79), has a particular interest in the area of neuroscience and its implications for an understanding of human identity, stemming from concern for her own grandmother who has Alzheimer's disease. This raises the question which many of us face when a person we care for is no longer who we want them or remember them to be. When a person's memory or physical state has deteriorated such that they cannot remember who we or they are, or relate to us as they used to. One might ask questions about whether identity depends upon a person retaining a memory of themselves. Digital traces might help to recall that person for us, even though they are still alive but apparently lost to us.

This is where it is important to consider the question of understanding identity as the sole and restricted possession of a single individual. It might be that once a person's memory has been lost, they are no longer that person. Watkin (2016, pp. 126–127) presents an alternative view and a critique of Malabou by suggesting that human identity cannot simply be reduced to the mental faculties of each individual in isolation, but that it is carried by and through relationships with others, even when that person can no longer function as they used to. A person is not just a lone individual or disembodied mind who ceases to have a recognisable identity when that mind has apparently departed, but that person is always what they are in relationship with others, and it is in those relationships that elements of their identity continue even when their normal functioning in those relationships have ceased. This then becomes another destabilising of the concept of human identity consistent with the ideas of Derrida and Stiegler.

This presents a much more holistic and realistic understanding of what it is to be human. If this is the case, then digital traces are even more inadequate and reductionist than already suggested. It is not only that one can never convincingly establish that a particular moment in time or stage in a person's life somehow captures their essential or original self, but also that anyone's identity is always carried in relationship to and with others. Re-presenting an individual life in whatever form is only a part of who and what they are or were, and a potential decontextualising of their identity that may even distort that life let alone fail to capture their impact upon others. If immortality is at least on one level about lasting impact upon others, then not being able to present that offers only a very attenuated version of that person.

One of the central arguments which is relevant to both identity and agency is that much of the current debate resorts to what is called a mind-body dualism. In other words, the body is understood as no more than a shell or container for the mind, and the brain is therefore capable of being separated from this shell in some way in the more extreme interpretations of human survival. There are other dualisms such as that between nature and culture; subject and object; reason and emotion; the material and the ideal; male and female. Once again as is evident in the work of Derrida, the objective is not to replace one with the other or reverse a supposed hierarchy, but to argue for a more complex and nuanced relationship between the two. In this case, the concern is to understand more deeply how it is that humans develop and learn by destabilising established notions of individuality and identity. There is always that 'more than' or excess of meaning that Derrida sought for, but now extended into other areas of human existence.

Two important figures in this discussion are the philosophers Deleuze and Simondon (for an excellent introduction to their work see Grosz, 2018, Chapters 4 and 5, respectively). The latter was an influence upon Deleuze and was particularly concerned with the technologies that increasingly pervade our lives. His interpretations of identity are relevant in this context, and from an educational perspective, to understand how humans learn, grow, and develop (Deleuze & Guattari, 2004). However, it is difficult to grasp that we can continue to change and develop in the light of new challenges and experiences and to recognise that we are in a constant process of becoming rather than being fixed or determinate in our views and attitudes.

Rather than talking about individuals as such, Simondon (In Crary & Kwinter, 1993, pp. 297–317) talks about the process of individuation. In order for us to continue to develop there has to be what he calls the pre-individual, that which remains open to further encounter and adjustment.

Rather than stability which would suggest that once we reach a particular stage in our lives it becomes less likely that we will ever see things differently, Simondon considers the idea of metastability, to make it clear that there is always scope for new practices and ideas to emerge as a result of our engagement in the world and with others. In other words, the idea that our identities and relationships with others are settled, stable, and determinate is to be challenged, and one must view those identities as in flux, shifting, and probably less stable than one prefers to imagine. Grosz describes the pre-individual:

> The pre-individual is the centre of Simondon's conception of being, but not a being composed of identities, things, substances. It is the metastable order from which beings, or rather becomings, engender themselves. Being, is for him, potential rather than actual (Grosz, 2018, p. 172).

If this is the case, and like Deleuze, Simondon is determined to promote ideas of becoming and an openness that allows for constant change and movement, then that question of which version of ourselves would be represented either through a digital trace or the construction of an avatar or disembodied continuation of the brain becomes a real problem. If a person is in a process of permanent development, but is also as an embodied and embedded being in a relationship with the world and with others rather than as a disembodied brain, what is the possible justification for freeze framing an individual life through the digital? These important philosophical perspectives of human identity present a serious critique of much that is now being presented as digital immortality. Through the work of these philosophers it is possible to recognise that a deeper understanding of what it is to be and become human requires the destabilisations that they present to us.

## AGENCY AND THE DIGITAL

There is a question about how and whether adding digital to terms such as trace, and immortality legitimately points to something new. If this is not the case then it would suggest that digital technology is no more than another mechanism by which each of these is produced. There would be no difference between a digital trace and any other sort of trace. In one way this takes us to the central idea about agency as it assumes another dualism or binary that the philosophers discussed here call into question.

Stiegler, for instance, argues that digital technology shapes and influences human practice and behaviour as much as humans shape and control the technology. This challenges the view that there is a clear and definitive distinction between subject and object. Hence it is not the case that humans as subjects employ or devise methods of deploying digital technology as an object of some description, but rather that both are already engaged in interactions which are 'more than' or in excess of what either is in themselves. When, for instance, a mobile phone is used to access emails or pictures, the person is not simply a human subject manipulating a humanly devised technology in order to achieve a specific aim, but they are in process of becoming something different that would not exist without that particular interaction. The common sense understanding is thus destabilised and raises the question of whether the specific technology being employed leads to beneficial or harmful consequences.

This understanding is important in two respects. First, the division between subject and object needs to be destabilised or deconstructed in the strict Derridean sense. Second, the proposal is that digital technology itself represents a serious step change in how humans function and develop. In other words, the technology is not simply of instrumental importance, but what philosophers call ontological significance, which means our very ways of being and working in the world. These two strands are closely related, however, the main danger in both cases is to avoid a form of determinism which would imply that things have to be that way. If that is not going to be the case then there needs to be a way in which we can see alternatives developing. Using the philosophical terminology of Malabou and Simondon, we need to find evidence of that metastability which allows for genuine change in the interactions formed by the human-digital technology interface.

The significance of this for an understanding of agency is that it is invariably so much more than a human subject manipulating or employing a non-human object, but instead forms part of what is called an assemblage which brings together the human and the non-human or what is known as distributed agency. Sitting down and playing a piano, for instance, presupposes a whole series of components and processes that go beyond the simply human, even though that engagement is what brings the music to life. This is obviously a non-digital example, although there is work on how the impact of the digital upon music production and performance is developing. What needs to be examined in the case of the digital and its impact upon practices of death and bereavement are the specific assemblages involved, how the human itself changes as a result of the interactions with the technology, and how that technology itself is shaping the humans in those interactions. In other words, digital technology is not a neutral tool which is just another mechanism by which humans address certain issues, but itself affects us as humans as and when we engage with it for those purposes. This is true of all technologies going back to the earliest days of human civilisation. The discovery of fire, the invention of the wheel, the developments stemming from the Industrial Revolution are all examples of the ways in which humans have changed as part of those assemblages and where the non-human has shaped the future of human development.

What then are the specific ways in which digital technology is shaping the human, particularly in the case of the attempts to engage with it in the context of immortality, death, and bereavement? If the digital is a step change at both an ontological and practical level, these issues should be identified and responded to appropriately. Returning to the example of the Facebook posting of my granddaughter as she was in her piano playing four years ago, some of this becomes clear. This posting has been created by the use of an algorithm devised and employed by Facebook in order to achieve a specific objective, that of engaging the continued attention of our family, presumably while also collecting information about us which can be used by others for marketing purposes. It is not then a neutral tool with innocent objectives. We as a family have no control over that algorithm, nor any knowledge of how it was developed or designed, let alone how it is then deployed. Yet its purpose is potentially to manipulate our behaviour and responses. When it comes to any aspect of the digital technology being employed in the immortality field, the same is true. Humans are in danger of becoming passive recipients of technologies used by others for what are essentially commercial objectives. Is that such a problem as long as we are aware of this?

According to Stiegler, one of the main arguments in this area is that these algorithms operate at such a speed that we do not have the time or opportunity to stand back and reflect critically upon what is happening (Stiegler, 2016, p. 140). Information or choices based on information being fed to us, is there instantly if we choose to be connected, and demanding instant responses unless we have the discipline to take time out and make more measured decisions. One of the concerns, for instance, about the impact upon young people of digital technology such as smart phones, is that they are so rapidly drawn into this way of functioning that they effectively become dependent on the technology itself. There is however conflicting research, but working in schools and talking to concerned parents who are not sure how to limit or monitor children's access to the technology, this is evidently a serious issue. The problem is how to find ways of addressing this while avoiding deterministic arguments or conclusions, which is why a deeper understanding of the specific assemblages and how humans are part of these in a distributed agency could be an important way forward.

Returning to the earlier arguments by which the philosophers attempt to disturb, disrupt, and destabilise established understandings and interpretations, the danger of employing digital technology in this context is that the algorithms being used effectively stabilise and therefore limit the possibilities for human identity and interaction. What is presented in digital traces are snap shots, frozen moments in time rather than the ongoing dynamic changes to which humans are subject; that metastability which is characteristic of a lived human life and can lead to surprising and unpredictable events. Once dead, one cannot know how a particular person might have continued in different and surprising ways, so even an avatar based on their life up until that point can hardly be an accurate representation of what they might have become.

Of course, if one believes in some form of post-death continuation one could argue that there is a form of continuing spiritual development inaccessible to normal human means, so creating an artificial form of that through digital technology is potentially misleading and a betrayal of what could otherwise be a different sort of interaction between the living and their departed loved one. Employing the digital in this context becomes a means of stabilising or constructing an unrepresentative human artifice through the use of algorithms thus effectively closing down or preempting the alternative futures that might have developed for this person. The legitimacy of this could be questioned even though there might be some beneficial outcome in terms of consolation for relatives and friends.

## CONCLUSION

The open question which remains to be researched and considered is whether it is possible for the digital technology to be both developed and employed in such a way as to enable that metastability and flexibility which is characteristic of human interaction with others, both human and non-human. Whilst the technology is so dominated commercially by Apple, Google, Facebook, Amazon, and even Netflix, it is difficult to know how genuine alternatives can be developed. This is a major political and practical challenge that will impact our lives in ways we have yet to fully appreciate and appropriately respond to.

It can be hoped that the sort of philosophical resources shared in this chapter will enable a more critical and constructive engagement with these human non-human assemblages, and that the processes of deconstruction or destabilisation shared will contribute to that end. That, however, will depend upon our capacity and willingness to stand back, take time, and create the spaces for critical reflection. It also demands a different conceptuality as hinted at in this chapter as we struggle to understand this rapidly changing and complex world which shapes us as much as we shape it. It has become clear that the concepts of agency and identity appropriately resist the freeze framing that occurs as a result of much contemporary deployment of digital technology.

## REFERENCES

Deleuze, G., & Guattari, F. (2004). *A thousand plateaus.* London: Continuum.

Derrida, J. (1997). *Writing and difference.* London: Routledge & Kegan Paul.

Derrida, J. (1998). *Of grammatology.* London: The Johns Hopkins University Press.

Derrida, J. (2013). *Dissemination.* London, Bloomsbury: Academic.

Grosz, E. (2018). The Incorporeal: Ontology. *Ethics and the limits of materialism.* New York: Columbia University Press.

Malabou, C. (2016). *Before tomorrow: Epigenesis and rationality.* Cambridge, UK: Polity Press.

Reader, J. (2017). *Theology and new materialism: Spaces of faithful dissent.* New York: Palgrave Macmillan.

Simondon, G. (1993). The genesis of the individual. In Crary. J., & Kwinter. S. (Eds.), *Incorporations.* New York. Zone Books.

Stiegler, B. (2013). *What makes life worth living: On pharmacology.* Cambridge, UK: Polity Press.

Stiegler, B. (2016). *Automatic society: The future of work.* Cambridge, UK: Polity Press.

Watkin, C. (2016). *French philosophy today: New figures of the human in Badiou; Meillassoux; Malabou; Serres and Latour.* Edinburgh, UK: Edinburgh University Press.

# CHAPTER 11

# Postdigital Afterlife

## *A Philosophical Framework*

Petar Jandrić

## CONTENTS

Introduction                                                     173
Immortality: A Postdigital Perspective                           176
The Ship of Theseus                                              178
The Problem of Continuity                                        180
The Problem of Similarity                                        183
Continuity and Similarity as the Basis for Normative
    (Practical) Solutions                    185
References                                                       186

## INTRODUCTION

This chapter examines recent definitions of immortality and offers a classification consisting of four different types of immortality: weak biological immortality, strong biological immortality, weak artificial immortality, and strong artificial immortality. Drawing from analyses of these forms of immortality, this chapter concludes that the challenge of achieving immortality, at our present stage of technological development, is postdigital. Philosophically, the problem of postdigital immortality comes down to two inter-related problems: the problem of continuity and the problem of duplicity.

*Digital immortality* can be broadly defined 'as the continuation of an active or passive digital presence after death' (Savin-Baden, Burden, & Taylor, 2017, p. 11). This definition encompasses a wide range of phenomena including post-mortem Facebook memorial pages (Frost, 2014) through 'artificially intelligent systems that could generate new commentary on media events in the style of a particular deceased person, for whom an online profile had been created before death' (Savin-Baden et al., 2017, pp. 11–12), to the not-yet realised dream of uploading person's personality and consciousness from their biological body to a different substrate including but not limited to digital circuits (Stillwaggon Swan & Howard, 2012, p. 249; see also Kurzweil, 2000). In Project Andros - Immortality! Rael (2015) offers the following classification of immortality:

> Definition: strong immortality - infinite life extension retaining ALL of the life form's native architecture. e.g.; an immortal human retaining the entire biological body.
>
> Definition: weak immortality - infinite life extension through artificial means while retaining PART of the life form's native architecture. e.g.; joint-replacement, cell-reparation/replacement, regeneration.
>
> Definition: artificial immortality - infinite life extension while retaining NONE of the life form's My R.Max android head on my RoboSapiens android body, simulated, native architecture. e.g.; encoding a human being's mind into an android robot but retaining none of the biological organism (Rael, 2015).

At present, Rael's strong immortality and weak immortality are out of human reach and can be discussed only as thought experiments. Artificial immortality, at least in some forms, could be viable in the foreseeable future and needs to be refined further.

In a recent paper, Savin-Baden and Mason-Robbie make a useful distinction between digital immortality and Digital Afterlife:

> 'Afterlife' assumes a digital presence that may or may not continue to exist, whereas 'immortality' implies a presence, in some form at least, *ad infinitum*. Whilst these terms may be used interchangeably, afterlife is a broader more flexible construct as it does not contain assumptions about the duration or persistence of the digital presence. (Savin-Baden & Mason-Robbie, in print).

The weaker notion of afterlife might indeed be better suited to the digital context. Avoiding the assumption of *ad infinitum* presence of life however, Digital Afterlife is conceptually different from immortality. Focusing on immortality, I offer some provisional definitions, although their wider consequences will need to be investigated in further research. These definitions are:

1. Weak biological immortality is infinite life extension in the human biological body using various artificial supplements (this definition would amount to Haraway's (1985; 1991) classical understanding of cyborg).

2. Strong biological immortality is infinite life extension in the human biological body.

3. Weak artificial immortality is Digital Afterlife presence *ad infinitum,* which includes both passive digital 'memorials' such as Facebook memorial pages and active artificial intelligent systems which simulate some aspects of person's behaviour after their death.

4. Strong artificial immortality is a transfer of full human consciousness from a biological body into a different (digital or non-digital) substrate.

At our present stage of technological development, the only feasible concept is weak artificial immortality—the remaining three definitions can be thought of only as thought experiments. However, weak artificial immortality cannot be discussed without strong artificial immortality, and weak biological immortality cannot be discussed without strong biological immortality. Drawing from insights into all forms of immortality, therefore, this chapter uses the postdigital perspective to examine the general problem of immortality.

The postdigital perspective describes a world 'where digital technology and media is [no longer] separate, virtual, 'other' to a 'natural' human and social life' (Jandrić et al., 2018, p. 893). It does not seek 'technical innovation or improvement, but considers digitisation as something that has already happened and thus might be further reconfigured' (Cramer, 2013). Inspired by various posthumanist traditions in various fields from the arts (i.e., Gibson, 1984) to sciences (Haraway, [1985]1991; Pötzsch & Hayles, 2014), the postdigital perspective accepts sociomaterial reconfigurations of relationships between human beings and technologies which 'conceptualise knowledge and capacities as being *emergent* from the webs of interconnections between heterogeneous entities, both human and nonhuman' (Jones, 2018, p. 47). Based on works of Latour, Fuller, and others, the postdigital perspective insists that the question of 'treating people and machines in a symmetrical way reaches all the way to questions of values and morality' (Peters & Jandrić, 2019, p. 203). Positioned as such, 'the postdigital is hard to define; messy; unpredictable; digital and analog; technological and non-technological; biological and informational. The postdigital is both a rupture in our existing theories and their continuation' (Jandrić et al., 2018, p. 893).

## IMMORTALITY: A POSTDIGITAL PERSPECTIVE

The concept of immortality, in all its forms, depends on a set of (more) general questions: What is a human being? Who can be considered human, and under which circumstances? During history, humankind has answered these questions in different ways. Arguably, slaves in ancient Athens (who could not freely move, work, or vote) were considered less human than their free, voting masters; in various places and historical periods, the same can be said for women, people of different races, and minorities. More often than not, these inequalities had been 'scientifically' justified. During the last few centuries, for instance, 'pseudo-scientific theories such as scientific racism, and their more proactive siblings such as eugenics, have been closely associated with poisonous social systems and politics such as slavery, apartheid, and fascism' (Peters & Jandrić, 2019, p. 198). Addressing the question of demarcation between humans and non-humans, Fuller writes:

'Human' began – and I believe should remain – as a normative not a descriptive category. It's really about which beings that the self-described, self-organised 'humans' decide to include. So we need to reach agreement about the performance standards that a putative 'human' should meet that a 'non-human' does not meet. The Turing Test serves to focus minds on this problem, as it suggests that any being that passes behavioural criteria that we require of humans counts as human, regardless of its material composition. While the Turing Test is normally presented as something that machines would need to pass, in fact it is merely a more abstract version of how non-white, non-male, non-elite members of Homo sapiens have come to be regarded as 'human' from a legal standpoint. So why not also say 'non-carbon' in the case of, say, silicon-based androids? (Fuller & Jandrić, 2019, p. 207).

Based on Fuller's argument, in a recent article Peters and I argue:

> Following Fuller's argument, our question becomes: under which circumstances should we accept living machines as (equal to) human beings? It is extremely hard to quantify humanity, and it would take genius of (at least) Alan Turing's calibre to give a satisfactory answer. Therefore, we finally settle at a more down to earth question: how should we treat living machines of the moment, and their potentially more advanced successors in the future? (Peters & Jandrić, 2019, p. 202).

Following this argument questions become: should (various kinds of) immortals be accepted as (equal to) human beings? How should we treat them?

Defined as infinite life extension in a human biological body, strong biological immortality is a clear case where immortals retain their humanity. Weak artificial immortality, both in the form of passive memorial pages and active algorithms, results in pale and incomplete images of a deceased person, not unlike late grandma's photo on the wall—therefore, it is a clear case of 'lost humanity'. However, other forms of immortality are more complex. From 'traditional' cyborgs, to a complete transfer of human consciousness from a biological body into a different substrate, we are facing different conceptual challenges including but not limited to radically different ways of functioning of different substrates. We have been transferring information between substrates for decades. First we transferred spoken word into writing, then we transferred various types of information into different media (music—gramophone, film—magnetic tape), and finally, during the second part of the 20th century, we digitised more or less all relevant information and made the computer into 'a medium of the most general nature' (Carr, 2011). According to Venter (2008), however, this process of abstraction has started to change direction.

> We're actually starting at a new point: we've been digitizing biology, and now we're trying to go from that digital code into a new phase of biology, with designing and synthesizing life. So, we've always been trying to ask big questions. 'What is life?' is something that I think many biologists have been trying to understand at various levels. We've tried various approaches, paring it down to minimal components. We've been digitizing

> it now for almost 20 years. When we sequenced the human genome, it was going from the analog world of biology into the digital world of the computer. Now we're trying to ask: can we regenerate life, or can we create new life, out of this digital universe? (Venter, 2008).

This change of direction is technical, scientific, and social. According to Peters, it is dialectically intertwined with an emerging form of capitalism. Bio-informational capitalism is 'the emergent form of fourth or fifth generational capitalism based on investments and returns in these new bio-industries: after mercantile, industrial, and knowledge capitalisms' and is 'based on a self-organising and self-replicating code that harnesses both the results of the information and new biology revolutions and brings them together in a powerful alliance that enhances and strengthens or reinforces each other' (Peters, 2012, p. 105). This mutually constitutive relationship between information and biology creates the postdigital condition where attempts at understanding immortality must take into account 'the difference between the continuous nature of biological existence, and the discrete ('on/off') nature of digital technology' (Jandrić et al. 2018, p. 893). Postdigital theorists have a general answer to this problem; they 'acknowledge the current state of technology while rejecting the conceptual shift implied in the 'digital revolution'—a shift apparently as abrupt as the 'on/off' 'zero/one' logic of the machines now pervading our daily lives' (Pepperell & Punt, 2000, p. 2). While it remains unclear how these opposing principles could exactly be reconciled, at our current stage of technological development—and in the context of bio-informational capitalism—a postdigital perspective may provide a productive lens for addressing the question of immortality.

## THE SHIP OF THESEUS

In 75 AC, Plutarch brings about one of the oldest thought experiments in Western philosophy—whether Theseus' ship, after it has had all of its parts replaced, retains its identity. Versions of this thought experiment include the grandfather's axe experiment (in which the son replaces the handle, the grandson replaces the blade, and the granddaughter asks whether it is still her grandfather's axe) and many others. If we replace each and every plank in the ship's hull with exactly the same type of wood and using the same level of craftmanship, the Theseus' ship paradox is a purely theoretical question. Whether it remains Theseus' or not, the ship remains just as seaworthy. This practical conclusion leads on to the next stage of the thought experiment:

> Suppose, though, that each of the planks removed from Theseus' ship was restored, and that these planks were then recombined to once again form a ship. Would this have been Theseus' ship? Again, a strong case can be made for saying that it would have been: this ship would have had precisely the same parts as Theseus' ship, arranged in precisely the same way. If this happened, then it would seem that Theseus had returned from Knossos in two ships. First, there would have been Theseus' ship that has had each of its parts replaced one by one. Second, there would have been Theseus' ship that had been dismantled, restored, and then reassembled. Each of them would have been Theseus' ship. Theseus, though, sailed in only one ship. Which one? (Hines, 2013).

This ancient problem reveals two distinct problems: continuity and duplication. The problem of continuity deals with the question: at which stage of repair, if ever, Theseus' ship transforms into something else? The problem of duplication asks: if we accept the ship's continuity, we will end up with two 'original' ships. Which ship, if any, is 'more original'? What is their relationship to each other? Human minds are more complicated than ships, yet the problems of continuity and duplication remain. In *The Age of Spiritual Machines: When Computers Exceed Human Intelligence* Ray Kurzweil recreates the problem of continuity in the context of artificial intelligence as follows:

> …if a person scans his brain through a non-invasive scanning technology of the twenty-first century (such as an advanced magnetic resonance imaging), and downloads his mind to his personal computer, is the 'person' who emerges in the machine the same consciousness as the person who was scanned? (Kurzweil, 2000)

If we accept that consciousness can be transferred from human brain to another substrate, we again bump into the problem of duplication. However, strong artificial immortality presented in Kurzweil's idea of transferring full human consciousness to a digital substrate is radically different from weak artificial immortality where algorithms simulate, and partially preserve, some elements of human consciousness. In the words of Stillwaggon Swan and Howard: 'If I will continue on as me, just in my duplicate, then death (for me) should not be a big deal. But if the duplicate were not the same as me—say there were even a subtle difference between us—then he would not be me' (2012, p. 249). In this way, weak artificial immortality retains the problem of continuity but avoids the problem of duplication. However, avoiding the problem of duplication does not answer the question of how we should treat weak postdigital immortals. Provided that differences between 'versions' of human consciousness transferred into different substrate(s) are indeed subtle, weak artificial immortality can still produce many practical issues. In the following analyses, therefore, I will replace the problem of duplication with the problem of similarity, illustrated in Table 11.1.

## THE PROBLEM OF CONTINUITY

The problem of continuity has been explored in literature quite extensively. In order to establish a frame of reference, let us start with a brief exploration of biological continuity in human beings. Cells in the human body have a finite life span; during the course of organism's life, individual cells continuously die off and get replaced by new cells. This fact has created a popular myth: 'Every seven years (or 10, depending on which story you hear) we become essentially new people, because in that time, every cell in your body has been replaced by a new cell.' However, Radford (2011) shows that this popular myth is not completely true:

> Red blood cells live for about four months, while white blood cells live on average more than a year. Skin cells live about two or three weeks. (…) Sperm cells have a life span of only about three days, while brain cells typically last an entire lifetime (neurons in the cerebral cortex, for example, are not replaced when they die) (Radford, 2011).

Human bodies do not replace themselves completely; from cradle to grave, there is at least some biological continuity.

Having established what happens in the human body, we can now move to a 'harder' problem of the relationships between the human body, thought, and consciousness. Arguably one of the most popular questions in the history of philosophy, the mind-body problem is out of the scope of this chapter. Whether we subscribe to one or another version of maintaining distinction between mind and matter (dualism), or to one unifying

TABLE 11.1   Thought Experiments on General Similarity and Similarity and Immortality

| | Thought Experiments on General Similarity | Thought Experiments on Similarity and Immortality |
|---|---|---|
| The question of ethics | Let us say that Kurzweil's Jack decides to move to another substrate (for instance, scan and upload himself into a computer) and to destroy his biological body after the act. Did Jack just commit suicide? And what happens if someone else (for instance, Jack's wife or child) destroys his biological body after the act? Did Jack's family commit homicide? | Let us imagine that artificial Jack decides to die. However, he is not able to delete his own consciousness from the computer and needs assistance. Does this case of 'assisted euthanasia' count as homicide? |
| The question of identity | Let us say that Jack decides to create several copies of himself and sends them to work. While his duplicates tirelessly do his job, Jack lounges by the swimming pool. Who should get paid for this work: biological Jack, artificial Jack(s), or all of them? And what happens when, after a while, the 'original' Jack and his duplicates develop different consciousness based on radically different recent life experiences? Has Jack 'branched' into two or more different people? | Let us say that Jack decides to scan his brain several times and upload these scans into several computers. Each 'artificial Jack' is different, because the brain scan was made in different points of Jack's life and under different circumstances. Which 'artificial Jack' should be kept after death of 'biological Jack'? If Jack's family decide to keep one 'artificial Jack' and destroy others, does that count as homicide? |
| The question of superiority | Let us imagine that 'artificial Jack' acquires some powers which 'biological Jack' did not have. He might be able to automatically retrieve Internet information during a conversation, do sophisticated mathematical analyses, speak foreign languages using automated translation programs, and so on. Let us now say that the enhanced 'artificial Jack' becomes superior to 'biological Jack' at making money and starts competing with Jack's biological (non-artificial) co-workers. Should such competition be allowed? | Let us imagine that 'artificial Jack' exists for centuries and amasses experience and wisdom which cannot be reached by mortals. This experience provides Jack with unfair advantage at the workplace. Should immortal Jack be allowed to compete with mortals? |
| The question of selection | Let us imagine that the availability of creating one's own duplicates is limited—for the sake of simplicity, let us assume it is too expensive. Who should be allowed to create a duplicate of themselves—those with money, those who can offer most to humanity, mortally ill children? | Let us imagine that the availability of achieving artificial immortality is limited—for the sake of simplicity, let us again assume it is too expensive. Who should be made immortal and under which circumstances? |

reality (monism), the problem of continuity remains: at which point (if any), during the natural process of cell replacement in the human body, one becomes a different person? Obviously, all people change with time; yet it is common knowledge that human consciousness has a continuity in spite of biological changes in our bodies.

Kurzweil (2000) applies the same logic to artificial changes in human bodies. If I have an accident and get an artificial knee, I am still the same person. A few years later, I can get a pacemaker, and I will still be the author of these words. With similar medical procedures, some of which are still out of human reach, I can replace my whole body (including my brain)—and I will still remain the same person. According to Kurzweil, there is no difference if these changes happen gradually or at once.

> Suppose rather than implementing this change a step at a time as in the above scenario, Jack does it all at once. He goes in for a complete brain scan and has the information from the scan instantiated (installed) in an electronic neural computer. Not one to do things piecemeal, he upgrades his body as well. Does making the transition at one time change anything? Well, what's the difference between changing from neural circuits to electronic/photonic ones all at once, as opposed to doing it gradually? Even if he makes the change in one quick step, the new Jack is still the same old Jack, right? (Kurzweil, 2000)

For Kurzweil, human consciousnesses can maintain continuity regardless of material setup, or substrate, in which it is hosted. Other theorists are not so sure. In his famous essay 'Facing Up to the Problem of Consciousness', Chalmers (1995) argues that functional approaches, such as Kurzweil's, are unable to explain the question: '*Why is the performance of these functions accompanied by experience?*' (italics from the original). According to Chalmers:

> This further question is the key question in the problem of consciousness. Why doesn't all this information-processing go on 'in the dark', free of any inner feel? Why is it that when electromagnetic waveforms impinge on a retina and are discriminated and categorized by a visual system, this discrimination and categorization is experienced as a sensation of vivid red? We know that conscious experience *does* arise when these functions are

performed, but the very fact that it arises is the central mystery. There is an *explanatory gap* (a term due to Levine, 1983) between the functions and experience, and we need an explanatory bridge to cross it. A mere account of the functions stays on one side of the gap, so the materials for the bridge must be found elsewhere (Chalmers, 1995).

For Chalmers (1995), cognitive science and neuroscience can only explain the performance of functions. Therefore, he argues that 'an analysis of the problem shows us that conscious experience is just not the kind of thing that a wholly reductive account could succeed in explaining', and that 'to account for conscious experience, we need an *extra ingredient* in the explanation'. Chalmers provides an account of various theories which indicate that the extra ingredient can be many things: chaos, nonlinear dynamics, nonalgorithmic processing, quantum theory, and so on. Whatever the extra ingredient is, however, its lack would definitely cause a rupture in continuity and Kurzweil's 'uploaded Jack' will not be the same person as the old, biological Jack. Because of this rupture, even the strongest definition of postdigital immortality does not meet the criterion of continuity.

## THE PROBLEM OF SIMILARITY

Using Chalmers' arguments, the problem of duplication defined in the Theseus' ship paradox becomes irrelevant for the problem of immortality. Artificial copy of Jack will never have the same consciousness as biological Jack, and it is clear which Jack is 'original'. However, problems related to similarity do not stop there, and can be exposed in several interconnected thought experiments. The experiments are classified into two groups: thought experiments on general similarity and thought experiments on similarity and immortality.

Thought experiments on general similarity:

1. **The question of ethics.** Let us say that Kurzweil's Jack decides to move to another substrate (for instance, scan and upload himself into a computer) and to destroy his biological body after the act. Did Jack just commit suicide? And what happens if someone else (for instance, Jack's wife or child) destroys his biological body after the act? Did Jack's family commit homicide?

2. **The question of identity.** Let us say that Jack decides to create several copies of himself and sends them to work. While his duplicates

tirelessly do his job, Jack lounges by the swimming pool. Who should get paid for this work: biological Jack, artificial Jack(s), or all of them? And what happens when, after a while, the 'original' Jack and his duplicates develop different consciousness based on radically different recent life experiences? Has Jack 'branched' into two or more different people?

3. **The question of superiority.** Let us imagine that 'artificial Jack' acquires some powers which 'biological Jack' did not have. He might be able to automatically retrieve Internet information during a conversation, do sophisticated mathematical analyses, speak foreign languages using automated translation programs, and so on. Let us now say that the enhanced 'artificial Jack' becomes superior to 'biological Jack' at making money and starts competing with Jack's biological (non-artificial) co-workers. Should such competition be allowed?

4. **The question of selection.** Let us imagine that the availability of creating one's own duplicates is limited—for the sake of simplicity, let us assume it is too expensive. Who should be allowed to create a duplicate of themselves—those with money, those who can offer most to humanity, mortally ill children?

Thought experiments on similarity and immortality:

1. **The question of ethics.** Let us imagine that artificial Jack decides to die. However, he is not able to delete his own consciousness from the computer and needs assistance. Does this case of 'assisted euthanasia' count as homicide?

2. **The question of identity.** Let us say that Jack decides to scan his brain several times and upload these scans into several computers. Each 'artificial Jack' is different, because the brain scan was made in different points of Jack's life and under different circumstances. Which 'artificial Jack' should be kept after death of 'biological Jack'? If Jack's family decide to keep one 'artificial Jack' and destroy others, does that count as homicide?

3. **The question of superiority.** Let us imagine that 'artificial Jack' exists for centuries and amasses experience and wisdom which cannot be reached by mortals. This experience provides Jack with unfair advantage at the workplace. Should immortal Jack be allowed to compete with mortals?

4. **The question of selection.** Let us imagine that the availability of achieving artificial immortality is limited—for the sake of simplicity, let us again assume it is too expensive. Who should be made immortal and under which circumstances?

This list of thought experiments is by no means exhaustive; with our limited understanding of technologies to come, the experiments are also not meant to be resolved. However, the experiments do indicate that the problem of similarity lies at the heart of various social, legal, and other arrangements related to postdigital immortality. Furthermore, even a briefest analysis of the thought experiments confirms Fuller's conclusion that the problem of similarity can be resolved only in the normative domain (Fuller & Jandrić, 2019, p. 207). Theoretical answers to these (and similar) problems should be sought in the realm of (philosophical) ethics, and practical answers should be sought in the realm of politics. Furthermore, the problem of immortality is a special case of the wider problem of technological enhancement of human beings. Therefore, recent attempts at formulating legal rights of cyborgs, such as the Universal Declaration of Cyborg Rights (DiEM25, 2017), and scholarly discussions about legal rights of cyborgs, which currently take place in journals such as *The New York Law Journal* (Lichtenstein, 2015), might provide useful directions for development of practical solutions for legal questions concerning immortality. Vice versa, immortality needs to be included in more general discussions and legal frameworks concerning technologically enhanced human beings.

## CONTINUITY AND SIMILARITY AS THE BASIS FOR NORMATIVE (PRACTICAL) SOLUTIONS

Immortality can mean many different things. Based on Savin-Baden et al. (2017), Savin-Baden & Mason-Robbie in Chapter 1 and Rael (2015), this chapter defines four different types of immortality: weak biological immortality, strong biological immortality, weak artificial immortality, and strong artificial immortality. Drawing from analyses of these forms of immortality, the chapter concludes that achieving immortality is a true postdigital challenge consisting of 'blurred and messy relationships between physics and biology, old and new media, humanism and posthumanism, knowledge capitalism and bio-informational capitalism' (Jandrić et al., 2018, p. 896). Philosophically, the problem of postdigital immortality comes down to two inter-related problems: the problem of continuity and the problem of duplication (as in the Theseus' paradox). From a functional perspective it is easy to agree with Kurzweil's idea that humankind will one day achieve the level of technological development which will enable the creation of artificial copies of human minds. Speaking of consciousness, however, continuity of human existence across the substrates will be broken unless we find a way to account for Chalmers' (1995) extra ingredient. Subscribing to Chalmers' theory of consciousness, the problem of duplication transforms into the problem of similarity. Solutions to thought experiments on general similarity and thought experiments on similarity and immortality clearly lie in the normative domain (Fuller and Jandrić, 2019) and need to be sought in realms of ethics and politics.

As technologies increase their capacities to come close to some forms of postdigital immortality (most notably weak artificial immortality), there will be a wide range of

> legislative conundrums of pre and post death (…) for example how the law should deal with any ensuing contracts and the legal framework for post-death presence, as well as legal deletion and legal protection. In the absence of a living, and identified actor, and without clear authority for virtual activity beyond death, mechanisms for pursuing liability in civil and criminal liability within a global jurisdiction is unclear (Savin-Baden et al., 2017, p. 179).

While this philosophical article cannot respond to these conundrums, it does point out that each and every problem related to immortality will inevitably involve the problems of continuity and similarity, and that legal issues associated with immortality need to be approached in relation to wider issues pertaining to cyborg rights.

## REFERENCES

Carr, N. (2011). *The Shallows: What the internet is doing to our brains.* New York: W. W. Norton.

Chalmers, D. J. (1995). Facing up to the problem of consciousness. *Journal of Consciousness Studies, 2*(3), 200–219.

Cramer, F. (2013). Post-digital aesthetics. *Lemagazine,* May 1. http://lemagazine.jeudepaume.org/2013/05/florian-cramer-post-digital-aesthetics/

DiEM25. (2017). Universal Declaration of Cyborg Rights. https://cyborgrights.eu/

Frost, M. (2014). The grief grapevine: Facebook memorial pages and adolescent bereavement. *Australian Journal of Guidance and Counselling, 24*(2), 256–265.

Fuller, S., & Jandrić, P. (2019). The postdigital human: Making the history of the future. *Postdigital Science and Education, 1*(1), 190–217. doi: https://doi.org/10.1007/s42438-018-0003-x.

Gibson, W. (1984). *Neuromancer.* New York: Ace Books.

Haraway, D. ([1985] 1991). *Simians, cyborgs, and women: The reinvention of nature.* New York: Routledge.

Hines, S. D. (2013). Theseus's Paradox. http://sdhinesbooks.blogspot.com/2013/09/theseuss-paradox.html

Jandrić, P., Knox, J., Besley, T., Ryberg, T., Suoranta, J., & Hayes, S. (2018). Postdigital science and education. *Educational Philosophy and Theory.* doi: https://doi.org/10.1080/00131857.2018.1454000.

Jones, C. (2018). Experience and networked learning. In N. BonderupDohn, S. Cranmer, J. A. Sime, M. de Laat, & T. Ryberg (Eds.), *Networked learning: Reflections and challenges* (pp. 39–56). New York: Springer International.

Kurzweil, R. (2000). *The age of spiritual machines: When computers exceed human intelligence.* New York: Penguin.

Lichtenstein, J. D. (2015). Rights of cyborgs: Is damage to Prosthetic a personal injury? *The New York Law Journal, 253*(56).

Levine, J. (1983). Materialism and qualia: The explanatory gap. *Pacific Philosophical Quarterly* 64:354–361.

Pepperell, R., & Punt, M. (2000). *The postdigital membrane: Imagination, technology and desire.* Bristol, England: Intellect.

Peters, M. A. (2012). Bio-informational capitalism. *Thesis Eleven, 110*(1), 98–111.

Peters, M. A., & Jandrić, P. (2019). AI, human evolution, and the speed of learning. In J. Knox, Y. Wang, & M. Gallagher (Eds.), *Artificial intelligence and inclusive education: Speculative futures and emerging practices* (pp. 195–206). Springer Nature. https://doi.org/10.1007/978-981-13-8161-4_12.

Plutarch (75 AC). Theseus. http://classics.mit.edu/Plutarch/theseus.html

Pötzsch, H., & Hayles, K. (2014). Posthumanism, technogenesis, and digital technologies: A conversation with N. Katherine Hayles. *The Fibreculture Journal, 23,* 95–107.

Radford, B. (2011). Does the Human Body Really Replace Itself Every 7 Years? LiveScience, 4 April. https://www.livescience.com/33179-does-human-body-replace-cells-seven-years.html

Rael, P. M. (2015). Project Andros - Immortality! http://intractablestudiesinstitute.org/ProjectAndros-longversion.pdf

Savin-Baden, M. (2019). (Post)Digital Afterlife? *Postdigital Science and Education.*

Savin-Baden, M., Burden, D., & Taylor, H. (2017). The ethics and impact of digital immortality. *Knowledge Cultures, 5*(2), 178–196.

Stillwaggon Swan, L., & Howard, J. (2012). Digital immortality: Self or 0010110? *International Journal of Machine Consciousness, 4*(1), 245–256.

Venter, C. (2008). On the verge of creating synthetic life. TED 2008. Retrieved February 8, 2018, from https://www.ted.com/talks/craig_venter_is_on_the_verge_of_creating_synthetic_life

# CHAPTER 12

# Digital Afterlife Matters

Victoria Mason-Robbie and Maggi Savin-Baden

## CONTENTS

Introduction     189
Psychological Aspects of Digital Afterlife     190
Legacy or Immortality?     190
Death, Mourning, and Netiquette     191
The Protection of Privacy     194
Digital Nomenclature in a Postdigital World     196
Moral and Ontological Questions     196
Technological Landscape     198
Conclusion     198
References     200

## INTRODUCTION

In writing this book, we sought to bring together experts from diverse fields who share an interest in Digital Afterlife and the wide-ranging issues that pertain to this. The perspectives represent a range of disciplines, and with this in mind, there is no unified framework for understanding the complexity of Digital Afterlife. However, it is possible to identify and discuss some of the common themes and shared understandings across these areas of inquiry. As always, we must avoid the parochialism that prevents us from seeing the wider context within which this issue is positioned and situated. Moreover, as a fast moving field, in the context of a changing sociocultural landscape, any conclusions are attenuated by the multitude of questions raised by the current status of the literature.

## PSYCHOLOGICAL ASPECTS OF DIGITAL AFTERLIFE

Certainly from a psychological perspective, we can identify thoughts we have about Digital Afterlife in the broadest sense, or specific to, our own or our loved-ones' situation. Indeed, when asked, people may hold a belief about their own and others digital presence including hypothetical scenarios that have not been encountered (e.g., the imagined loss of a loved one, which in a sense becomes a thought experiment). The emotional consequences, including unforeseen or unexpected reactions, must be considered when making sense of data from people faced with either the loss of a loved one or when people are asked to consider their thoughts and feelings around others having access to their own digital legacy. There is undoubtedly an emotional impact of choosing (or not) to retain a digital presence after death, and of encountering the digital presence of a loved one after death. There is a long tradition of psychologists focusing on behaviour as the only aspect of human nature that is directly observable (Watson, 1913), as opposed to mental or emotional states which are not directly observable and reside in the so-called 'black box'. From this perspective at least, whilst it is possible to verify the concept of Digital Afterlife because our digital footprint remains as a potential source of data, it is not possible to prove the concept of digital immortality because it is not directly observable or measurable. However, with respect to our *actual* online behaviour and plans regarding own digital legacy, these aspects of our digital lives can be subjected to empirical inquiry. Although our thoughts, feelings, and behaviours are key dimensions of human experience, these are underpinned by philosophical understandings of ranging complexity, and the changing cultural, technological, and legal landscape.

## LEGACY OR IMMORTALITY?

In the broadest sense, the desire for immortality is not new, and we know that great writers, thinkers, and artists have immortalised themselves and those they depict in their work. That these objects exist after their death represent a form of immortality as they are not forgotten, even by those who did not know them, or who did not live at the same time. Shakespeare's famous sonnet 18 tells us that for as long as people are reading and seeing the lines of the play, life is given to the character, and Juliet will not be forgotten. Thus she is very explicitly immortalised in the written word for all to see and hear. Clearly most of us are not fictional, and are not Juliet, but the same notion of being immortalised through our words, voice or pictures remains the same. But living on like artists and the characters they represent through their work, whilst in some way immortalising and concreting their status in the minds of the living, does not have the profound emotional impact that the personal experience of encountering the form of our loved ones has upon us—both in the physical and digital spheres.

Of letters, Goethe (1749–1832) described them as 'the most significant memorial a person can leave' (Sebag Montefiore, 2018). Whether this is true today is a matter of debate since, according to public discourse, surveys show the decline of handwriting (Chemin, 2014), and by implication letter writing; having been replaced by alternative forms of electronic communication. The speed and pace of letter writing involves time for thought and reflection, whereas an email or text can be written and sent without careful consideration. Questions of privacy are raised in terms of the wishes of the deceased, and the impact on loved ones of discovering communication that was not intended for their eyes. Permanence of such electronic communication is assumed, and *form* matters: if we were to digitise our letters, would they be more permanent in this form? Such an intentional act would suggest that we wish our letters to be preserved and perhaps read by others.

Intentionality is important because arguably, much of our digital footprint or legacy is unintentional because we tend to share a narrative, or curate our lives shaped, in the moment, by how we want to be seen by others. In particular, with respect to self-presentation, Goffman's (1959) ideas about the desire to present ourselves in such a way that we receive positive evaluations, and to meet the expectations of others is still highly relevant and has been used to explain social behaviour on the Internet (Hogan, 2010). Furthermore, psychologists tend to conceptualise intentions as the antecedents of behaviour (Ajzen & Fishbein, 1970), and they are not necessarily coherent or rational. Intentionality is of practical importance here too, because much has been said in this book about the importance of communicating our wishes to our loved ones to make their lives easier when we are gone. Many of us may intend to set up *Legacy Contacts* or a digital executor; however, our intentions are not realised, perhaps through anxiety around thinking about our own demise.

## DEATH, MOURNING, AND NETIQUETTE

Whilst we are all likely to experience the death of a loved one, and to mourn in our own idiosyncratic way, such mourning is subject to many personal, situational, and cultural influences. Similarly, so-called netiquette—behaving appropriately online—may also change according to these influences. Indeed as none of our actual or online behaviour occurs in a situational or cultural vacuum, we need to be conscious of how mores shift over the passage of time, as something deemed appropriate today, may not be tomorrow.

Just as the idea that burial plots exist 'in perpetuity' has now been transformed into a finite period due to restrictions on space and financial concerns. There is a certain irony that digital legacy services set up to safeguard the digital legacies of their clients have since folded. There are also potential issues with Facebook's *Legacy Contact*, as this is dependent on the contact being willing and able to maintain the page of the deceased for years to come. We are reminded of the potential challenge that future historians will face when trying to access data that is no longer available. We may also wonder how they will interrogate and make sense of any data that are available in order to make sense of the past, as aspects of our lives that are salient to us now, may be trivialised and even ignored as irrelevant by future generations. Our desire to leave our own digital legacy to be experienced by others as our Digital Afterlife, may be typical of the self-aggrandisement of people living in the 21st century. What is certain is that as online activity surpasses the writing of written diaries, it is less likely that written diaries of the historical importance of Samuel Pepys 17th century diary will be discovered.

The blurring of life and death is something that has been important for ancient humans as well as ourselves. Indeed, the Ancient Egyptians provided the dead with wares for their afterlives (e.g., Shabti dolls) suggesting an ongoing relationship with the dead. Similarly, the Inca venerated their dead by bringing them out and feeding them. Essentially, their relationship with the deceased continues after the death and they continue to interact with them, which has parallels with the continued interaction with a person's Digital Afterlife once they have died. Here, the offline life ceases, but there is a sort of continuity of the online existence. An interesting metaphor comes to mind when considering the setting in stone of death (through inscriptions on graves) and the finality of this, which is now somehow breached by the so-called digital zombie. Death is quite literally no longer set in stone. Bassett (2015) describes digital zombies as being the online dead who are re-animated and socially active. Indeed, this conjures up an image of a zombie walking through a dark graveyard, which would hint at a place of unrest and fear as opposed to rest and peace. Sherlock (2013) discusses how these 'posthumous representations' contribute to a form of symbolic immortality. Thus, when discussing the immortality aspect of Digital Afterlife, a central question becomes: are we talking figuratively or literally?

Comparing the anticipatory fear of second loss with Victorian mourning jewellery Bassett (Chapter 5) provides a useful metaphor, with the image fading each time the locket is opened, that is, each time it is looked at and thought about. Importantly, it is carried around with us, just like the Digital Afterlives of our loved ones are carried around with us on our mobile devices. According to Bassett, the fear of second loss creates a new form of anxiety in that it becomes a form of anticipatory grief at the prospect of losing data from a loved one. Thus we see a shift of perspective from the anticipated needs and wishes of the dead, to careful consideration of the emotional state of the bereaved. Moreover, there is a central need to consider the emotional aspect of our experience with respect to Digital Afterlife, not just our attitudes or what we actually do or intend to do. Such a need requires ongoing conversations between people, despite cultural taboos around the discussion of death and dying. It also requires an engagement with the companies that control the way our data will be used when we die.

Rachman (2016) suggests that people are motivated to document their experience at the end of life because it is a way of enduring when physical existence is not possible in death. In this volume, the example of Randy Pausch is given, a Carnegie Mellon professor who shared his experience at the end of his life following a diagnosis of pancreatic cancer. He described the sharing as akin to putting himself in a bottle to wash up in the future for his children. This metaphor could of course be de-constructed; although deciding to put a message in a bottle is an intentional act, actually finding a message in a bottle is a rare occurrence which one does not choose to do (although one does choose whether or not to read the message). In contrast, the children of a deceased parent may choose to explore the digital legacy of their parent (should they be able to access it) such that anything unexpected would be in the content rather than in the actual finding of the message. In contrast to the death of a parent, the challenges faced with managing social media when a young person dies suddenly are critical, particularly given the idiosyncratic nature of grief. The concepts of emotional rubbernecking (DeGroot, 2014) and memorial trolling (Phillips, 2015) appear to be an emergent and potentially unavoidable and harmful aspect of the online milieu. That a person's grief could be unexpectedly hijacked, causing more harm, is a troubling aspect of this new reality.

Decision-making regarding the private or public expression of grief becomes complex in this new context. Consequently, an exploration of the netiquette of dealing with death online is important as such norms are dynamic and subject to cultural influence. Sabra (2017) found inconsistent attitudes towards emotional displays on Facebook. Similarly, Wagner (2018), in a review of 25 articles, found that although norms on social media are generally consistent with traditional norms, they are changeable and negotiated between users. In particular, Wagner identified three dominant themes related to grief expression and mourning practices: first, norms on how social media are used to express these; second, norms on the content and form these take; and third, reacting, regulating, and interacting with those who are expressing grief and mourning practices. This is further evidence that norms are not static, and that we should consider perspective, that is, the person being mourned, the mourner, or the people encountering and responding to the grief and mourning of the bereaved. In addition to perspective, context is important, for example what is normative for our Digital Afterlife now, is likely to shift and change in response to the changing landscape in which it is situated.

## THE PROTECTION OF PRIVACY

Many of the authors in this book tackled the complex issue of postmortal privacy, by addressing the personal, social, and legal dimensions. Although there is a need for a new legal framework to address issues about digital assets and posthumous privacy, some useful suggestions have been outlined for people thinking about how to manage their digital estate. For example, advice on appointing a digital executor to manage our digital legacies, and making use of the *Legacy Contact* function within Facebook.

With respect to the issue or privacy, it seems that even when a person dies, their 'informational body' (Floridi, 2014) or aspects of self and identity should be treated with the dignity and respect worthy of a human regardless of whether they are living or not. Essentially, privacy is equated with dignity, yet postmortal privacy covers a wide and complex set of digital material left by individuals when they die. The status of these assets is elevated since they relate to a person's self and identity. In this volume Rycroft and others discussed legal frameworks and the call for more clarity and development in the law. The need for legal solutions that protect the privacy and wishes of the deceased, rather than the application of traditional views of digital assets as property is called for. It is this tension between the priority we give to the rights of those who are gone and those that are left behind that highlights the complexity of decision-making regarding our digital legacies. If a person chooses for their social media accounts to be closed on their death, they are exercising their rights, but if the bereaved experience a second loss as a result of being unable to access the accounts of their loved ones, this may increase their suffering. Here a tension exists between the rights, wishes, and desires of each party.

It is important to consider whose perspective or viewpoint we are considering when thinking about the issue of digital immortality. Alignment between the wishes of those leaving their digital legacy behind and the bereaved encountering this legacy may vary. Indeed, it may also be more specific as there could be aspects of our digital footprint that we are happy to share, but others that are intensely private and thus blanket 'access all areas' may not be appropriate. Again, this echoes the problem concerning private physical effects such as letters, and whether or not we are happy for them to be shared on our death. Recently, a number of books have been published on notable letters from both living and now-deceased people (e.g., Sebag Montefiore, 2018), and even if the estate of a deceased person has given permission for a letter to be published, it may still be against the wishes of the deceased person when they were alive (if they had been asked!). And so again, we come back to the issue of who's view we give priority to, and the status we give to the presumed wishes of the dead.

The potential for creating a Will on a mobile device is now possible and there are different types of digital asset. Monetary, sentimental, social, and intellectual value are just some of the key categories that digital assets can be seen to occupy. Rycroft discusses a range of practical issues regarding access to the digital assets of a deceased person including that if no paper trail exists, then some digital assets may never be identified and accessed. Thus, any financial, sentimental, or other such value to the loved ones will be lost. The investment that companies have put into lawyers drawing up terms and conditions in their own interests are apparently met with an uninformed 'tick here' in agreement by the users who are potentially unaware of what they are signing up to and whose interests they serve. It is clear that there is potential tension between the rights of the user to privacy, and the interests of the family and friends who may wish to access the digital assets of their loved ones for a variety of reasons. Access rights to online material after a person has died remain a challenge when passwords are not known. The Data Protection Act (1998) and the General Data Protection Regulation (2018) relate to living persons only, and as terms and conditions are overly complex and to many, unintelligible, there is also an issue about digital literacy. A list of useful steps to ensuring that your beneficiaries can access your digital assets is included by Rycroft. These practical suggestions are invaluable for considering the potential impact on our loved ones of trying to identify or navigate any digital assets, whether of financial or sentimental value.

## DIGITAL NOMENCLATURE IN A POSTDIGITAL WORLD

It seems we are faced with a rapidly increasing vocabulary to describe the various aspects of Digital Afterlife and thanatechnology (a term originally used by Sofka, 1997). Jandrić and colleagues (2018) argue that we are now in a postdigital world, as the digital is now a taken for granted aspect of our existence and is no longer seen as separate or different from our natural human behaviour. Such co-existence of co-dependence encapsulates contemporary society, but simply applying the word digital to a range of terms: immortality, legacy, footprint, and so on does not imply a universally shared or understood meaning. Such meanings are not static, but will evolve as intellectual and vernacular understandings merge and shift. We argue that the term afterlife is broader and more flexible and does not make assumptions about our digital lives existing *ad infinitum.* However, in principle at least, immortality in the digital sphere is possible, but does such existence—stored digitally—require a viewer? This becomes a metaphysical question about unperceived existence (similar to Berkeley's 18th century idealism). If our digital immortal or digital legacy does not reach the lofty heights of Aristotle or Shakespeare it is unlikely that, after our loved ones are also deceased, anyone will take much of an interest.

## MORAL AND ONTOLOGICAL QUESTIONS

The pertinent moral questions are likely to change as society adapts and accepts new forms of digital technology. The moral status of the digital material left behind, if considered to be part of Floridi's informational bodies as it relates to identity and selfhood, may be treated on a par with physical remains (Floridi, 2014). The status of so-called thanabots or avatars, may depend on when they were created: pre or posthumously. Thus the temporal element of our decision-making could impact on the way such entities are treated. Furthermore, in Chapter 10, Reader highlights the tendency for digital footprints to be frozen in time once a person dies, and how this alters the ongoing relationship that the living have with the person who has died.

Deconstructing the concepts of afterlife and immortality helps us to avoid making assumptions about how these notions will impact upon us. In particular, the language we use to describe aspects of Digital Afterlife is some distance from the emotions that such encounters engender, whether expected or not. When a person dies their digital trace is in some way stabilised so that they remain frozen in time. Whether they are a child or an older person, their living selfhood ceases, and it is only possible to predict or imagine how they would have changed or developed in the physical world. Since our interactions with others shape and form part of our identity, the concept of identity is destabilised rather than it being something continuous that we possess. Immortality is thus re-defined as being the impact we have on others. Such destabilisation and deconstruction leads us to question the notion of digital immortality as somehow a continuation of our physical selves in the digital realm. Indeed, when we cease to have an impact on others, does our afterlife cease?

Ideas surrounding the postdigital have gained traction in recent years in the sense of the digital as a taken for granted aspect of human experience (Jandrić et al., 2018). A consideration of ethics, identity, and the status of the Digital Afterlife or a digital immortal help flesh out (pun intended) the issues of creating a digital copy or duplicate of oneself. Jandrić makes an important distinction between the functional copying of human minds on the one hand, and the problem of the continuity of human consciousness on the other, which would be broken if transferred to another substrate. This reminds us of the nature of embodiment in its literal sense of being within a body, and the idea of an embodied agent comes to mind as opposed to other interfaces for interacting with a digital immortal (e.g., via a computer interface). Indeed in the concept of embodied cognition, the body of the organism shapes the different aspects of cognition (Rosch, Thompson, & Varela, 1991). With this in mind, if the Digital Afterlife or digital immortal of ourselves or others is not embodied, unlike for example, the character Rachel in Cass Hunter's *The After Wife*, it will be more closely aligned with the online experiences that we have grown accustomed to, which in a sense are disembodied. Again such though experiments raise questions about perspective. First in terms of embodiment: what does it feel like to live in my body, and how does my body shape the way I learn and interact in the world?, and what is it like to interact with you (in whatever form you are in); and second, in terms of selfhood: who am I?, and what are my thoughts about you as a being? Thus thoughts around 'me and 'I' are arguably as important as thoughts about 'you'.

## TECHNOLOGICAL LANDSCAPE

The possibilities and time scale of what is and what is not currently possible in terms of developing an actual digital immortal reminds us of not only the potential pace of development, but also the thorny and inherently philosophical notion of consciousness and selfhood. With respect to this is the tantalising issue of how natural language conversations are likely to be possible with a digital immortal by the 2030s such that it would be impossible to distinguish between a person and the digital representation of that person through interacting with them. Of course, this raises the question of how we distinguish between a digital immortal that has been programmed to argue for its own existence, from one where this is an emergent ability resulting from its own subjective experience of itself as an entity. That sentience could be non-binary, for example, people with Alzheimer's disease may have fragmented sentience (Kanov, 2017) and digital immortals may be more or less sentient than each other is an intriguing possibility. The backdrop to these technological and philosophical questions is the potential financial cost implications of maintaining a digital immortal over time. Certainly at this stage, a number of companies that purport to enable Digital Afterlives in its many forms have been created and some of these are no longer operating (a somewhat intriguing irony).

Furthermore, at a practical level, the issue of intentionality arises again; our Digital Afterlives are either constructed and narrated whilst we are living for ourselves and the living and are not explicitly intended, or consciously constructed as becoming our digital legacy; or we utilise the services of a company to create a digital immortal of ourselves. In the case of the latter, this may co-occur with the former, but is most definitely a conscious and intentional act. In addition, as we highlighted in Chapter 1, a distinction is made between those who preserve their own or another's Digital Afterlife, those that mediate the experience of others, and those who receive or encounter the Digital Afterlife of a deceased person.

## CONCLUSION

One of the most striking aspects of collating this book has been the disciplinary differences between the contributors, which serves to remind us of the very broad and diverse reach of Digital Afterlife. Psychological, sociological, legal, philosophical, and technological approaches have been included, and it could be argued, are of equal importance in understanding the complexity of Digital Afterlife which is likely to impact on every person who is in some way digitally connected. Its existence has emerged as a bi-product of technology and human behaviour, and it is timely that we should be discussing its many dimensions. In particular, this volume has shown that we should be mindful of the different perspectives; those who create and leave their own digital legacy, those who support the creation of the legacy (e.g., social media platforms), and the recipients of the digital legacy of others. The interests of these three groups may not always be aligned.

Digital Afterlife can be approached from many disciplinary perspectives and can be viewed through a purely theoretical lens or investigated empirically as this volume illustrates. Complex and evolving, the social, psychological, and moral questions raised by this exciting aspect of contemporary society require ongoing investigation. For the incidental footprint left through our social media use, as Rycroft (Chapter 8) points out, Facebook will be left with a great number of accounts of deceased people by the end of the 21st century (if such platforms still exist) and this has thought-provoking implications. For our intentional decisions, such as in the creation of an active digital immortal of ourselves, this has further implications. At a practical level for both of these potentially co-existing versions (incidental and planned), cloud (or other) storage, its existence, cost, accessibility, and compatibility are all potentially finite and thus permanence is called into question.

Although there may well be exciting technological possibilities, these come with a set of potentially evolving ethical and moral questions about rights and responsibilities. Furthermore, the ideas raised in this book highlight the need to raise public awareness of some of the issues we may face in terms of our Digital Afterlives to protect ourselves and our loved ones from any legal or emotional harm, through increasing digital literacy. There are also many questions that we need to ask ourselves as individuals and as members of society about what happens to our data after we die, so that we can make informed choices—at least within the scope of our current understanding—despite cultural barriers to discussing death and dying.

In a sense, reflecting on the way that the work of great writers and artists has been immortalised in the creations they left behind—shared and remembered for generations—our own ability to leave a digital footprint for others to see democratises the process, and removes it from the realm of the privileged. Thus political questions, in addition to moral and ethical ones abound. We may ask for example, does our digital immortal or the general presence of a Digital Afterlife have to be useful? Can it inflict harm (financial, psychological)? As Burden argues, the big challenges for a digital immortal are to appear as human, and to be general purpose. However, we must also consider the acceptability to all parties concerned.

Our lives are shaped by and shape the creation of our Digital Afterlife as the digital has become a taken for granted aspect of human experience. At a practical level, cost of data storage, changing data storage systems, and so on all mitigate the likelihood of our digital presence existing in perpetuity, in addition to questions about whether this presence needs to be experienced or viewed by another. Whether we create accidental or intentional digital memories, our intentions, decisions, and actual behaviour has psychological consequences for ourselves and for society. What is clear from considering the many perspectives shared in this book is that whilst a Digital Afterlife is a possibility for most of us due to our ongoing digital presence, immortality is only a theoretical possibility given the impossibility of empirical certainty. Essentially the foreverness of forever is in question.

## REFERENCES

Ajzen, I., & Fishbein, M. (1970). The prediction of behavior from attitudinal and normative variables. *Journal of Experimental Social Psychology*, 6, 466–487.

Bassett, D. (2015). Who wants to live forever? Living, dying and grieving in our digital society. *Social Sciences*, 4(4), 1127–1139.

Chemin, A. (2014). Handwriting vs typing: Is the pen still mightier than the keyboard? The Guardian. Retrieved from https://www.theguardian.com/science/2014/dec/16/cognitive-benefits-handwriting-decline-typing

DeGroot, J. M. (2014). 'For whom the bell tolls': Emotional rubbernecking in Facebook memorial groups. *Death Studies*, 38(2), 79–84. doi: 10.1080/07481187.2012.725450.

Floridi, L. (2014). *The fourth revolution—How the infosphere is reshaping human reality*. Oxford: Oxford University Press.

Goffman, E. (1959). *The presentation of everyday life*. New York: Anchor Books.

Hogan, B. (2010). The presentation of self in the age of social media: Distinguishing performances and exhibitions online. *Bulletin of Science, Technology & Society*, 30(6), 377–386. https://doi.org/10.1177/0270467610385893.

Hunter, C. (2018). *The After Wife*. London: Trapeze.

Jandrić, P., Knox, J., Besley, T., Ryberg, T., Suoranta, J., & Hayes, S. (2018). Postdigital science and education. *Educational Philosophy and Theory*. 50(10), 893–899. https://doi.org/10.1080/00131857.2018.1454000.

Kanov, M. (2017). *'Sorry, what was your name again?': How to use a social robot to simulate Alzheimer's disease and exploring the effects on its interlocutors*. Stockholm, Sweden: KTH Royal Institute of Technology.

Phillips, W. (2015). *This is why we can't have nice things: Mapping the relationships between online trolling and mainstream culture.* Cambridge, MA: MIT Press Books.

Rachman, T. (2016, January 25). Meeting death with words. Available on https://www.newyorker.com/culture/cultural-comment/meeting-death-with-words.

Rosch, E., Thompson, E., & Varela, F. J. (1991). *The embodied mind: Cognitive science and human experience* (Paperback 1992 ed.). MIT Press. ISBN 978-0262720212.

Sabra, J. B. (2017). 'I hate when they do that!' Netiquette in mourning and memorialization among danish Facebook users, *Journal of Broadcasting & Electronic Media*, 61(1), 24–40. doi: 10.1080/08838151.2016.1273931.

Sebag Montefiore, S. (2018). *Written in history: Letters that changed the world.* London: Weidenfeld & Nicholson.

Sherlock, A. (2013). Larger than life: Digital resurrection and the re-enchantment of society. *The Information Society, 29*(3), 164–176.

Sofka, C. J. (1997). Social support 'internetworks', caskets for sale, and more: Thanatology and the information superhighway. *Death Studies, 21*(6), 553–574. doi: 10.1080/074811897201778.

Wagner, A. J. M. (2018). Do not Click "Like" When Somebody has Died: The Role of Norms for Mourning Practices in Social Media. Social Media + Society. https://doi.org/10.1177/2056305117744392.

Watson, J. B. (1913). Psychology as the behaviorist views it. *Psychological Review, 20*, 158–177.

# Glossary

**Augmented reality** The live view of a physical world environment whose elements are merged with computer imagery; thus it places emphasis on the physical, so that information from virtual space is accessed from within physical space. An example of this would be the projection of digital 3D objects into a physical space.

**Avatar** The bodily manifestation of one's self or a virtual human in the context of a 3D virtual world, or even as a 2D image within a text-chat system.

**Chatbots** Software programs which attempt to mimic human conversation when communicating with another (usually human) user. The Turing test is a standard test of the maturity of chatbot technology. Chatbots may also be used to control 3D avatars within a virtual world, 2D avatars on a website, or exist as participants within text-only environments such as chat rooms. Chatbots are conversational agents which support a wide range of natural language and extended conversations, rather than just question and answer or command and response.

**Digital Afterlife** The idea of a virtual space, where information, assets, legacies, and remains reside as part of the cyber soul.

**Digital death** Either the death of a living being and the way it affects the digital world or the death of a digital object and the way it affects a living being.

**Digital endurance** The creation of a lasting digital legacy and being posthumously present through digital reanimation.

**Digital inheritors** Those who inherit digital memories and messages following the death of a significant other.

**Digital legacy** Digital assets left behind after death.

**Digital mourning labour** This is activity undertaken by corporate brands who use social media to share (and gain from) emotions of grief and nostalgia about dead celebrities.

**Digital remains** Digital content and data which were accumulated and stored online during their lifetime that reflect our digital personality and memories.

**Digital resurrection** The use of dead people in media after death.

**Digital traces** Digital footprints left behind through digital media.

**Pedagogical agents** Virtual humans used for education purposes.

**Posthumous personhood** The idea of a model of a person that transcends the boundaries of the body.

**Second death** The deletion of digital remains.

**Second life** A persistent, shared, multi-user 3D virtual world launched in 2003 by Linden Lab. Residents (in the forms of self-designed avatars) interact with each other and can learn, socialise, participate in activities, and buy and sell items with one another, without any constraints of game play.

**Second loss** The loss experienced due to the deletion of digital remains.

**Technologically mediated mourning** The use of social networking sites to mourn and memorialise those who have died physically.

**Text chat** The means of communicating by text message, and specifically in immersive virtual worlds by typing a response to another avatar in-world rather than using voice. Text chat may be private, public, or in a closed group.

**Text-to-speech** The techniques and technology which can convert text (typically generated by a computer, but possibly also scanned from a page of text) to audible speech.

**Thanatechnology** Any kind of technology that can be used to deal with death, dying, grief, loss, and illness.

**Virtual humans** Software programs which present as human and which have behaviour, emotion, thinking, autonomy, and interaction modelled on physical humans.

**Virtual humanoids** Simple virtual humans which present, to a limited degree, as human and which may reflect some of the behaviour, emotion, thinking, autonomy, and interaction of a physical human.

**Virtual reality** A simulated computer environment in an either realistic or imaginary world. Most virtual reality emphasizes immersion, so that the user suspends belief and accepts it as a real environment and uses a head-mounted display to enhance this.

**Virtual sapiens** Sophisticated virtual humans which are designed to achieve similar levels of presentation, behaviour, emotion, thinking, autonomy, and interaction to a physical human.

# Index

Note: Locators in *italics* represent figures and **bold** indicate tables in the text.

## A

Access, to digital remains
  access by proximity, 116–118, *117*
  awareness to existing online tools, 118, *118*
  online activities, 115–116, *116*
  potential fiduciary, 119–120, *120*
  reasons for and against allowing, 120–122, *121*
  wish to allow or deny, 118–119, *119*
Access by proximity, 110, 116–118, *117*
Access rights to data, 135–137
Accounts, 5, 8, 32, 35, 36, 39–43; *see also* Posthumous accounts
Actions, digital immortal (DI), 150, 153
Administration of Estates Act, 131, 135–136
Adult education programs, 70
Afterlife, 1, 12, 15–16, 52–54; *see also* Digital Afterlife
*The After Wife* (Hunter), 197
Agency, 168–171
Age of Apocryphal Immortality, 30
Age of Forbidden Death, 28–29, 30
Age of Spectacular Death, 30
*The Age of Spiritual Machines: When Computers Exceed Human Intelligence* (Kurzweil), 179
Alzheimer's disease, 198
Analogue data, 110
Apple, 137
Application programming interfaces (API), 149, 150

Architecture, digital immortal (DI), *145*, 145–146
Ariès, P., 28–29
Árnason, A., 41
Arnold, M., 77–78
Artificial general intelligence (AGI), 155–156
Artificial immortality, 174
  strong, 175
  weak, 175
Artificial intelligence, 12, 31
Artificial Intelligence Markup Language (AIML), 148, 149
Artificial sentience (AS), 156–157
Assemblage, 169–170
Assisted immortality, 58, 80, 96
Augmented coffins and tombstones, 12
Augmented eternity, 61
Augmented reality, 76
Authenticated permissions, 150
Authoring process, digital immortal (DI), 151–152
Autobiography, 41
Avatars, 31, 78–79, 196
  creators, 21
  digital immortal (DI), 146, 150, 152
  as virtual property, 111

## B

Baby Internet, 29
Baecker, R. M., 84
Bassett, D., 22, 64, 192, 193
Belief-Desire-Intent (BDI) model, 150
Bell, G., 79
Bentham, J., 92

Bereaved people, 2, 4, 5, 64
   digital material use and experience, 43–54
   digital media and, 12, 15
   fear of second loss, 22, 81–86
   grief theory and, 5, 39–40
   Internet ghosts and, 77
   posthumous accounts of their dead, 5, 39–43
   sites of memory and, 113
   technology-mediated connection and, 58, 62, 77
   thanatechnology and, 76
   well-being of, 12, 15, 20
Bereavement, online communities of, 65–67
Bereavement counsellors, 4, 21
'Be Right Back' episode of *Black Mirror*, 31, 152
Berners-Lee, T., 34
Biography, 40, 41
Bio-informational capitalism, 178, 185
Biological immortality; *see also* Artificial immortality; Immortality
   strong, 175
   weak, 175
Black box, 190
*Black Mirror* (television show), 31, 152
Boellstorff, T., 76
Bollmer, G. D., 77
Brown, G., 96
Burden, D., 149, 156

C

Canada, 101
Cann, C. K., 77, 78
Capitalism, 178, 185
CaringBridge, 60
Carroll, E., 60
Chalmers, D. J., 182–183, 186
Chatbot systems, 148–149
Chauvet, L. M., 16
Christian/Christianity, 15–16
Cloud computing, 157–158
Cognitive science, 183
Commemoration, 6, 12, 22, 65, 85, 108, 112, 113–114, 120–121

Communities of remembrance, 65–67
Community death education opportunities, 70
Computer-assisted web interviewing (CAWI) system, 115
Computer Misuse Act, 135
Consciousness, 179–180, 182–184, 186
Constructivist grounded theory, 44
Consumer Rights Act 2015, 139
Contemporary grief theory, *see* Grief theory
Continuing bonds, 40, 61–64
Continuity
   problem of, 180–183
   similarity and, 185–186
Continuous development, 151
Conversation, digital immortal (DI) and, 148–152
   actions, 150
   creation and authoring process, 151–152
   influence, 152
   internal narrative, 151
   memory, 149–150
   meta-management, 151
   motivation, 150–151
   natural language conversation, 148–149
   sensing, 149
Conway, H., 93
Coping with death, 113–114
Counterparts, 17–18
'The Crafting of Grief' (Hedtke and Winslade), 41
Creation process, digital immortal (DI), 151–152, 154
Creators of Digital Afterlife, 21
Crypto-currencies, 130
Cuminskey, K., 22
Cyberconsciousness, 79
Cyberspace, 66

D

Daden, 20
Data
   access rights, 135–137
   digital *vs.* analogue, 110

intellectual property, 111
kinds of, 110–111
personal, 111
property, 111
Data mining, 12, 152
Data Protection Act, 135, 195
De Abaitua, M., 156
Dead, resurrection of, 77–79
DeadSocial, **13**, 17
Death
beliefs about sentience and agency
after, **63**
coping with, 113–114
exposure to, 28
Death Cafes, 58
Death Positive Movement, 58
Death-tech industry, 16–20
Daden, 20
DeadSocial, **13**, 17
Eter9, 17–18
Eternime, 19
LifeNaut, 18–19
DeGroot, J. M., 66
Delete-after-death policy, 32
Deleuze, G., 167, 168
Derrida, J., 163–166, 167
Digital Afterlife, **13**
concept of, 12
creation, impact of, 22–23
creators of, 21
features of, **13–14**
immortality fantasy and, 29–30
overview, 1–9
perspectives on, 20–22
psychological aspects of, 190
religion and, 15–16
social and psychological impact, 15
transition from life to, 58–59
Digital asset management, 60–61
Digital assets, 6, 7, **91**, 109, 111, 127–131
data security and access rights, 134–139
financial value, 130
intellectual value, 131
law reform, 139–140
legal and practical issues, 131–134
'"new" new property,' 90–93
propertisation of, 90–93
sentimental value, 130

social value, 131
steps to be taken to protect, 140–141
Digital autobiographies, 35
Digital creators, 63, 79
Digital death, **13**, 83, 89, **91**
'Digital Death Day' events, 58
Digital Death Survey (DDS), 61, 62, 63
'Digital Dust' website, 60
Digital endurance, 5–6, **14**, 81
Digital estate planning, 58, 60–61, 70
Digital etiquette
netiquette, 191–194
posthumous, 22
Digital executor, 17, 36–37, 191, 194
Digital footprints, 162
Digital hoarders, 36
Digital immigrant, 29
Digital immortal (DI), 7, 144–159
architecture, *145*, 145–146
artificial sentience (AS), 156–157
current offerings, 147
developing conversation, 148–152
developing generality, 155–156
developing meaning, motivation, and
internal narrative, 152–155
developing sentience, 156–157
development stages, 148–157
esoteric approaches to, 148
infrastructure and payment, 157–158
overview, 144–145
passive, 146, *146*
types of, 146–147
Digital immortality, 1, 75
artificial intelligence and, 58
defined, 91, 173–174
platforms, 79–81
Digital inheritors, **14**, 63, 64, 79
Digital legacy, 5, **13**, 30–35, 109
as loaded concept, 35
Digital Legacy Association (DLA), 60
Digital literacy, 139–140
Digital material
grief and, 42, 43
narrative about, *see* Narrative
research on, 43–51
Digital media, 12
preservers of, 21
receivers of, 22

Digital memories, 21, 64, 76, 78–86, 165, 200
Digital mourning labour, **14**
Digital native, 29
Digital nomenclature in postdigital world, 196
Digital objects, 43; *see also* Digital material
Digital personality, 6, 108; *see also* Digital remains
Digital photographs, 130
Digital Railroad, 33
Digital remains, 6–7, 108–123
  access to, 115–122
  concept, **13**, 108
  in context, 108–109
  overview, 108
  physical and, 28–29
  terminology, 109–110
Digital Republics Act 2016, 101
Digital resurrection, **14**
*Digital Sociology* (Lupton), 76
Digital survivor advocacy, 67–68
Digital traces, **13**, 162–163
Digital *vs.* analogue data, 110
Digital zombies, 77–79, 192
Direct authoring, 151
Directed conversation, 151
Distributed agency, 169
Documenting end of life, 59–60
Dow, E. H., 96
Duplicity/duplication, 173, 179–180, 183–186

E

Egan, G., 157
Electronic communication, 53, 191
Electronic Communications Privacy Act of 1986 (ECPA), 99
Eliza Nine, 18
Emotional life insurance, 63
Emotional rubbernecking, 66, 193
End of life documentation, 59–60
Episodic memory, 150
Esoteric approaches to digital immortal (DI), 148
Etern9, 1, 17–18, 147

'Eternilisations,' 18
Eternime, 19, 31, 78–79, 147
Ethics, question of, **181**, 183, 184
Eugenics, 8, 176
Experiential empathy, 66, 67

F

Facebook, 1, 20, 27, 32–35, 78, 83
  access to digital remains, 118
  accounts of deceased people, 29–30, 199
  data security and access rights, 138–139
  delete-after-death policy, 32
  digital assets, 134
  digital remains, 32
  emotional displays on, 194
  emotional rubberneckers, 66
  legacy contact (LC) feature, 114, 134, 141, 192, 194
  memorialisation features, 32
  memorial pages, 174, 175
  traces, 164–165
  users, 134
'Facing Up to the Problem of Consciousness' (Chalmers), 182
Fear of second loss, 81–85, 193
*Felicific calculus,* 92
Financial value, digital assets with, 130
First World War, 162
Flickr, 33
Floridi, L., 76, 81, 82, 93, 94–95, 97, 196
Forbidden death, 28–29
Forget locket, 85
France, 101
Fuller, S., 8, 176–177
Funeral home, 28
Funeral-tech tutorials, 17
Future and second loss, 85–86

G

Gambling, 130
Gaming, 130
Gazzard, H., 138
General Data Protection Regulations (GDPR), 98, 112, 135, 195–196

Generality, digital immortal (DI), 155
Gibbs, M., 77–78
Goethe, 191
Goffman, E., 191
GoneNotGone, 63
Gonzalez, E., 67–68
Gooder, P., 16
Google, 114, 118, 122, 134
    access to digital remains, 118
    inactive account manager (IAM), 114
Grandfather's axe experiment, 178
Grattan, S., 93
Gray, J., 79
Grief, 57–58
    bond continuation and, 40–41
    digital objects in, 43
    material objects in, 42
    posthumous storying, 41
Grief counselling, 41
Grief theory, 5, 39–40
Grief tourists, 67
Grosz, E., 167, 168
'Growing Up Digital,' 140

H

Hagiography, 49–51
Hedtke, L., 41
Himsworth, M., 137
Hjorth, L., 22
Hospice/palliative care, 70
Howard, J., 180
Human(s)
    consciousness, *see* Consciousness
    identity, 166–168
    *vs.* non-humans, 176–177
Hunter, C., 197

I

Identity, 166–168
    question of, **181**, 183–184
Immortality, 190–191, 197
    achieving, 185
    artificial, 174–175
    fantasy of, 29–30
    *vs.* legacy, 190–191
    postdigital perspective, 175–178

two-way, 61
types of, 173, 174, 175
Inactive account manager (IAM), 114
Industrial Revolution, 170
Informational bodies, 90, **91**, 194
    postmortal privacy, 96–97
    post-mortem privacy, 94–95
Infrastructure, digital immortal (DI),
    157–158
Intellectual property, 111
Intellectual value, digital assets with, 131
Internal narrative, digital immortal (DI),
    151, 154
Internet, 34
    engagement with death, 113–114
Internet ghosts, 77–78
Intestacy Rules, 131–132, 137
ITunes, 132

J

Jackson, M., 78
Jacobsen, M. H., 30
Jandrić, P., 8, 19, 196, 197

K

Kamarinou, D., 111
Kasket, E., 20, 23, 60, 64, 70, 83, 89, 103
Kasky, C., 68
Kastenbaum, R. J., 58, 80, 96
Kinds of data, 110–111
Klass, D., 61–62
Kohn, T., 77–78
Kondo, M., 31
KonMari method, 31
Kübler-Ross, E., 53–54
Kurzweil, R., 179, **181**, 182, 183, 186

L

The Land Registry, 129
*Last Lecture* (Pausch), 60
The Law Commission, 129
Laws/law reforms
    digital literacy, 139–140
    post-mortem(al) privacy, 98–102
    in United States, 140

Lawyers, 21
Leddy, K., 61, 62, 64
Legacy
    *vs.* immortality, 190–191
    as loaded word, 35
    meaning of, 36
Legacy contacts, 32, 114, 134, 141, 191,
        192, 194
Legal issues, 7, 127–141
    data security and access rights,
        137–139
    digital assets, *see* Digital assets
Leland, J., 58
Libel, 131
LifeNaut, 1, 18–19, 147
Life-planning tutorials, 17
Literature, on posthumous digital
        material, 40–43
Litton, R. J., 78
London Cemetery Company, 30
Lupton, D., 76


**M**

Machine-learning based systems, 148
Malabou, C., 166, 169
#MarchForOurLives, 67
Marjory Stoneman Douglas High School
        (MSD), 67–68
Maslow's Hierarchy of Needs, 150
Mason-Robbie, V., 149
Massimi, M., 84
Masterson, A., 63
Material; *see also* Digital material
    in grief, 42, 43
McMahon, F., 137
Mediators, 21
Memorial trolling, 66–67, 193
Memory; *see also* Digital memories
    digital immortal (DI), 149–150
    (web)sites of, 113–114
Memory creators, 21
Mental Capacity Act, 135
Meta-management, digital immortal (DI),
        151, 153–154
Metastability, 168, 171
Michels, J. D., 111

Microsoft Research, 79
Migration, digital immortal (DI), 158
Millard, C., 111
Mindclones, 79
Mindfile, 18–19, 79
Mindware, 18, 79
MIT Media lab, 61
Mobile phone, 169
Monkhouse, B., 78
Moral questions, 196–197
Motivation, digital immortal (DI),
        150–151, 153
Mourning, 5, **14**, 191–194
#MSDPickUpAPen, 67
Music libraries, 130


**N**

Nansen, B., 77–78
Narrative, 42, 44–53
    harmful hagiography, 49–51
    internal, digital immortal (DI),
        151, 154
    protecting, material relativised to,
        48–49
    as relational strength, 44–48
Natural language conversation, 148–149
Netiquette, 191–194
Neuroscience, 166, 183
#NeverAgain, 67
New Elysium, 89
New(ish) property, **91**, 94
'"New" new property,' 90–93, **91**
*The New York Law Journal,* 185
Norris, J., 60


**O**

Obar, J., 133
*The Observer,* 33
Oeldorf-Hirsch, A., 133
Öhman, C. J., 81, 82, 94, 95
Onlife, 76
Online communities of bereavement,
        65–67
Online memorial candles, 12
Online voyeurs, 66

## P

Parent–teacher associations, 70
Passive digital immortal (DI), 146, *146*
Pausch, R., 59–60
Payment, digital immortal (DI), 157–158
Perpetuity, 30
Persona creators, 21
Personal data, 111
Peters, M. A., 177, 178
Pew Research Center, 59
Pharmakon, 163
Phillips, W., 66
Photo-based avatar, 18
Photograph albums, 130
Physical and digital remains, 28–29
Platforms, digital immortality, 79–81
Postdigital immortality, 173
Posthumous accounts, 5, 39–43
    digital objects in, 43
    material objects in, 42
Posthumous avatars, 82
Posthumous digital etiquette, 22
Posthumous digital material, 39–54
    discussion, 51–54
    hagiography and, 49–51
    literature and background, 40–43
    relationship with the deceased and,
        46–48
    relativised to protect narrative, 48–49
    research and findings, 43–51
Posthumous personhood, **13**
Posthumous privacy, 112
Posthumous representations, 77
Postmortal privacy, 6, **91**, 95–98, *97*
    informational bodies, 101–102
    laws, 98–102
Post-mortem privacy, 6, **91**, 93–95
Pre-individual, 167–168
Prensky, M., 29
Preservers of digital media, 21
*The Prince* (Machiavelli), 156
Privacy
    posthumous, 112
    postmortal, *see* Postmortal privacy
    post-mortem, 6, 93–95
    protection of, 194–196
    questions of, 191
Problem
    of continuity, 180–183
    of similarity, 183–185
Procedural memory, 150
Processing power, digital immortal
        (DI), 157
Propertisation of digital assets,
        90–93
Property data, 111
Pseudo-scientific theories, 8, 176
Psychoeducation, 64
Psychological impact of Digital
        Afterlife, 15
Psychological perspective, 190
Public schools, 70

## Q

QR codes, 12
Question
    of ethics, **181**, 183, 184
    of identity, **181**, 183–184
    of selection, **181**, 184, 185
    of superiority, **181**, 184

## R

Rachman, T., 59, 193
Rael, P. M., 174, 185
Reader, J., 16
Receivers of digital media, 22
*The Red Men* (De Abaitua), 156
Relationship, 44–51; *see also* Narrative
Religion, 15–16
Religious leaders, 20, 21
Remembrance, communities of, 65–67
Research, on posthumous digital material,
        43–51
Resurrection, 16, 77–79
    digital, **14**
Resurrection of the dead, 77–79
Revised Uniform Fiduciary Access to
        Digital Assets Act (RUFADAA),
        100, 101, 140
Romano, J., 60
Rothblatt, M., 79
Rycroft, G.k, 195, 196, 199

**S**

Sabra, J. B., 194
SafeBeyond, 63
Savin-Baden, M., 149, 156
Scientific racism, 8, 176
Second death, **13**, 64, 81, 82–83
Second Life, 76
Second loss, **13**, 64
    fear of, 81–85, 193
    future and, 85–86
Security, data, 134–139
Selection, question of, **181**, 184, 185
Semantic memory, 149
Sensing, digital immortal (DI), 149
Sentience
    digital immortal (DI), 156–157
    fragmented, 198
Sentimental value, digital assets
    with, 130
Service providers (SPs), 79–81
Shakur, T., 78
Shanahan, M., 148
Shavit, V., 60
Sherlock, A., 77, 78, 192–193
Shiluv I²R, 115
Ship of Theseus, 178–180
Similarity
    continuity and, 185–186
    immortality and, 184–185
    thought experiments on, 183–185
Simondon, G., 167–168
Sites of memory, 113–114
(Web)sites of memory, 113–114
Social death, 81–83; *see also* Second loss
Social impact of Digital Afterlife, 15
Socially active digital zombies, *see*
    Digital zombies
Social media, 4, 27–37, 131
    in coping with impending death and
        loss, 65
    digital legacies, 30–37
    overview, 27–28
    physical and digital remains, 28–29
Social networks sites (SNS), 110
Social value, digital assets with, 131
Sofka, C., 66, 76

Sophia (humanoid robot), 19, 147
Stiegler, B., 163–164, 166, 169, 170
Stillwaggon S., L., 180
Stokes, P., 64, 81–83
Story/storying, 5, 40, 41, 43, 52
Stroebe, M., 41
Strong artificial immortality, 173, 175,
    179, 185
Strong biological immortality, 173, 175,
    177, 185
Strong immortality, 174
Superiority, question of, **181**, 184
Survivor advocates, 67; *see also* Digital
    survivor advocacy

**T**

Technological landscape, 198
Technologically-mediated, digital
    mourning labour, **14**
Technologically mediated mourning, **14**
Terasem Movement Foundation, 18
Text-chat application, 146
Text-to-speech, 146
Thanabots, 82, 196
Thanatechnology, 5, 76, 196
    bereaved people and, 76
    digital grieving, 85
    digital zombies, 78
    grief and, 58–68
    overview, 57–58
    posthumous memories and messages,
        79–81, 83
    practices of remembrance, 77
Thanatology, 57–58
Thanatosensitive design, 68–69
Theseus, 178–180
Thompson, R., 137
Traces
    Derrida on, 163–166
    digital, **13**, 162–163
Transformation Strategy 2017 to 2020
    (UK Government), 129
Trolling, 66–67
Twitter, 67–68
Two-way immortality, 61, 79–80

## U

Ulguim, P., 80
Uniform Access to Digital Assets by
        Fiduciaries Act (UADAFA),
        100–101
Uniform Law Commission (US), 140
Uniform Law Conference of Canada, 100
Unintended consequences, 23
United States
    law reforms, 140
    post-mortem(al) privacy laws, 99–100
Universal Declaration of
        Cyborg Rights, 185
University of Worcester,
        United Kingdom, 20
US Electronic Communications Privacy
        Act of 1986 (ECPA), 99
Users' perspectives, 108–109
    access to digital remains, 115–122
U.S. Model Law, 108
US Restatement (Second) of Torts, 99
US Uniform Law Commission, 100

## V

Venter, C., 177–178
Virginia Tech massacre of 2007, 32
Virtual assistant (VA), 1, 17, 151
Virtual human, 2, 20, 21
Virtual life coach (VLC), 151

Virtual persona, 20, 21, 147, 149, 154; *see
        also* Digital immortal (DI)
Virtual property, 111
Virtual reality, 15, 76, 96
Virtual sapien, 21

## W

Wagner, A. J. M., 15, 22, 194
Wallace, J., 85
Walter, T., 40–41
Watkin, C., 166
Weak artificial immortality, 173, 175, 177,
        179–180, 185, 186
Weak biological immortality, 173, 175, 185
Weak immortality, 174
Willis, B., 132
Winslade, J., 41
*With the End in Mind* (Mannix), 35
World Wide Cemetery, 29
World Wide Web, 58

## Y

Yahoo!, 99
YouTube, 29, 60, 110

## Z

Zombies, *see* Digital zombies

Milton Keynes UK
Ingram Content Group UK Ltd.
UKHW031532071024
449327UK00005B/120

9 780367 337919